Kerrie Hide is a mystical theologian, spiritual director, formator and retreat giver whose lifelong work interweaves theological, scholarly, and deep heart wisdom about contemplation from the Christian mystical tradition. She is the author of the award-winning *Gifted Origins to Graced Fulfilment: The Soteriology of Julian of Norwich* and many articles on contemplative prayer. Kerrie received her doctorate in 2000, was a lecturer in theology for eighteen years at the Australian Catholic University and spiritual director at St Mary's Tower's MSC Retreat Centre for nine years. Writing with lucidity and ease, Kerrie's work is unique in that it combines the nuanced and attentive listening of an experienced spiritual director with the mystical eye of a seasoned theologian.

Kerrie Hide

Love's Oneing

A Book About Contemplation

Austin Macauley Publishers™
LONDON * CAMBRIDGE * NEW YORK * SHARJAH

Copyright © Kerrie Hide 2022

The right of Kerrie Hide to be identified as author of this work has been asserted by the author in accordance with sections 77 and 78 of the Copyright, Designs and Patents Act 1988.

All rights reserved. No part of this publication may be reproduced, stored in a retrieval system, or transmitted in any form or by any means, electronic, mechanical, photocopying, recording, or otherwise, without the prior permission of the publishers.

Any person who commits any unauthorised act in relation to this publication may be liable to criminal prosecution and civil claims for damages.

A CIP catalogue record for this title is available from the British Library.

ISBN 9781398452282 (Paperback)
ISBN 9781398452299 (ePub e-book)

www.austinmacauley.com

First Published 2022
Austin Macauley Publishers Ltd®
1 Canada Square
Canary Wharf
London
E14 5AA

For Dawn and Bernie

Thanking is a tender quality that pours forth from the heart of God. My gratitude flows to so many. I wish to thank my students who were so part of the creativity of the early years when I first began to explore the beauty of Julian's Oneing. At the same time, I must thank my directees who are living this journey of oneing so deeply, so fully with so much love. Their luminous wisdom and insights into contemplation continues to enrich my life and indeed, the noosphere.

I am so grateful to Sr Joanne Fitzsimons OSC, Sr Madeline Duckett RSM, Sr Catherine Hefferan RSM, Sr Margaret Collis RSM, Sr Patty Andrew OSU, Sue Gesell, Rev Dr Sarah Bachelard and Fran Hegarty for encouraging me to write and make accessible the content of my retreats. They are so at home in love's silence and live from these depths of contemplation.

And I must extend a special heartfelt thank you to Dr Robyn Fitzgerald, who spent many hours praying with these ponderings, sharing invaluable insights and assisting with editing, thus enabling the book to be completed. Our many conversations of the heart inspired the insights that were emerging to become words on the page. Finally, I am deeply grateful to my husband, Col, whose love is endlessly enriching.

Contents

Introduction	i
Part One: Beholding in Oneing	**1**
Chapter I: Beholding and Oneing in the Ground of the Heart ~ Julian of Norwich	*3*
Chapter II: Following Love's Stirrings ~ The Author of the Cloud of Unknowing	*29*
Chapter III: The Birth of the Word ~ Meister Eckhart	*55*
Part Two: Suffering in Oneing	**83**
Chapter IV: Flowing Sinking Enjoying ~ Mechthild of Magdeburg	*85*
Chapter V: In the Vulnerable Embrace of Love ~ Clare of Assisi	*113*
Chapter VI: At the Time of the Rising Dawn ~ John of the Cross	*141*
Part Three: Communion in Oneing	**169**
Chapter VII: Centre to Centre ~ Pierre Teilhard de Chardin	*171*
Chapter VIII: Enstatic-Ecstatic Communion ~ Beatrice Bruteau	*199*
Chapter IX: A Holy Wholeness ~ Ilia Delio	*227*

Introduction

May they be one.
John 17:21

Here is a book about contemplation — in which the soul is oned to God.[1]

These opening words from the *Cloud of Unknowing* hold the essence of this book. My desire is to draw together the pattern of wisdom that has informed my ever-growing appreciation that we are one and in a relationship of oneing in God. The book seeks to shed light on how we become consciously aware, behold with a unitive, or oneing consciousness, and express the wisdom that arises from this oneing. The book is an interweaving of the wisdom of nine mystics from the Christian tradition that have helped continue to answer the original question of my life-long research on Julian of Norwich, that Julian asks at the end of her showings, "What was God's meaning?"[2] The response she receives fills the universe with hope as she comes to behold and see: "Love is God's meaning."[3] Together, yet uniquely, Julian of Norwich, the *Cloud of Unknowing* author, Meister Eckhart, Mechthild of Magdeburg, Clare of Assisi, John of the Cross, Pierre Teilhard de Chardin, Beatrice Bruteau and Ilia Delio give us a glimpse of how the Christian contemplative tradition offers a luminous view of our oneness in God and potential for awakening a unitive, or oneing consciousness.

---

[1] *The Cloud of Unknowing and the Book of Privy Counselling,* ed. Phyllis Hodgson, Early English Text Society. (London: Oxford University Press, 1955), 1. These are my translations.

[2] *The Writings of Julian of Norwich*, A *Vision Showed to Devout Woman and A Revelation of Love,* eds. Nicholas Watson and Jacqueline Jenkins (Pennsylvania: Pennsylvania State University, 2006). Hereafter, S is for Showings, chapter and line numbers are given. Roman numerals indicate the short text. These are my translations. S: 16.86.11-12.

[3] Ibid., S: 16.86.17.

Each mystic offers us a multi-coloured palate of translucent metaphorical language, that arises from the silence of the ground of the heart and has its own distinctive nuanced way of describing mystical union, or oneing, and the transformation in consciousness that occurs through contemplation. Each author contributes to this overview of the Western Christian version of what is today called non-dual consciousness. Each shows how the practice of contemplative prayer imparts increasing union with God, that transforms consciousness from reliance on the cognitively dominated thinking of the conscious mind, to the unitive perceptivity, or what I call, a oneing-heart awareness. Each bequeaths some luxuriant colours that enable us to paint a multihued canvas of how, in Mechthild's words, we are "written into the book of the Godhead, painted in our humanity,"[4] and are evolving in our capacity to see translucently from the core of our existence in Christ, in the Trinity of Love. Each seer takes us into the holomovement of the evolutionary flow of Love's oneing, enfolding and unfolding in creation, until we realise the fullness of our oneness, behold, and truly see that the soul is indeed oned to God.

Placing us within the ground of our heart, and attuning our heart ways of knowing, to the point where Silence speaks the Word, not only within our own soul, but within the wholeness of creation, these mystics offer us a way of contemplation that awakens an abiding unitive heart, or oneing consciousness. I understand the term mystic to describe a person who experiences the presence of God, perceived in conscious awareness as either presence, or absence.[5] In this sense, we are all mystics. This book seeks to situate each of the mystics in her, or his cultural, historical environment, behold in the silence of open receptivity and ponder how each distinctively contributes to the rise of the consciousness of our intrinsic unity in the divine, in this twenty-first century. Critically, we will explore the complexifying of consciousness as articulated in these texts that assists us to live in the oneing consciousness of the Christ and contribute to the contemporary quest to enable non-dual consciousness to evolve. We will fine tune how to see, beholding blindly from within the oneness of our shared identity in Christ, in the Trinity of Love, in our time.

In her celebrated book, the *Unbearable Wholeness of Being*, the contemporary mystic, Ilia Delio highlights how we are at a crossroad in understanding the

---

[4] See, *Mechthild of Magdeburg: The Flowing Light of the Godhead,* ed. Frank Tobin (New York: Paulist Press, 1998), 108.

[5] While in pure contemplation there is no experience, no reflexivity, or knowing that we know, I use experience, in the sense of perceiving in conscious awareness.

implications of our wholeness in God, and the evolutionary movement of how we are one. She urges us to see love as the fundamental energy of evolution, reminding us that we must discover the still point of love within us that empowers us to do new things. "Our challenge today," Ilia affirms, "is to trust the power of love at the heart of life, to let ourselves be seized by love, to create and invent ways for love to evolve into a global wholeness of unity, compassion, justice and peacemaking."[6] Inviting us into a future full of Love's newness and freedom, poignantly Ilia reminds us that:

> The way forward is the way inward — to recover the mystical dimension of life beginning in the human heart as that heart extends into the cosmos. We need to find the Omega centre within us, that depth of love that makes each of us unique and distinct, that God-centred love which holds us together moment to moment and constantly creates us anew.[7]

This recovery of the mystical dimension of life is crucial for the future of our planet as we currently face this climate crisis moment. We must discover the Omega centre that holds the potential creativity necessary to evolve and is the source of our future oneness in God. Searchingly, we must dissolve the dualisms that haunt our future growth in unity.

As David Applebaum recognises, this necessitates uncovering the awakened state of Christ awareness, that shatters the most fundamental dualism, and "break[s] the dualism of all dualisms, that between God and his creature, the self, the 'I'."[8] We must return to, and see from within, our original oneness in love, in Christ, in Love's Trinity. We must rediscover how to enter into the ground of our heart, in the divine heart and consciously participate in the newness of the fullness of divine love evolving. This includes embodying how the inner universe and outer universe are one verse of love. I understand heart to be the centre, the luminous,[9] spacious energy field of pure oneness, that is within our deepest interiority, extending into the cosmos. I will address this heart journey into contemplation that reclaims the Omega centre within us frequently, considering questions such as: What is contemplation? How does each mystic help me/us deepen my/our practice, of contemplation? While responses to these

---

[6] Ilia Delio, *The Unbearable Wholeness of Being: God Evolution and the Power of Love* (New York: Orbis Books, 2013), xxv.
[7] Ibid., 182-3.
[8] David Applebaum, in Reiner Schürmann, *Wandering Joy: Meister Eckhart's Mystical Philosophy* (Great Barrington: Lindisfarne Books, 2001), x.
[9] "Luminous" is a word I use often as it is infused in light and points to the uncreated light of the divine within our *nous* and the noosphere.

questions are always evolving, nonetheless, ancient wisdom is inscribed in our heart and the mystics in this book offer such wisdom for today's contemplatives.

Contemplation as Oneing

This book is a beholding of contemplation, as oneing. Literally, *con–templ–ation,* derived from the Latin *contemplatio,* is from *con* – to go within, *temp* – to create time and space, to gaze, ponder, or study, within the *temple (templum).* Contemplation is to go within, to look at God within the temple of the heart. The Greek term adopted, *theōria* (θεωρία), from *theōrein,* again stresses to gaze at something intently.[10] However, as the catholic tradition of contemplation unfolds, contemplation loses the sense of looking at God, reflexively as subjective-objective knowing that we know, and becomes beholding in total awareness of God, or oneness with God. Contemplation is beholding until there is only one beholding. In contemplation we are absorbed within the loving of divine contemplation, within Love's oneing. All that we will explore about contemplation as oneing is held in the celebrated oneing prayer of Jesus that resounds from the luminous pages of John's gospel. Jesus, who identifies himself as the Word spoken from the silence of divine contemplation, utters this haunting prayer, shortly before he walks the way of the cross. He prays from the depths of his heart: "Father, may they be one (ἕν *hen*)" (Jn 17:21).

Jesus longs for us to live in this oneness of contemplation. His words are infused with unbounded presence, as they create a oneing field from the intimacy of Jesus being one with the source of his being, that he calls his Father. Reciprocally, this eternally creative Silence who speaks the Word, or consciousness of the Father, is in Jesus. As Jesus continues to pray, "just as you are in me and I am in you," we see that oneness is not a static condition. To be one includes the dynamism of oneing, in the reciprocal indwelling of one in another. Jesus invites us to abandon all into the intensity of this "I in you and you in me" union, continuing to stress that we all share in this same oneness. Jesus desires for us to know this "complete oneness." His timeless words echo throughout the centuries: "May they also be in us … May they be one as we are one – I in them and you in me – so that they may be completely one" (Jn 17:21). In contemplation we discover

---

[10] *The New Dictionary of Catholic Spirituality,* ed. Michael Downey (Collegeville: Liturgical Press, 2001), 209-210.

this "I in you and you in me," oneness that is intimately personal and expansively cosmic.

In a later text, *Pistis Sophia*, Mary Magdalene and John the Virgin, are a powerful example of what Jesus means by being completely one, as their loving is so full, unconditional, absolute, that Jesus comes to say: "I am they and they are I."[11] Jesus desires that our consciousness be so turned within, grounded, stable, oned, that the energy of love evolves into oneing and we love from the overflowing fullness of this oneing. This fullness is the fullness we have already received; the grace upon grace (Jn 1:16) the Holy One gives us, and the eternal fullness of joy continually flowing in us. The energy field is potent, intoxicating, puissant, as Love's desire for our oneing infuses light. This light imbued from the one who says, "I am the light of the world" (Jn 8-12), is an eternally luminous light that darkness cannot overcome (Jn 1:15). Received in contemplation through our oneing in love, this enlightenment, enables us to behold the face of the one who is divine desire, "to come and see" (Jn 1:39). We see by beholding, by oneing.

When, in silence and stillness we turn into the ground of our heart, lean into the silence of the Word spoken from the divine silence, yield beyond into naked awareness, repose in open receptivity and awaken the eye of our heart that is nakedly aware, in the illuminating darkness, we realise the energy of the divine desire expressed in this prayer is already within us. We become immersed in the desire of Jesus. We become his desire. We become one with him and so participate in this original loving of the divine contemplation that speaks the Word. In the chapters that follow, we will seek to illume the multifaceted gift of being one in contemplation and attend to the dispositions that predispose us to these graces.

Beatrice Bruteau reminds us that at the heart of the mystic discovery, "we are all one, and that One is unconditioned, unlimited, and undefined."[12] This original, limitless, indefinable oneness and its many derivatives, "*one*," "*oonying*," "*ones*," "*onyd*," "*oned*," points far beyond numeration, and carries us into the ineffable. In this way, "oneing" leaves more room for nuance and ambiguity, than the most commonly used phrase, "union with God," conveys. Moreover, as

---

[11] Herbert Christian Merillat, "When the Two Become One," 1997. http://gnosis.org/thomasbook/ch24.html

[12] Beatrice Bruteau, *Radical Optimism: Practical Spirituality in an Uncertain World* (New York: Crossroad Publishing, 2002), 64.

years of commitment to contemplation strengthens this oneing consciousness, this ineffable knowing by being one, demolishes an onto-theological foundation of the divine life, that limits God to an analysis of being, towards establishing what we might call a metaphysics of oneing, that is ever inclusive and expansive. This metaphysics of oneing, as we will see, holds together in creative union, the wisdom of contemplation that takes us into the apophatic waters of dark unknowing, along with a humble struggle to centre in Love and be filled with divine Wisdom, with Logos, and the desire to find some language that is finely nuanced and ever inviting of a deeper, richer articulation of our oneness. Thus, I wish to suggest that "oneing" holds within it our original oneness and the dynamism of the intimacy of being one in God, along with the ever-*kenotic* emptiness of the yet to be fulfilled intimacy of our oneing. We are one and yet must be open, empty, responsive to this invitational oneing.

"Oneing" vibrates with the amorising energy of Love's evolutionary impulse that arises in our awareness as we abandon subject-object seeing and become more intensively reflexively conscious. In being one with God in contemplation, we know that we know, in the unknowing of the intense single-pointed reflexivity of subject within subject, as one "I." "Oneing" points to the fluid ground of Christic consciousness within human nature and within all creation. "Oneing" highlights the intimacy of the soul's journey in God, along with the dynamism of the holomovement that creation is, that quantum physics expounds, and the meaning that arises from holographic wisdom. With care not to naively relate this oneing consciousness that emerges with all the intricacies of the field theories that quantum develops, never-the-less, the primordial, energetic, fluid, open, boundless nuances of the contemplative term oneing, enables it to become a container word, expressing our original oneness and the endless oneing of the divine creativity.

When the eternal consciousness of oneing awakens within us, a rich, vivid tapestry of inter-relatedness and inter-connection emerges. We feel our bodies open into a limitlessness as we become one in Christ Omega, one with each other, one with the earth, one with the universe. Within this oneing dynamism everything belongs. Paradox is welcomed, as opposites embrace in an ever-creative dialectical tension that infuses deeper oneing. Shadow is integrated, transformed and transfigured, so that the evolutionary future of our oneing in Love can enhance our world. A faithful commitment to contemplation and reflection on the heart-wisdom that emerges from our onening in spiritual direction, intentional communal contemplation, along with the deep study of the wisdom of mystical texts can inform this urgent need for a more nuanced Christian contemplative wisdom.

A Hermeneutic of Beholding

When, years ago, I entered into the depths of Julian's showings, the whole question of the meaning of suffering and salvation haunted me. By suffering I mean to be afflicted by, or endure physical, emotional, sensual, heart, soul pain, as physical, emotional and spiritual pain are interconnected. Suffering was often considered a punishment from God. And the predominant interpretations of the reason for the incarnation focused on God becoming human as a response to human dysfunction, rather than the original desire of God to love and express God's self in the finite. Our natural oneness in God that incites our desire to contemplate and be one with God, seemed to be lost in doctrinal formulations. Yet, I knew intuitively the incarnation had to originate in the origin-less divine desire to love and share love. It could not be a second order response to the problem of sin in the world.

During this time, Julian immersed me in the mysterious beauty of beholding and oneing, until I came to behold from the depths of where I am endlessly grounded and rooted in God, the energy field of oneing that is this ground. Guided by the wisdom of Julian's way of beholding, of entering into stillness and silence, being, participating in, and holding the One I beheld until there was only beholding, I developed a hermeneutic of beholding to explore her understanding of salvation as oneing. I came to behold the exquisite beauty of our oneing in the Trinity, from our original oneing in being, to oneing through the cross and oneing through the Holy Spirit. This oneing in the Trinity endlessly draws us into the joy and bliss of living, enfolded, enclosed, *beclosed* in the Trinity, as the Trinity is enfolded, enclosed, *beclosed* in us.[13] Gradually, over the years, as this reciprocal enclosing – *beclosing* has become more intensely reflexive, the whole nature of beholding within beholding, is drawing me deeper and deeper into oneing.

This book grounds the practice of contemplation in a hermeneutic of beholding, so that beholding from within our oneness in God creates a boundless canvas of oneing that is foundational to the painting that emerges. This oneing is

---

[13] See, Kerrie Hide, *Gifted Origins to Graced Fulfilment: The Soteriology of Julian of Norwich* (Collegeville: Liturgical Press, 2001).

ontological. It is fundamental to all that is. Our oneness in God, in the endlessly oneing of love, is the source of consciousness. Oneing is the originating foundation, the golden string that holds everything together.[14] It is not possible for us to exist separately from God, or from creation. We indwell one another within the dynamism of oneing. We are an alling. It follows then that our interpretation must begin from within beholding in contemplation, from within the infinite intimacy of our original oneness in God. When in contemplation, we lean into this oneness, coincide, delicately attend from within, beholding, continuous waves of illuminating intimacy deepen and expand our being in one another, in the Word, until we are filled with the Word. This infuses an ineffable sense of presence, of grounding in the heart of God. This loving from within the heart's ground, infuses a love-knowledge that comes from a profound being within one another. Our aware-ing-self, who is gazing, dissolves in beholding. We subjectively be-hold. We become the beholding. In this beholding we are infinite, hollow and fertile in the spaciousness of the heart. We are the oneing.

As this oneing in the Word immerses us in silence, drawing us beyond all discursive language, a new heart-language arises that imparts unitive seeing. Meaning then arises from this ground of mutually indwelling each other. Martin Laird names this contemplative vision that arises as *"logophasis,"* emphasising how as all subject-object dichotomies dissolve, we become filled with Logos.[15] Laird describes how as we abandon:

> thoughts and concepts in poetic gestures of *aphaeresis* in order to enable union by the grasp of faith, concepts are also the paradoxical result of such letting go and union. For in the grasp of faith the soul places her mouth on the fountain of the Bridegroom, and her mind is bewedded with knowledge however indistinct and tentative. Her mouth is filled with words of eternal life."[16]

This way of interpretation through beholding and oneing involves engaging with the text in a way that takes us into the silent ground the words arose from, releasing our usual ways of knowing into the ground of love, awakening a contemplative gaze, being and holding the fruits of the gaze in our hearts, until we behold from within beholding. We behold from within our oneing, bewedded with the knowledge that arises through love, however delicately and darkly.

---

[14] Ibid., see, Ch. 9.
[15] Martin Laird "'Whereof We Speak': Gregory of Nyssa, Jean-Luc Marion and Current Apophatic Rage," *Heythrop Journal* Vol. 42, No.1, 2001, 4.
[16] Martin Laird, *Gregory of Nyssa and the Grasp of Faith: Union, Knowledge, and Divine Presence* (Oxford: Oxford University Press, 2004), 144.

Although it is customary to dismiss this Logos seeing as being indescribable, and it is, there are nuances to this Logos fullness of the divine Silence that speaks the Word infused with Wisdom in our hearts. In my experience, Logos fullness awakens Sophia-Wisdom.

This fullness imparts an abiding sense of ever-grounding trust in Love's continual incarnating, infusing an abundance of meaning. This way of knowing through beholding in such a way that the Word says itself through our words and deeds, we could also say, creates a metaphysics of oneing. We abandon the metaphysics of subject-object seeing and our oneing in the Word becomes the first principle of interpretation. The grace of contemplation informs our vision and action. And importantly, as Laird affirms, the discourse that emerges is not language that seeks to understand God, but language that is full of God. This wisdom that arises from our union in the Word, in the *perichoresis* of Trinitarian loving, colours how we see, how we speak and what we do. We see from within the conception of the divine in the human. We see from within expectancy. We see with hope. In the oneness of illumined realisation, we know we are ever knit in the knot and oned in the oneing of divine love continuing to incarnate through us. We know we are evolution becoming conscious of itself. We know we are One.

Interpreting the Texts

Thus, the interpretation of the mystical texts in this book is located within this hermeneutic of beholding. As interpreter of the texts, grounded in the ground of the texts, I bring my own voice to sing in harmony with each mystic present in the text, who speaks from his or her own experience and historical time, drawing on unique vocabulary, images and cultural mores. While I invite you, the reader, to be aware of their cultural distance, I will not increase this distance by analysing their writings through a subject-object polarity. Rather, I invite you to behold in the way the author who wrote the text beholds, to ponder, to ruminate, to plunge into a subject-subject harmony. Within this dynamism of oneing in the ground of the text, I invite you to enter the text as subject, ever attentive to the dance between silence, word and silence, as the text speaks out through you. Together, as the text continues to reveal itself, we can then appropriate wisdom about contemplation, relevant for this pivotal turning point in evolution. Paul Ricoeur, in his seminal writings about hermeneutics, reminds us that to appropriate a text (*aneignung*), is "'to make it one's own,'" so that "interpretation brings together, equalises, renders contemporary and similar."[17] In meeting these mystics in the field of oneing, we seek to enter into their original intentions as much as possible, and at the same time, expand our consciousness as reader by actualizing the meaning of the text in our lives. "Appropriation," Ricoeur reminds us, "is a dialectical concept: the counterpart of the timeless distanciation."[18] The language of these mystics is timeless. Because they composed their texts from the ground of contemplation, they continue to speak from the hidden depths of this ground, in the heart-language of contemplative knowing. Each mystic invites us to join in the dialectic of unknowing and knowing, in the ongoing revelation of divine love. It is here we meet, in this revelatory moment, in the intimacy of oneing in the divine. Together, we evolve in God. Importantly, Ricoeur reminds us, the appropriation of a text is not an act of possession. Rather it is an act of dispossession.[19] It is intrinsically *kenotic*. Our egoic conceptual mind must yield into unknowing, into love, into an evolving interpretive oneing consciousness in the ground of consciousness itself, that is divine Love.

In entering into this revelatory moment that is the oneing of contemplation, the wisdom that arises from this ground of consciousness has an essential contribution to make to the ongoing task of theology, to utter words about the mystery of divine Love, as faith seeks understanding. Sarah Coakley upholds this foundational nature of contemplation for any theological expression of the divine mystery. All we say must be informed by contemplation. Reason must be expressed in relation to grace and continue to be transformed by the ongoing revelation of Spirit infusing wisdom. I am reminded of the seminal words of Evagrius, "If you are a theologian, you will truly pray. And if you pray truly, you are a theologian."[20] Similarly, Jean-Luc Marion's post-modern perspective that theo-*logy* must be *theo*-logy concurs as the *theo*-logian, is not taught, "since it (*the logia*) is encountered by mystical union. And yet, one must speak *of* him."[21] Marion affirms that what we speak must be words filled with Logos, filled with love. The Word must speak directly through a heart that is emptied and oned to

---

[17] Paul Ricoeur, *Hermeneutics and the Human Sciences*, trans. and ed. John Thompson (Cambridge: Cambridge University Press, 1983), 185.
[18] Ibid.
[19] Ibid.
[20] See, Evagrius the Solitary, "On Prayer," in *The Philokalia: The Complete Text Compiled by St Nikodimos of the Holy Mountain and St Makarios of Corinth*, Vol. 1, trans. G.E.H. Palmer, Philip Sherrard and Kallistos Ware (New York: Faber and Faber, 1979), 62.
[21] Jean-Luc Marion, *God Without Being,* trans. Thomas Carlson (Chicago: University of Chicago Press, 2012), 185.

God. Marion stresses that we must abandon every linguistic initiative to the Word, in order to let ourselves be said by the Word, "as the Word lets himself be said by the Father – him, and in him, us also … our language will be able to speak about G⊗d only to the degree that G⊗d, in his Word, will speak our language and teach us in the end to speak it as he speaks it – divinely, which means to say in all abandon."[22] In this abandonment into contemplation, in silence and stillness, the Word speaks the Word's self in us. Contemplation and the wisdom that arises from contemplation is essential to any Christian theology.

Sarah Coakely further qualifies that this privileging of contemplation necessary to any theologising is not a quest to simply authenticate religious experience. Rather, it demands:

> an attentive openness of the whole self (intellect, will, memory, imagination, feeling, bodiliness) to the reality of God and of the creation. Through the 'interruption' of the Spirit, the authority of the revelatory Word is continually and freshly encountered and expounded – by a 'reason' which is itself in process of disclosure. It follows that *théologie totale* involves an ongoing journey of purgative transformation and change.[23]

Hence, the attentive openness of our whole self to the Logos within us, and within all creation, which transforms our intellect, will, memory, imagination, feeling, and bodiliness, is indispensable in this process of disclosure. And I would accentuate that the contemplative knowing of heart-awareness that arises from the ground of oneing, is irreplaceable. Illuminating the wisdom that infuses as we become more reflexively turned into the ground of our heart, abandoned into the indwelling Word, who is one with the Silence who speaks the Word, is pivotal. Seeing from within the oneing love of the threefold loving of Silence-Word and Spirit within us, is the only way we can truly be present in the revelatory moment. We must humbly see through the eyes of the One who is revelation. In this abandonment to the revelatory moment, these mystical words need soft candlelight shone on them so they may glow if they choose, reveal their luminous transparency, or be allowed to touch us in the darkness of obscure love-knowledge. In the sacred spaciousness of the dancing silence, the Beloved speaks the Word in us as readers, as beloveds, as "I," personally and communionally.

---

[22] Ibid., 173.
[23] Sarah Coakley, *God, Sexuality, and the Self: An Essay 'On the Trinity'* (Cambridge: Cambridge University Press, Kindle Edition, 2013), 88.

The Writer

Each of these mystics is significant in my journey of discovering my Christic nature. I write as a married woman deeply enriched by the love of my husband and friend in communion. This sacred marriage creates an ambiance for the mystical marriage, and in the timeless sense of *oneing,* I experience the two as one, not separate. Both enhance each other. Both enable me to evolve into the love that is the ground of all being. As a small child, I had a sense of the Holy Mystery that became ever present to me in my sacred place under the daphne bush. Its beauty and aroma would fill my senses, immerse me in love and infuse a feeling of oneness as it carried me beyond time into eternity. Over the years as I've entered into Silence, I would encounter Jesus of the gospels. I lived with him, experienced his absence, suffered and died with him and spent time in the tomb of many dark nights. Senses and spirit were darkened and filled with love, until the deep inner recesses of my heart opened and I discovered an abyss of Love. Jesus became Beloved, *my* Lover. There was a long phase of meeting in the wine cellar, as Jesus became the Christ in a gradual infusing of one in another. Slowly, gently, two lovers no longer met. We met as one. My heart-self awakened, my heart-self lost in the Christ-self, lost in each other. Now, we/I see darkly, through one eye of love, we/I see from oneness, we/I see all is one love.

My spiritual, theological formation is grounded in the showings of Julian of Norwich, as I lived in her *showings* for many years while writing my doctoral thesis on her understanding of salvation. In this research, I developed a soteriology of oneing that explored how the whole cyclical journey from God to God is an evolutionary oneing of all things in God, from our gifted origins until our graced fulfilment. Put simply, the way of soteriology is the way of oneing love. When I began my research, I was struggling to understand how the journey to self and the journey to God are one and the same journey. Julian appreciated how it is easier to know God than it is to know our own soul. I remember clearly the day my understanding expanded, when I was pondering Julian's words, "in the first we have our being." Our being is in Unmade-Love. My being, my substance, my essence is in God, and God is in my sensuality. I am knit to God in the making. This endless, creative point where I am knit began to stir within me. The psalmist sang with the voice of endless love: "In the womb before the dawn, I begot you" (Ps 110.3). Light poured through my being enclosing and be-closing me in the endless oneing of the Trinity, beyond, and now, in space-time. My whole identity changed. I discovered myself as belonging to and participating *in* Christ. From the mystical infusion in my Beloved, I awoke in the Trinity breathing in the breath of Trinitarian loving. My sense that all creation is breathing in this creative dance of Trinitarian Love begetting Love expanded. In recent years, the continual pouring out of love and Christic consciousness encourages me to delight in a future filled with the dance of *oneing*, as Omega expands in consciousness and enables all of us, in communion, to see in the fullness of Love that "all shall be well".

This book gathers together insights from many years as a theologian at Australian Catholic University, from the wisdom of the many students I have taught and from the decades I have spent as a spiritual director accompanying directees and giving retreats to beautiful people deeply engaged in this mystical journey of love. As I have been writing this book, I often walk to a trickling creek with my dog, Mollie. The luminosity of Presence infuses me in stillness, Logos-Sophia numinously shines through the grey green bush. The silence of eternally rooted trees grounds and draws me into the being of Love. Delicate intricate spiders' webs sparkle and centre me in in their empty centre. Against the buzz of distant traffic, the water captivates my attention as it ripples, bubbles and sings – calming, releasing, purifying my consciousness. A goanna gazes as I dance Tai Chi. Fish gently glide in circles, dragonfly wings dance in transparency. Birds sing announcing the *point de vierge* of this contemplative moment. Silence, stillness, nature's enstasy drawing me deeper into the point of oneness. Nature's ecstasy expanding out in circles of love, family, spiritual companions, the suffering of the world, all drawn into this oneing. All is held in Omega. Aboriginal spirits share their song-lines of wisdom, inviting me into dream-time. All is in All – one being, one ground of Love in Love evolving, endlessly creating one Love. In the afternoons, I join the Contemplative Evolution Network in meditation, as we seek to unite with the suffering of the world and create a contemplative noosphere.

This Book

While there are a growing number of excellent books on contemplation, few have explored a praxis approach that begins in life experience, and then leads into an in-depth study of a range of classical Christian mystic texts, drawing out implications for a contemporary growth in the practice of contemplation and rise of nondual consciousness. The book is written in response to a growing number of mature contemplatives already steeped in the central movements in the journey of being one and living in the dynamism of oneing in God, who have asked me to write this, because they seek more nuanced wisdom on the how to nurture heart-awareness, discern and foster a more stable contemplation. Although contemplation is neither a skill, nor a method, but a gift of grace, there are within the Christian mystical tradition a reservoir of delicate nuances that enable the seeker to nurture and fine-tune responses to the presence of the Spirit which we will explore. While remaining true to the published texts, wherever possible, I have tried to integrate inclusive language, so we may behold all humankind within the *Imago Dei*. This is not simply a preference, but a theological necessity for any words about the Mystery of Love must humbly seek to reflect the oneing of the One.

The chapters are organised thematically within the rhythm of the paschal mystery, with three main sections *Beholding in Oneing, Suffering in Oneing, Communion in Oneing*, that highlight central movements in the journey of being one and living in the dynamism of oneing in God. As the reader enters into this dynamism, the implicit transformation of the paschal movement draws the reader into a deep transformation in Christ, crucified, risen and continuing to incarnate through us. Following this introduction, the first section of the book *Beholding in Oneing*, lays the foundations for the reader to awaken a way of contemplative beholding. Julian's way of beholding and her teaching about how prayer ones the soul to God, along with the *Cloud of Unknowing* seer's blind beholding of the stirrings of love within our heart, prepare the reader to enter into the ground of the birth of the Word in the soul that Meister Eckhart exquisitely illuminates. With this awakening of the Logos/ Sophia within, the reader is then ready to gaze with the eye of love on the mystery of suffering in love, in the second section, *Suffering in Oneing*. Mechthild of Magdeburg's *kenosis* of flowing light and Clare of Assisi's mirror of the cross that becomes the mirror of eternity, offer a way to live the cycle of dying and rising. The dark nights of John of the Cross extend this insight into personal and communal suffering and prepare the reader for the rising dawn of resurrection luminosity. In the third section of the book, *Communion in Oneing*, we highlight Pierre Teilhard de Chardin's exploration of the role of creative union in the rise of unitive consciousness, along with Beatrice Bruteau's development of enstatic-ecstatic Trinitarian communion consciousness. Ilia Delio, then invites us to embrace the holy wholeness of our oneness in Omega love, so that this holographic vision informs our every-day awareness.

These thematic ponderings are reflections to encourage prayer, to invite deeper rumination of the love we dwell within. Each chapter elucidates how, when we draw on the language of heart yearnings, poetry and theological insights that flow from prayer, we are encouraged to go deeper, to risk a further pouring out of our heart in love, to trust the oneing. Our awareness of how all of reality is impregnated in divinity magnifies. Each of these mystics inspire us to undergo the necessary dyings and risings that free us to enter into the ground of Christ consciousness into the evolving oneing consciousness of the Trinity. A *contemplatio* at the end of each chapter then enables the wisdom of each mystic to be embodied and lived.

I

Beholding in Oneing

I

Beholding and Oneing in the Ground of the Heart

Julian of Norwich

I want those you have given me to be with me where I am.

John 17:24

When a soul comes into itself, and abides in beholding,
the beholding is blissfully set in God,
wonning (dwelling) within the soul.
For humanity's soul is God's very wonning place.[1]

The radiance of a humble purple crocus stretching through melting snow, holds my memory of Norwich. It was a dark time in my life, a winter season where there were many dyings, when I made a pilgrimage to Julian's cell. To have this time with Julian was precious to me, so my longing, my desire, my deepest yearning was to yield into the promise of the darkness until it carried me into the mysterious, depthless, endlessly fertile way of oneing. I did not know how, but I knew to trust that this was the path I must take. Day by day, I sat with Julian, one

---

[1] *The Writings of Julian of Norwich*, A *Vision Showed to Devout Woman and A Revelation of Love*, eds, Nicholas Watson and Jacqueline Jenkins (Pennsylvania: Pennsylvania State University, 2006), S:16.68.25-29.

with her in the ground of her womb-like cell and garden, filled with the wound of her longing. Words in my journal touch into my felt sense:

> In the darkness of an unquenchable wound of longing, I follow Julian's stirrings, beholding an abyss of opaque darkness that seems depthless, endless. Like an anchoress enclosed in her room, there is a loneliness that feels overwhelming, as if it will never release me. Yearning, searching, seeking, I long for your oneing love to enfold me.

Days turned into night and into day, as I surrendered into the loneliness and waited in the silence of Julian's cell, in the gentle sunlight of her garden, and in the stillness of the Catherine room in Norwich Cathedral, with my wound of longing exposed and gaping. I yearned for the gift of oneing. Spring came, as bulbs and yellow kerria blossomed. The blackbird's song caressed my spirit and I found myself gently, softly infused in spring's warmth of hope, in a gentle oneing.

I returned to Julian's cell eighteen years later. This time, I felt my whole being transformed into a luminous emptiness that was so very intimate, expansive, embracing. I had a sense of the exchange of love taking place in the eye of my heart, in my way of seeing, of beholding. The yearning felt empty, beyond longing, until mysteriously the eye of my heart was drawn to behold in beholding, to be the beholding in the oneing, and open into an abyss of absence that felt so fertile, so loving. I write in my journal:

> I feel the oneing, the translucency of being in one another, the *noughting* awareness of turning into you my Beloved, the ground of my being, the ground of my prayer. You draw me into yourself, into the closed, enclosing of the Trinity. Infused in you, Beloved, my Christic lover, I feel the point of pure stillness, the exquisite silence, the love making of the turning, that opens into love infusing love, in a spacious enfolding, embracing, enclosing in one another.

> We intertwine in the luminous sharing of love, creating a love knot, as every point of our oneing kisses, radiates and expands, breathing radiant beauty endlessly. Our Christic being knows the gift of *noughting* that is oneing, an opaqueness that is resplendent, an intimacy that dissolves. The busy noise of life continues all around Julian's cell, yet the silence infuses and strengthens and creates a harmonious sense of all of life impregnated in Love's silence. In the soft light of Julian's cell, the world becomes radiant, shining like droplets of water touched by the sun. "All our living is prayer," Julian says, in this graceful oneing.

Julian has shared with me so much about beholding and oneing and continues to teach me how to turn all that I am into the infinite enfolding Trinitarian love within the depthless depths of my heart, so that I may live within the flowing light of Wisdom's stirrings. Julian's way of beholding and her teachings about how prayer ones the soul to God, offer us a trustworthy path to follow as we seek to become filled with the Word, who is also Wisdom-Sophia, and awaken to see from within the mind of Christ within our own heart. Julian is a gifted English mystical visionary with profound insights into the oneness of Love. She is unique in her ability to enable us, as Ilia Delio says: "to engage evolutively in love."[2] Hence, Julian's profound mystical insights will create the foundations for all we will read about Love's oneing as the book unfolds.

Julian of Norwich – Beholding Love

Light shines through every word of Julian's *Revelations of Divine Love*. Like the vibrant colours of stained-glass windows illuminating the dark interior of a cathedral, her words infuse us in light revealing the multi-layered facets of our soul oned in God. Though we have little historical detail about Julian's life (1346-1420), because of her vibrant theology of Christ as mother and the powerful image of a dead child lying in the mud, scholars tend towards thinking she was a married noble woman, who later in life became an anchoress attached to St Julian's Church Norwich. Julian composes her texts at the eve of reformation, in turbulent times like our own, where from the midst of enormous communal heart ache, fear, loss of trustworthy leaders and the continued articulation of a punitive theology, she encounters the unconditional love of the Christ. She tells us how, when she was thirty, she had a severe illness where she thought she was going to die. As she lies in a darkened room, lingering in the *pointe*[3] between life and death, she beholds the tender face of Christ, on a softly carved bone crucifix. She portrays how as she sets her eyes on the cross, a radiance emanates from the face of Christ. Julian becomes immersed in the presence of Christ, which she identifies as a showing. When she recovers, she writes of her *Revelation of Love*, in a short text, that has an immediate, visual quality. After many years of re-entering these showings in contemplation, she composes her long text that is a spiritual and theological masterpiece. She writes

---

[2] Ilia Delio, *The Unbearable Wholeness of Being: God Evolution and the Power of Love* (New York: Orbis Books, 2013), 196.
[3] S: ii.42.

of her encounter with divine love, in beautiful Middle English, for her "even-christians." "Even," emphasises communion, equality in our oneing in the Christ, and the centrality of our relational identity. These showings that Julian receives, move her so deeply into oneness in Christ, that this same homely and courteous love pours out from her heart to all. She speaks from the mutual indwelling of the oneing of her heart, one in the communal human heart, one in Christ's heart.

This Chapter

In this chapter, we will focus on what Julian teaches us about beholding and seeing from within the ground of the heart and the foundational insights she has into human-cosmic becoming as oneing.[4] Initially, we will explore how she teaches us to behold and see by beholding in beholding and then focus on her threefold way of prayer that ones us to Christ our ground, who becomes the deep wisdom of the Trinity our mother. We will then see how in this oneing we are closed and enclosed in the Trinity, as the Trinity is enclosed in us. This will help us illume how Julian's beholding and oneing enlightens our understanding of contemplation and contemplative practice.

Beholding Julian's Showings

All Julian's showings are a beholding. They are a contemplation on love. They begin in the dark with a bodily sight that she describes in fleshy detail: "Suddenly, I saw the red blood trickling down from under the crown of thorns, hot and freshly, plenteously and lively, just as it was when the garland of thorns was pressed into his head."[5] We can picture the crown of thorns, the flow of the red blood trickling, and the pathos on the face of the vulnerable, wounded Christ. Although Julian draws us into the imagery of this flow of love pouring out, she reminds us that this sight is "without any *meane* (cause)."[6] This sight of the wounded Christ has no origin, it comes from God. It is a showing of love, that draws her into Christ, to behold, to be present to and to participate in this "great

---

[4] When I first explored a soteriology of *oneing* in the 1980's as far as I knew, *oneing* was not part of the general spiritual vocabulary. Oneing was translated as union, so I needed to argue a case for adopting the term. Now, thanks to the journal of Richard Rohr titled *Oneing*, the term has become part of contemporary spiritual vocabulary. See Hide, *Gifted Origins to Graced Fulfilment: The Soteriology of Julian of Norwich* (Collegeville: Liturgical Press, 2001), 52-54.
[5] S: 1.4.1-3.
[6] S: 1.4.5.

oneing between Christ and us."[7] While, one could dismiss these showings as mere visionary literature, Julian's choice of the word "showing," alerts us to the ongoing revelatory nature of this bodily sight that leads to words forming in her understanding and beyond into spiritual sight and more spiritual sight.[8] She invites her readers to behold and see how, in seeing a bodily sight of her wounded Lover's head bleeding, "in this same time," she sees a spiritual sight of Christ's homely loving. Her phrase "in the same time" reinforces a timeless, space-less, sense of presence, where multiple layers of Love's meaning spontaneously unfold. Simultaneously, she is drawn beyond words, into the silence of oneing, and beholds how this wounded one, "is our clothing, who for love, wraps us, winds around us, embraces us, hangs about us, and encloses us, in a tender love that never leaves us."[9] This wrapping, winding, embracing, enclosing movement of Christ endlessly enfolding us flows throughout her whole text. All her showings, she says "are grounded and oned"[10] in this sight of Christ, wounded, risen and enfolding humankind.

So, this is how we must behold Julian's showings, from within this being enfolded within the Christ, within the showing. As we enter into this embrace, into the text, there is an implicit fluidity, a flow, that draws us into an endless oneing. Gradually, as the showings continue, we see how at the same time we behold the suffering of the wounded body of Christ and the spiritual sight of Christ's homely loving, we behold the Trinity. There is a multilayered infusing sense of Christ's homely love that fills our heart with joy. In this enfolding love, we are wrapped and enfolded in Christ in the Trinity. Thus, Julian awakens our sensual imagination, until in the beholding we are drawn into an enclosure in the Christ, that immerses us in the secret depths of spiritual in-sight that continually unfolds the depths of Trinitarian loving. Julian keeps us present, grounded in the present moment, be-holding. She gives us time and space to behold, to be and to hold, to become one with all that we perceive.

Beholding

At the beginning of Julian's showings, Christ says, "behold and see."[11] For Julian, beholding involves seeing deeply, seeing with the eye of our heart,

---

[7] S: 8.18.11.
[8] S: 1.9.28.
[9] S: 1.5.1-5.
[10] S: 1.6-7.
[11] S: 1.35.

"beholding spiritually, marvelling in unmeasurable love."[12] Julian's beholding is Ecce Ecce, beholding the wounded one, with echoes of centuries of lovers of Christ beholding, pouring into this beautiful word. Beholding is seeing from the point of our shared identity in Christ where we are knit and oned. For Julian then, beholding is contemplation. To behold, is to be and to hold all that we encounter in a loving abiding, mutual indwelling, until we are the beholding and behold from within beholding. Beholding is intrinsically kenotic as it involves noughting, emptying ourselves of all conceptualisations, as we pour out our heart in love. Therefore, if we desire to awaken this way of beholding, we must enter into silence, yield into the desire of our Beloved, awaken the soft penetrating gaze of the eye of our heart, turn into the flow of the loving of our Beloved, lingering, surrendering, softly remaining and resting our vision in a malleable darkness. Gently, almost motionlessly, attentive to the stirrings of Love's vibrational energy, beholding then opens us into the organically enfolding, embracing, enclosing movement of Love's oneing in us. Beholding affects us at a spiritual and cellular level, transforming us into the subject of our beholding, changing every particle of our being through the light of grace that is organically within us, until we are the beholding. As the solitary Maggie Ross observes: "Silence and beholding are our natural state."[13]

Julian provides a brief, yet prevailing example of this way of beholding in the spiritual sight of Christ's wounded heart. After some dynamically vivid, intensely conversational scenes of Christ's dying, this showing of the risen Christ, who is still on the cross, has a heightened numinous, luminous quality about it, as the risen Christ exudes "glad cheer."[14] In this showing, the risen one, whose face is shining with joy, looks into his wounded side and beholds. Julian carefully describes how, "with his sweet looking, he leads the understanding of his creature by the same wound, into his side within."[15] Here we see highlighted a critical movement in this way of beholding that is essential for us to appropriate if we are to understand her text. So, let us now enter into this showing with Julian and behold. Notice how the beholding begins with Julian's gaze meeting the gaze of the Christ, until she is drawn into the "sweet looking" of Christ, so that she

---

[12] S: 1.6.46-47.
[13] Maggie Ross, *Writing the Icon of the Heart: In Silence Beholding* (Abington: The Bible Reading Fellowship, 2011), 11.
[14] S: 10.24.1.
[15] S: 10.24.1-2. This beholding mirrors Jn 19:34, where the soldier pieces Christ's side with a lance. Julian would be familiar with the many illuminations of this moment in John. This wound is also associated with the cleft in the rock, becoming a resting place for one praying, Sg 2:14.

beholds from within his beholding. As eye meets eye, and the looking becomes one loving beholding, Christ takes her into his wound, into his vulnerability, into his heart. Julian's beholding is an intensely *kenotic noughting*, as she pours out all her love, her whole being and enters into the darkness of Christ's wound, his pain, his suffering. She empties into the hollow, into the emptiness, until she dwells within the heart of Christ. There is a pure silence in the text, ineffable being in one another in the wound, the oneing, as Christ's looking draws her into his gaze. Julian's heart-perception is drawn deeper, until her understanding is one with Christ's understanding. Her understanding arises from within the depths of the heart of Christ. There is an unspoken sense that Julian's understanding, her heart-wisdom, has entered into, has become one with Christ's understanding, Christ's heart-mind. For Julian, to understand, is to be drawn into the same sweet looking as the Christ's, to behold, to pour out her heart until in ineffable wisdom, she perceives as Christ perceives, understands with the same heart-mind as the Christ. She receives the gift of ineffable spiritual sight.[16]

Julian invites us into a profound *kenosis* of allowing our understanding, or the mind of our heart, to be drawn into the heart of Christ, so that our looking and Christ's looking become one "sweet looking." This is how we must behold and see, from the ground of our shared identity, that we received in our first creation, when we were knit and oned in Christ. Simultaneously then, just as Julian's Christ draws her within, into a single vibrant luminosity, she invites us, her readers, to behold and see: "a fair and delectable place large enough for all humankind, …to rest in peace and love."[17] In the mystical depths of heart understanding, Julian beholds and sees that all humankind are at rest in peace and love, in Christ. Here, we see how beholding the bodily sight of Christ, yields into words forming in her understanding, into more and more spiritual sight. The

---

[16] As Julian uses the term, "understanding" there are resonances of Augustine's memory, understanding and will, the image of the Trinity within the mind of our soul. See, *De Trinitate* XIV in Barry Ulanov, *Prayers of St. Augustine* (Minneapolis: Seabury Press, 1983), 127. When Julian speaks of words forming in her understanding, or her understanding being drawn within, she is referring to the knowing that arises from the mind of her soul that is within the midst of her heart, which we have in God in our first making. She also speaks of understanding as knowing by reason, or being answered in her reason. This reason is more in keeping with the *nous,* intellect, eye of the soul, or inmost mind of the heart that understands divine truths by immediate experience, intuition, or simple cognition. In the Orthodox tradition *nous* is not to be confused with *dianoia*, reason that functions through formulating abstract concepts and arguing conclusions. See, *The Philokalia: The Complete Text Compiled by St Nikodimos of the Holy Mountain and St Makarios of Corinth*, Vol. 1, trans. G.E.H. Palmer, Philip Sherrard and Kallistos Ware (New York: Faber and Faber, 1979), 362. Thus, understanding arises from: "the clear light of our reason, and the steadfast mind which we have of God in our first making, at the time our soul is inspired in our body and we are made sensual" S: 14.56.12-13.

[17] S: 10.24.3-7.

wounded-risen body of Christ becomes "the body of Christ," in the deeply Pauline sense of communion in the Christic body.

In contemporary language, we could say Christ consciousness awakens in Julian. In an intense oneing in love, she becomes one with Christ, the ground of Love, one with all humankind at rest, one with the luminous presence, who says: "See, how I love you."[18] The light of grace arises in her awareness,[19] as she sees with the heart-perception of her shared identity with Christ in the ground of her soul. Julian beholds and sees that in the innermost vision of who we are, all of humanity rests in peace and love in the heart of Christ. This is our home, our everlasting dwelling. In short, this way of beholding is entering into, and indwelling the heart of Christ until, in silence beholding, we are oned.

Perceptively, Julian affirms how Christ is present to us, oneing us within the Christ self, in a way that enables understanding to arise from our being within one another. There is no object of beholding. No separate me beholding. There is one beholding. In this one beholding, what overflows into our understanding makes us more like Christ. Thus, I would suggest, beholding is always about becoming one with Christ. It forms our Christic identity. Importantly, this Christic identity is a dynamic identity, a oneing identity, so that ontologically our being in Christ is fluid, active, enfolding, enclosing, always evolving. For Julian, the understanding that arises from this beholding and oneing is what we might call, "the oneing consciousness of the mind of the soul of our heart." This oneing consciousness is not so much a heart awareness, as "heart-awareing." As our heart awareness blossoms, the realisation in the very substance of our love-knot being oned in God, infuses a sense of indefinable ceaseless peace, silence, joy. We simply are in pure consciousness, pure existence. In the bliss of sheer presence, our love is consummated in the one who is all in All (Col 3:11).

Abiding in Beholding and Oneing

We may ask, how do we prepare to awaken this way of beholding? Julian's response is clear: "Prayer ones the soul to God."[20] Julian gives us a threefold flowing, enfolding, enclosing movement, or way of entering into the silence of beholding, by responding to the desire of Christ and turning into the ground of our heart. Initially, Christ says to us, "I am the ground." "First, it is my will."

---

[18] S: 10.24.15-16.
[19] S: 16.78.2-3.
[20] S: 14.43.1.

Secondly, Christ describes the manner and how we should pray by turning our will into his will, enjoying. Thirdly, the fruit and end of our prayer is to become one and like Christ in all things.[21] In this gentle flow, we are simply drawn by the desire of Christ, to turn into the ground of our heart, into the presence of the Christ, enjoying. This turning into Christ makes us one and Christ-like. Julian affirms: "when a soul comes into itself, and abides in beholding, the beholding is blissfully set in God...*wonning* (indwelling) within the soul. For humanity's soul is God's very *wonning* place."[22] We abide in beholding, until our whole being is "*set,*" still, abiding in God. Hence, with our awareness stably in God, *wonning* or indwelling, there is no separate me beholding. There is only one beholding. Observe also, how "*wonning,*" incorporates the enstatic, silent, still, sitting, dwelling, of being within one another with the dynamism of "oneing," emphasising how oneing infers indwelling. In turning into the oneing in our heart's depths, our natural indwelling within divine love is illumed by the light of grace, until we see from within this *wonning*. Each of the three flowing movements in Julian's prayer of oneing is critical for this *wonning* to illuminate our conscious awareness, so we will focus on each in turn.

I am the Ground

Christ's words "I am the ground,"[23] are foundational, the caveat, for Julian's way of prayer, infusing each of the three movements. Therefore, we will explore its meaning before we turn to the three-fold way, for it is in this ground of our shared identity that mystical union takes place. When we come to prayer, nakedly, fully and homely,[24] to behold, Christ addresses us personally, saying "I am the ground." Christ identifies himself as "I," subject of our heart. This "I" is the (*I it am,*) the "I am," the One who Is, Presence, pure consciousness, "the one who is our being, the one who is our meaning, the one who is all."[25] This initial awareness that Christ is our ground is so central to all that we will explore about contemplation. Indeed, Wolfgang Rielle suggests, that "*grounde*" is the leitmotif

---

21   S: 14.42.1-8.
22   S: 16.68.25-29.
23   S: 14.41.8. Denise N. Baker, in "The Structure of the Soul and the 'Godly Wille' in Julian of Norwich's Showings," *The Medieval Mystical Tradition in England, Exeter Symposium VII*, ed. E.A. Jones (London: DS Brewer, 2004), 38, suggests this ground echoes Augustine's "fundus animae memoria." Literally, "fundus" is the deepest part of an organ, what is farthest from the opening, such as a uterus. See, https://en.wiktionary.org/wiki/fundus.
24   S: 1.5.29.
25   S: 12.26.7-11.

of the Long Text.[26] We will see how in identifying Christ as our ground, Julian affirms humankind's oned identity in Christ, and our ongoing dynamic grounding, or oneing in the ground.[27] "I am the ground" becomes a mantra, calming, stilling, calling us to prayer, drawing us deeper into the ground of our heart, into the heart of Christ, into a homely oneing in Christ our ground.

In this ground of shared identity in Christ, we are so one, that our oneness extends not only to what Julian calls our substantial soul, but also in the sensual dimension of our soul. As we saw with the showing of the heart of Christ, Julian draws us into the ground of our soul, where we are at rest in God:

> God (Christ) is nearer to us than our own soul. For God is ground in whom our soul stands, and God is the means who keeps the substance and the sensuality together so that they shall never be separate. For our soul sits in God in true rest, and our soul stands in God in sure strength. And our soul is naturally rooted in God in endless love.[28]

Julian invites us to linger with this sense of Christ as the ground of our soul, to truly know how in this ground, it is not possible for either our substance, or sensuality, to be separated from Christ. They are together, oned in Christ. Substance and sensuality are important terms for Julian, for in our substance in God, "we are who we are."[29] Julian upholds the mutual indwelling of our substance in God when she says: "Our soul is made to be God's *wonning* (indwelling), and the *wonning* of our soul is in God, who is unmade. It is a high understanding inwardly, to see and to know that God…dwells in our soul. And an even higher understanding to see and to know that our soul…dwells in God in substance."[30] This mutual *wonning* of God in our substance is so in God, that Julian can say, "I saw no difference between God and our substance. It is as if it

---

[26] Wolfgang Rielle, *The Middle English Mystics* (London: Routledge and Kegan, 1981), 156.

[27] Julian's ground language resembles Meister Eckhart's use of "ground-grunt," where he says: "God's ground is my ground and my ground is God's ground," but her foundational principle of being knit and oned in Christ in substance and sensuality has a stronger sense of distinguishing us as a unique person, in Christ, in communion with all humankind, than we will see in Eckhart's more undifferentiated ground-grunt. See, *The Complete Mystical Works of Meister Eckhart*, trans. and ed. Maurice O'C Walshe (New York: Crossroad, 2009), 109. Scholars speculate as to whether Julian was influenced by Eckhart as there was a Dominican priory in Norwich in her day that may have kept his writings.

[28] S: 14.56.9-12.

[29] S: 14.54.12. We will see that substance is a term used by John of the Cross to describe our essence.

[30] S: 14.54.8-12.

is all God."[31] In contemporary terms, our substance is our essential, true-self, or what I identify as our heart-self. And importantly, for Julian our substance is not a thing, or a place, but the image of Christ, that places us in the Trinity. Our substance is our eternal Christic identity, our Christic consciousness that arises from our subsistence in Christ our ground. This oneness in substance is common enough in mystical literature, but Julian is unique in her way of drawing us beyond all soul-body splits, to perceive how, in Christ, our substance is never separated from our sensuality. She wants us to know this oneness in Christ in the ground within ourselves. Remarkably, Julian affirms the holiness of our sensuality, as she delights, "God is in our sensuality. For in the same point that our soul is made sensual, in the very same point is the city of God. Never leaving our sensual soul, God dwells blissfully without end."[32] This oneness in sensuality occurs when, "God knit Christ to our body in the maiden's womb, took our sensual soul and in the taking enclosed us in him."[33] Our substantial soul eternally oned in Christ is knit to our sensuality at the moment Christ becomes flesh. At this point, through our oneness in Christ, the image of the Trinity is knit into the centre-point of our sensual-soul. Our sensuality is the dwelling place of God.

And critically, for contemplation, substance and sensuality are now "together," knit and oned in Christ our ground. It is when we become blind to this essential unity of substance and sensuality in Christ, live in the illusion that our sensual-self is all there is, that the nothingness of sin manifests in and through our sensual wounding. In this feeble state, we suffer from the distortions caused by the split, a suffering we will explore in following chapters.[34] As we receive the gift of contemplation, we must be attentive to this feebleness, always knitting what feels separate, to Christ.[35] Hence, Julian says to us, "if we would have knowledge of our soul, and come to dalliance within, it behoves us to seek it in our God, in whom it is enclosed."[36] Julian encourages us to live in the unity of our substance and sensuality in the ground of our soul that is enclosed in Christ, in God. Her choice of the word dalliance, suggesting romance, intimacy, making love within

---

[31] S: 14.54.13.
[32] S: 14:55.20-24.
[33] S: 14:57.35-37.
[34] See, Hide, *Gifted Origins*, 97.
[35] S: 16.78.29.32.
[36] S: 14.56.14-15.

our soul, invites us to dally, to linger, to enjoy being within the ground of our soul enclosed in Christ.

Julian gives another glimpse of our oneness in the ground of our soul, when she describes how, "the mid-person would be the ground and head of this fair kind out of whom we all come and in whom we are all enclosed, and in whom we will all go."[37] There is a lovely play on imagery here, as she sees "our soul made of God and in the same *point* knit to God."[38] This point is the eternal point of our origin, "the blessed point from whence we come from God."[39] This point, where we are knit to God, mirrors Julian describing the point between life and death and her later saying she saw God in a point.[40] Eloquently, she further portrays this point as like being knit to God, "with a knot so subtle and so mighty that it is oned into God. In this oneing it is made endlessly holy."[41] This luminous love-knot is rich in multiple illusions that expand our appreciation of how Christ is our ground. While the knot concretely evokes a knot that unites two threads, it is also the knot tied between lovers, the knot in marriage, the knot of the inner kiss of oneness, the luminous knot of pure transcendence, the knot where paradox meets, the cosmic knot, the translucent spark, where the human and divine are oned. Moreover, although the imagery of the point and the love-knot has some resemblance to the *synderesis*,[42] as the knitting in the knot is the point where human and divine consciousness one, for Julian it is far more. This love-knot is the ground where we are endlessly in oneing love, in the mid-point of the Trinity.

---

[37] S: 14.53.25-28.
[38] S: 14.53.33.
[39] S: 14.63.4. For Julian, humanity shares in God's being without being God, for God is unmade being who shares being with us.
[40] S: 3.11.1; S: 16.81.4.
[41] S: 14.53.49-52.
[42] In brief, the *synteresis* (*synderesis*) emerged from St Jerome's (347–419) exegesis on Ezekiel's vision of the four living creatures (Ezek 1:4-28). Jerome identifies the fourth creature, the eagle, with *synderesis*, the spark of conscience which was not extinguished from the breast of Adam when he was driven from Paradise. The *synderesis* (a misspelling meaning to guard closely) was then identified with the *scintilla conscientiae*, the spark of conscience, the natural faculty of knowing, and choosing God. See, *Encyclopedia of Philosophy*, ttp://www.iep.utm.edu/synderes. Peter Lombard (d.1160) later paraphrases Jerome and speaks of the *scinitilla rationalis*, the spark of reason in the *intellectus,* the intellect of our spirit that knows God darkly. Subsequently, Thomas Gallus (1200-1246), places this highest point of contemplation within the *affectus,* the aspect of our spirit that is affected towards God. Hence, this spark becomes *scintilla affectus*. However, for Thomas Aquinas (1224/5-1274) the *synderesis* was the light of conscience that never dies. Thus, on one hand the *synderesis* is identified with the spark of reason that guides us to choose the good, and on the other, with the zenith of love in contemplation. Julian's point, love-knot and godly will, creatively knit the *scintilla affectus, scintillia rationalis* and *synderesis* as conscience together. See, Baker, "The Structure of the Soul," 47.

Ever-enclosed within this knitting enfolding oneing of the love-knot, we are one mysterious entwining of love. We indwell within a love-knot of oneing: "knit in the knot and oned in the oneing and made holy in the holiness."[43] Julian explicitly identifies the awakening of this point with contemplation when she says: "It is God's will that we set the point of our thought in this blissful beholding as often as we may, and stay there within, with God's grace. For this is a blessed contemplation to the soul who is led by God, that delights God."[44] As we set the point of our thought in beholding, Cynthia Masson suggests that the point, "acts as a point of access to the divine…as a point of access to the apophatic realm."[45] While this is true, in the sense that in setting all our thought into this oneing point, all cognitive perception dissolves, for Julian, this apophatic heart-mind realm has its own Christic consciousness. Julian invites us to behold from within this ground, to awaken what I will call a *"Christic ground awareness."* While this is "high and imperceivable,"[46] to our discursive mind, we do perceive through the unitive wisdom of love-knowledge within the ground of our heart that we are one. We will now explore this threefold, enfolding movement in prayer, where we will see how this *Christic ground awareness* naturally awakens in contemplation.

Turning Our Will, Enjoying and Oneing

First, It Is My Will

"First, it is my will,"[47] Christ affirms. These reassuring words of Christ, "It is my will, I make you *beseek* it and you do *beseek* it,"[48] encourage us to come to prayer whether we feel barren and dry, or filled with desire, because it is the will, the desire of Christ that stirs our desire and invites us to *beseek*. I maintain the Middle English, *be-seek*, because for Julian, literally *be-seeking,* is being, and seeking oneness in contemplation. Seeking has the quality of longing, searching, desiring. *Be-seeking* is not, as many suggest, petitionary prayer. In fact, Julian describes *be-seeking* as, "the true gracious lasting will of the soul, oned and

---

[43] S 14.53.53-54.
[44] S: 15.64.39-42.
[45] Cynthia Masson, "The Point of Coincidence: Rhetoric and the Apophatic in Julian of Norwich's Showings," *Julian of Norwich: A Book of Essays*, ed. Sandra McEntire (New York: Routledge, 1998), 163.
[46] S: 14.43.18.
[47] S: 14.42.4.
[48] S: 14.41.8-9.

fastened into the will of our God, by the sweet inner work of the Holy Spirit."[49] In be-seeking, we abandon ourselves to the Spirit within us, in an exquisite dance between being filled with desire, feeling the absence of the One we are seeking, *noughting*, yearning, feeling empty, until the absence itself fastens our will to the will of Christ. This fastening of our will awakens what Julian calls our "godly will," that is so whole and safe in Christ, it naturally wills as Christ wills.[50] This godly will contrasts with what Julian calls our "beastly will," that arises when our sensuality is split from our substance. Like a wild beast, this will is uncontrolled, unpredictable, capricious. We could identify this beastly will with a scattered, unfree, disturbed mind that is disconnected from the ground of our soul. So, the choice to *turn* our will, that arises from Christ's longing, involves the knitting and oneing of our beastly will into our godly will until, set in the point of beholding, there is only one divine will. This turning is a returning, a knitting, enfolding, centring into the point of our original oneness. Julian affirms, how in this prayer as we are so "oned into the sight and beholding of our Lover, … we pray only as God stirs us at the time."[51] Praying only as the Spirit stirs us incites joy.

Second, Turning Our Will, Enjoying

In this responsive turning our will into Christ's will, there is a delicate dance between being active and passive, as we turn and set the point of our thought in a blissful beholding, in the ground of our heart. Thus, turning is a loving, recollecting, enfolding, reflexive movement, a centring within, that knits every particle of our being into the eternal love knot, where substance and sensuality are one. The awareness of our discursive mind, senses, and all that feels feeble, turns into this indwelling, until there is no self-consciousness in the point of beholding, as "all our intent and all our might is set whole in beholding."[52] In other words, we become single pointed, silent, still, grounded, oned. Gradually, in the oneing, we see God in a point as the oneing of holographic vision arises in the mind of our heart. In this Christic ground awareness, we behold from our oneness in Christ, in the ground of our soul. One in this translucent beholding, Christ prays in us. Set, absorbed in Christ, seeing shifts from beholding Christ as

---

[49] S: 14.41.24-25.
[50] S: 13.14; 14:53.15.
[51] S:14.43.18-21.
[52] S:14.43.17-18.

the object of our awareness, to beholding from within the ground of our soul oned in Christ. We see as Christ sees. We behold from oneness.

This encircling into the point of the love-knot, that awakens a Christic ground awareness naturally becomes enjoying, as we reflect Christ's joy. We enjoy each other until we: "clearly know ourselves and fully have God, truly seeing, fully feeling, spiritually hearing, delectably smelling, sweetly swallowing ... until we see God face to face, homely and fully.[53] Julian shows us how, although any sense of this oneing in the ground occurs imperceivably, within the ground of our heart, and is not registered by our conscious mind, our perception is transfigured. We receive luminous touchings of grace. Wisdom-love knowledge arises in our heart's mystical senses, exuding joy. In *beseeking*, wisdom arises from the spacious silence of pure presence, awakening Christic ground awareness that gradually flows through the heart senses, into our consciousness mind, as we see, feel, hear, smell and swallow God. In a natural, homely way, these heart senses immerse us in a "face to face" encounter, or we might say, "face in face." In the ground, we understand that we participate in the fullness of divine love. While this endless oneing comes to fulfilment in being born into eternal life, we live in the joy of oneing now, ever becoming one and like Christ in all things.

Third, One and Like Christ

Hence, beholding Christ's light-filled words: "I am the ground," following the stirrings of love and turning into the ground that is Christ, into the dynamism of oneing and enjoying, transforms us. We become enfolded, closed, be-closed in Christ, creating what Maggie Ross calls "*en-Christing*."[54] In this enfolding, enclosing, en-Christing, we become not only the image of Christ in our ground, but like Christ in all things in our living. Julian's way of beholding opens us to the healing of any splits between substance and sensuality, and between the knowing of our heart and our conscious mind. Julian is quite unique in how her Christology of the ground then unravels, for as the flow between our Christic ground awareness and her conscious mind strengthens, she sees that Christ crucified and risen, is the deep wisdom of the Trinity our mother. Contemplation infuses an awareness that we participate in the divine nature and transcendent knowing of Christ as the deep wisdom of the Trinity. We become "wise in

---

[53]   S: 14.43.40-43.
[54]   Maggie Ross, *Silence: A User's Guide* (London: Darton, Longman and Todd), 3.

mind."⁵⁵ As well, we know the tender love and mercy of the enfleshed Christ continually giving birth to us. We realise Christ is ever present, ever birthing, evolving, becoming more flesh, more human, more love, in us. We discover the deepest identity of ourselves, in substance and sensuality oned in Christ. Ultimately, there is only one "I," one Christic identity.

Julian takes us into the mutuality of our *wonning* in Christ our ground, stressing how: "our very Mother, in whom we be endlessly born, we never shall come out of him … for we are enclosed in him and he is enclosed in us."⁵⁶ Thus for Julian, to be endlessly born, is to live in this rhythm of mutual indwelling, so that our whole life shimmers brightly with this pattern of inter-penetrating Love energy. Julian places us in this closing-enclosing dynamism:

> The almighty truth of the Trinity is our Father, for he made us and keeps us in him. And the deep wisdom of the Trinity is our Mother, in whom we are closed (*be closed*). The high goodness of the Trinity is our Lord, and in him we are closed (*be closed*) and he in us. And we are closed (*be closed*) in the Father and we are closed (*be closed*) in the Son, and we are closed in the Holy Spirit. And the Father is enclosed (*beclosed*) in us, the Son is enclosed (*beclosed*) in us and the Holy Spirit is enclosed (*beclosed*) in us, all mighty, all wisdom, one God, one Lord.⁵⁷

In the ineffable luminous vastness of the ground of our heart, we live within a closed, yet enfolding, enveloping, enclosing, encompassing, encircling relationality of being in one another. Julian's choice of language, closed and be-closed, enables her to convey the paradoxical nature of this enclosure. "Closed" stresses permanence, showing how human nature is knotted, fastened, sealed, locked within the depthless depths of the enstatic, mutual indwelling of the divine Lovers. Similarly, "be" or "en-closed," conveys a sense of ongoing inter-penetration and exchange that we experience through the Father creating and keeping us, Christ as deep wisdom and mother giving birth to us and the Spirit infusing us in goodness. In the deepest truth of who we are, in the depths of the

---

55   S: 14.53.32.
56   S: 14.57.42-43. Meister Eckhart, as we will see, also relates this being inborn to being enclosed and locked in the Trinity. See, *The Complete Mystical Works of Meister Eckhart*, trans. and ed., Maurice O'C Walshe (New York: Crossroad, 2009), 286.
57   S: 14.54.23-26. I have maintained the distinction between closed and be-closed made in the Paris text of Julian's Showings, as "*closed*" emphasises enstatic being within oneself, while "*beclosed*" evokes the dynamic ecstasy of continual self-sharing that we will explore with Beatrice Bruteau. See, *A Book of Showings to the Anchoress Julian of Norwich, Part Two*, eds. Edmund College and James Walsh (Toronto: Pontifical Institute of Medieval Studies, 1978), 563.

point of the love-knot, in the soul in the midst of our heart, we dwell within the closing, enclosing *oneing* of this ground of Trinitarian Love infusing us with might, wisdom and goodness.

As we become wise in mind, as Trinitarian consciousness becomes stronger in us, the might of the creativity of the Father and the deep wisdom of the Mother integrate with the goodness of the Spirit. This integration of masculine and feminine attributes within our essential goodness is critical to the awakening of our heart-mind and the arising of a oneing consciousness. Moreover, we see, how for Julian, words that form in our understanding, or what we come to know through reason,[58] arise from the deep wisdom of Christ who is our mother, making reason also a feminine principle, as well as the traditional masculine Logos energy within us, enabling us to integrate Word and Wisdom. We come to know from within this Trinitarian indwelling that is an enclosing. Truth, wisdom and goodness become ours as the image of the Trinity is illumed in our soul. Julian celebrates our enclosure in this Trinitarian identity reminding us that "it is Christ's liking to reign in our understanding blissfully, and sit in our soul restfully, and to *wonne* in our soul endlessly, working us into him."[59] Christ longs for us come to this blissful understanding, that infuses spiritual sight and more spiritual sight, beyond what words may say. From the ground of this restful indwelling, understanding arises infused with the joy of oneing.

Julian's Oneing

"Prayer ones the soul to God,"[60] Julian says so simply. Prayer is love oneing in us, until we are "oned and like our Beloved in all things." All our living is prayer, is a oneing. And so this vivacious word oneing and its derivatives: *"one,"* *"onying,"* *"ones,"* *"oned"*, becomes the essential principle of mystical union that holds all Julian's showings together. She shows us how we are so grounded in this oneing in Christ, in the unmade love of the Trinity, that the threefold movement of "love unmade, love made and love given"[61] is ever active within us, enfolding, enclosing, again-making. We come to know irrevocably how love unmade is God, Love made is our soul in God, that is constantly gifted with

---

[58] S: 15.67.23. Julian's reason then, is not the formulation of abstract concepts and arguments, but our capacity to understand divine truths through Christ deep wisdom and mother.
[59] S: 14.57.46-48.
[60] S: 14.42-43.
[61] S: 16.84.8-12.

virtue. This unmade, made, given love is the light of love, the love energy, the oneing, the ever-creative, vivacious grace that we are. "This light is so large," Julian says, "that we can clearly see our blissful day."[62] This Christic light that illuminates our heart in oneing, enables us to see as Christ sees. We can only know this luminous oneing by being the oneing, being a flow of love, unmade, made and given love. Thus, the classic definitions of oneing as being joined, or united, fall short of conveying the original creative dynamism and fluidity of the oneing that is love unmade, made and given. Used alone, these terms are too dualistic to convey the point of the original knot of love where we are oned in God, the wisdom that arises into consciousness from the ground of this original unity and the way our whole lives are transformed into Christ.

Julian's oneing holds within it our original oneness and the dynamism of the intimacy of being one in God, along with the *kenotic noughting* of having nothing between us and God and the emptiness of the yet to be fulfilled intimacy of our oneing. "Oneing" vibrates with the ever unitive, luminous energy of love that arises in our awareness as we turn into the ground, become more reflexively conscious, and know that we know, as subject within subject. "Oneing" points to the fluid ground of Christic consciousness within human nature and within all creation. "Oneing" highlights the dynamic of the holomovement that creation is, that quantum physics expounds, and the meaning that arises from holographic wisdom that we will explore later. "Oneing" holds how our centre unfolds into a boundless presencing of all things in a holomovement that feels like love breathing. This presencing has a sense of being fused and yet differentiated, with the oneing made up of the unique beauty of every point of being, creating a substance-sensuality-soul-body-spirit identity in Christ. "Oneing" returns us to our natural state of being oned and at the same time oneing in a ceaseless, being-in-one-another. "Oneing" naturally integrates the shadow of disturbances that scatter and work against our oneing. Its powerful unfolding, enclosing, be-closing forceful energy is unlimited in its capacity to one all things into our heart, into the holy wholeness of our original being in the Trinity. "Oneing" is the ever-unitive flow of unmade love, made and given in the endless divine-human-earth-cosmos, heart-body-mind in the inflowing-outflowing of enclosure in the Trinity. Though Julian would not know the term, oneing is naturally evolutionary.

As Julian draws us into beholding from within this mutual enclosure into an infusing abiding, awakening our Trinitarian identity, wise in mind, we know how

---

[62] S: 16.84.2-3.

all shall be well. The prayer of thanking arises. Again, Julian's words carry us into the prayer they portray, when she delights in how: "Thanking is a true, inward knowing, with great reverence and lovely wonder, turning ourselves with all our might into the working that our Beloved stirs in us, enjoying and thanking inwardly."[63] Notice the repetitive movement of going within the depths of the ground of our heart, turning into the stirrings of our Beloved, enjoying and thanking inwardly with all the wisdom of our heart awareness awakened. This gracious word, thanking, holds within it, Julian's whole way of prayer. Julian shows us how to live our life as a thanking, offering us so many invitations for our present-day living. Julian infuses us in this endless gratitude assuring us that when we finally see in the fullness of the Trinity, we will say with one voice: "Ever-loving Trinity, blessed must you be. For all is well."[64] Christ longs for us, "to take the meaning that arises from this enlightening of his precious love and to fasten it faithfully in our heart."[65]

Illuminating Contemplation

In contemplation we are oned to God, Julian affirms. Her way of beholding and seeing from this oneness that inspires words to form in our understanding, as spiritual sight continues to unfold, lays the foundations for all the mystics that follow. Silently, delicately she draws us into the knitting and oneing that enfolds, encloses, ones us in Christ, in the Trinity, as the Trinity encloses us. Her threefold way of responding to Christ's desire to turn our will into Christ's will enjoying, and become one and like Christ, returns us to the ground of oneness in Christ, awakening Christic ground awareness. Her words enfold us into Christ, into Love's mothering deep wisdom, giving birth to a oneing heart-awareness, as the silence of unmade love continues to create, and make-again our onening identity.

Therefore, as we in the twenty-first century seek to nurture a contemplative practice that will prepare us for the gift of contemplation, we must come to the showings with an open-hearted receptivity, an interior silence, and a preparedness to pour out our love in *noughting*, to the point where we lose ourselves in the one who says, "I am the ground." It is from our shared identity, knit in the love knot and oned in oneing, that the understanding of deep wisdom arises and words can form in our understanding. Christian Wiman perceptively

---

[63] S: 14.41.45-47.
[64] S: 16.85.12.
[65] S: 16.70.20-21.

warns, "what sort of understanding could be emptier than one that diminishes or erases the moments that made understanding essential in the first place? What discipline more dubious than learning to see every logical flaw in the light that once mastered you?"[66] So we must soften the scrutiny of the logical mind disconnected from our heart, that interprets by separating and dividing. Julian calls us to behold from within our oneing in Christ and understand with our heart, wise in mind, with the might, wisdom and goodness of the Trinity. Four foundational insights emerge.

First, Julian teaches us how to behold. Her way of beholding is a rhythmical oneing and *noughting* until all that we are is turned within, set within Christ. This way of beholding shifts the ground of our identity from our self, into Christ, into our mutual enclosure in the Trinity. As we turn within and centre in the point where we are knit in a love-knot and oned in the oneing, in the point where love unmade becomes love made, and stabilise in this closed, enclosing loving within the Trinity, oneing consciousness emerges. We behold from within beholding. We become one beholding. We become wise through the deep wisdom of Christ our mother, as we are reciprocally enclosed in each other. Julian teaches us how to turn into this Christic ground oneness, be transfigured in the oneing, and sensitively attend to the touchings our heart-senses perceive. In this transfiguration, all that feels feeble, split, distorted, is knit and oned in the oneing, enabling us to become whole in Christ, oned. Christ is crucified and risen, deep wisdom and mother, the mid person of the Trinity, the Omega point of oneing.

Thus, Julian's beholding creates a reciprocal flow between conscious and unconscious, dissolving splits between "kataphatic" and "apophatic" knowing and unknowing, as beholding enhances a dialectic between conscious and unconscious. Beholding prepares us for the transformation in consciousness that grace infuses, as we shift beyond the limits of the discursive mind and receive access to the spacious, loving ground of the onening awareness of our heart mind. When, we are nurtured through regular beholding in stillness and silence, if words do rise in our understanding, they arise from this sacred point of love unmade, becoming love made, in Christ. This Christic understanding sees from our oneness, not our division, always pointing beyond into ineffable mystery. Beholding gives us access to our natural enfolding, embracing, en-Christing,

---

[66] Christian Wiman, *My Bright Abyss: Meditation of a Modern Believer* (New York: Farrar, Straus and Giroux, Kindle Edition), 76-78.

enabling the wisdom of heart-knowing to naturally flow into daily conscious awareness.

Second, there is no body-soul split in Julian's way of prayer. Rather, contemplation re-turns, knits, ones us to the ground of our soul in Christ, where substance and sensuality are oned as we participate in Christ, in *hypostatic union*,[67] in his humanity and divinity. This way of prayer divinises us, reuniting our sensual ways of knowing to our substantial, or heart-self. Thus, Julian's oneing infuses a dynamic, transcendent, sensually attuned knowing, that heals the split between our reactive beastly will and our godly will naturally one in Christ. As well, oneing naturally integrates the masculine and feminine divine attributes into a mature self-image that truly expresses the essential oneing of the Trinity. Her Christology, of Christ as deep wisdom and mother, who is mother of nature, mother of mercy and mother of grace, enables us to reclaim Christ as Sophia-Wisdom and integrate this with the Logos-Word.

In the chapters that follow, I will show how the restoration of the lost feminine deep wisdom-mother aspect of our Christic consciousness is essential to contemplation. We recall how for Julian, our sensuality, how we express ourselves as masculine and feminine in the world, is eternally knit and oned in the love-knot in Christ. When the feminine is eradicated from the Christological ground of our identity, part of our sensuality is split from our substance, which results in a distorted vision of who we are in Christ. Furthermore, this disturbance in our soul, makes it difficult to behold in stillness and silence. When the deep wisdom of Christ as mother, as eternal womb, is restored to us, our original face in Christ is recovered. This restoration is critical for us personally and communally, especially at this time of crisis. It resonates with the neo-feminine consciousness Beatrice Bruteau develops, which we will explore, that is endlessly participatory and inclusive, because it arises in us from within the ground of Christ. When we are in the oneing, in Christ deep wisdom and mother, in the union of the masculine and the feminine, we are free to live in joy. There is a radical reconstruction of how we live relationally.

Third, Julian's vibrant and dynamic oneing love as the source of all being, places all that we will say about our relationship with divine love within a metaphysics of oneing. She establishes the ontological (the nature of our being) knit and oned in Christ in the Trinity and existential (how we live now) oneing in the Trinity.

---

[67] The union of Christ's humanity and divinity in one *hypostasis*, or existence.

In Julian's vision, we are one and in an endless relationship of oneing that is dynamic, creative, evolutionary love, amorising creation through the threefold, inpouring-outpouring, enfolding-unfolding, enclosing-*beclosing* of love unmade, made and given. We must claim this oneing identity and become the oneing. Though Julian would have no sense of contemporary physics, she knows our divine life in the wholeness of the Godhead deeply. And we will see the endless sharing of love that oneing powerfully conveys is resonant with quantum physics' emphasis on the wholistic movement of enfoldment and unfoldment, that David Bohm identifies as a "holomovement." Julian offers us wisdom that flows from the wholeness of the divine that is absolutely abundant, creating more abundance. Her way of prayer returns us to our ground in Christ and encloses us in the Trinity. Julian's foundational nature of oneing, constitutes a true henology of the ground that is ours to live. All that she reveals about oneing, is shown by love and given in love, so that we may truly know, "love is God's meaning."[68]

Fourth, currently, in this evolutionary moment, we have a pivotal role to play in enabling the incarnation to continue in and through us personally and communally. We will see as the book unfolds, how central contemplation is to this awakening of a communal Christic mind that is an expression of the divine desire. When we see together from this oneness, in communion, in the flow of enclosing Trinitarian love, our world becomes oneing love. Julian encourages us to live from the ground in the heart of Christ, with passion, and to allow life to happen to us, in all its beauty and terror, knowing that in all things, we are continuously knit and oned in love. She affirms how fidelity to stillness, silence and beholding in the ground of our heart places us in the midst of divine desire, in the loving source and ground of our being, in Christ who says to us, "I am the ground." In the ground we are the oneing. Julian affirms, as Christ says to us:

> "It is I." That is to say, "It is I, the might and goodness of Fatherhood. It is I, the wisdom and the kindness of motherhood. It is I, the light and grace that is all blessed love. It is I the Trinity. It is I the unity. It is I, the high sovereign goodness of all manner of things. It is I who makes you love. It is I who makes you long. It is I, the endless fulfilling of all true desires."[69]

This "I" is the wounded and risen Christ, whose words resound with eternal love. Christ, who is "I" is our essential "I" the ground of our being, the ground of our

---

[68] S: 16.86.14.
[69] S: 14.59.11-15.

longing, the ground of our loving. Christ is the unity. Christ is the oneing. And the repetition of "I" is so intimate, inclusively loving, invitational for us to embody these Trinitarian qualities of might and goodness, wisdom and kindness, light and grace. As Julian grounds us in our Christic nature, may we be the beholding and the oneing in the one who is "I."

I invite you to conclude this reflection by beholding in the ground of your heart as Julian teaches us, before we join Julian's contemporary, the author of the *Cloud of Unknowing*.

Praying Contemplatively

"And then we can do no more than behold Love, enjoying, with the most powerful desire to be all one-ed in Love and attend to Love's wonning (indwelling), enjoy the loving, and delight in the goodness."[70]

Embracing Stillness

Listening into your delightful words,
whispered from the depths of your Silence:
"*I am the ground*"
I behold.
Tenderly awakening the eye of my heart,
I turn into you Beloved, ground of my being,
as the inner depths of my longing
calls out for us to be one in your *oneing*.
I knit and weave and turn into You
attending to your loving, delighting in your goodness
enjoying your Presence.
Oneing-loving-enjoying.

---

[70] S: 14.43.33-35.

Ruminating on Scripture

Behold, my servants will sing out of the joy of their hearts.
Isaiah 65:14.

The Music of Silence

Beholding, silence infuses tenderly.

Contemplatio

Julian says so simply "prayer ones the soul to God." She invites you to *beseek*, to come to prayer, yearning to be oned into the sight and the beholding of your Beloved, enjoying with loving wonder and such great sweetness and delight that you can only pray as Love stirs you at this time.[71] Find a quiet place then, where the silence that is the ground of your heart can flow through you effortlessly. Settle, still and become sensitive to the music of silence, feeling yourself open into a loving beholding. Become attentive to this soft, luminous seeing with the eye of your heart, the gentle beholding of beholding.

As silence ripples, calms and sooths your body, your mind, your soul, listen to Love's words whispered in the depths of your heart, "I am the ground." Arising from the ground of Silence, resounding with primordial creativity, Love's silent words, "I am the ground," resound with sonic presence, like a mantra, ringing in the universe.

"It is my desire," the Beloved murmurs, softly, gently, invitingly; "that you turn into me, into the depths of my heart, enjoying." Tenderly turn within into the ground of silence, knitting and oneing every particle of your being into the point of pure presence into the ground of your heart, into the oneing of silence.

---

[71] S: 14.43:18-22.

In the oneing, in the being and holding, in beholding, yield into a lingering, soft enfolding, closing and enclosing.

Feel yourself one in this enfolding, closing, enclosing oneing love. Enjoy soaking in the infusing oneness.

Allow as much time as Love invites, to abide in the silence of this enfolding, closing, enclosing, oneing love.

Thanking is an inner knowing filled with wonder. As you feel the Beloved draw you to finish, give thanks for this loving presence, remaining centred in the ground of your heart enjoying the presence of Love in all things.

Blessing

Beloved Ground of my Soul,
May your oneing love flow in and through me
creating peace, harmony and wholeness
as earth sings her love song to you this day.
I live today in deep gratitude
for this evolutionary journey of Love's oneing.
Amen.

II

Following Love's Stirrings

The Author of the Cloud of Unknowing

The Holy One promised to dwell in a cloud.
2 Chronicles 6:1

I greatly commend the wisdom of this lysti (desirous),
sleiȝt (wise) working
which is the radiant wisdom of the Godhead,
graciously pouring into humanity's soul,
knitting and oneing us into God's self,
and giving us spiritual sight.[1]

Autumn light was shining through a window into my lounge room as I sat by a warm, glowing open fire. The dancing flames allured and urged me to become attentive to the stirrings of love in my heart. As the flames frolicked, I felt a kindling of desire arising from the ground of my heart, inciting a yearning to begin a more formal practice of meditation. My way of contemplative prayer at that time was to enter into the depths of my heart, into my inner wine cellar and abide in loving awareness, simply beholding the Beloved. Now I felt called to add a practice of meditation to help calm my wandering mind and enable me to become more stable in the silence of the ground of the heart. As I attended to the stirrings, there seemed to be an opening in my heart, a flow of luminous love that flooded through me. "Take o word and wrap it in desire," my intuition, guided

---

[1] Translations are my own from *The Cloud of Unknowing and the Book of Privy Counselling*, ed. Phyllis Hodgson. Early English Text Society (London: Oxford University Press, 1955) and *Deonise Hid Divinity and Other Treatise on Contemplative Prayer Related to the Cloud of Unknowing*. ed. Phyllis Hodgson. Early English Text Society (London: Oxford University Press, 1955). Page numbers, chapter numbers for the Cloud of Unknowing only, and line numbers are referenced. C *Cloud of Unknowing*, PC *The Book of Privy Counselling*, DS *The Discernment of Stirrings*, EP *The Epistle of Prayer*, HD *Denys's Hidden Divinity*. PC: 145.3-5.

by the *Cloud of Unknowing* author, gleaned. This was the gift of my prayer word, arising from the ground of my consciousness. The prayer word was joy. This little word, joy, has been my companion ever since. Now, luminously infused into the depthless ground of my heart, the enfleshed prayer word, organically activates, gathers and holds my attention, turning me towards, and into, the love that abides in the centre of my heart. I breathe while reciting the little word whenever my attention wavers from my Beloved at the centre. Like a shaft of light piercing through the darkness, the word draws my wandering mind into my heart, while it continues to centre me in the ground of all Love. Here there is one silence, one spaciousness, one luminous simplicity of loving awareness.

For many years, the delightful author of the *Cloud of Unknowing* corpus has been my companion in meditation practice, which he calls the "lovely work of prayer." I believe daily commitment to this lovely work essential in keeping me balanced and still. Over time, this creative contemplative soul has taught me so much about the nuances of meditation, and the changes that take place in our consciousness. I find that his explicit teaching about how we are oned to God in contemplation through naked, blind beholding affirms Julian's insights into beholding. His wisdom about how to recognise the stirring of love within our spirit, within the loving dark awareness of beholding in a cloud of unknowing is invaluable. The author is a trustworthy guide, especially when we go through phases of distractions. He prudently leads us through these turbulent waters and shows us the way into a deeper awareness in how love continues to draw us home to our original oneness. With the lightness of heart of a wise contemplative, he encourages us to follow the stirrings of love, place all our ways of knowing in a cloud of forgetting, and pierce the cloud of unknowing, into God. This fertile, word "God," used frequently throughout all the letters, is like a seed waiting to germinate within our spirit. This word naturally imparts a sense of divine presence, in this eternal naked moment where God is, "for there is no name, no feeling, no beholding more, in accord with God's everlastingness, than can be seen and felt, in the blind, lovely beholding of this little word 'is'."[2] When this contemplative whispers the word "God," he draws us into a translucent simplicity, to be present to the Presence, until there is only "isness," only God. He prepares the ground of our heart so that in contemplation, we may be, "knitted and oned in grace and in spirit, to the precious being of God, in God's self, only

---

[2] PC: 143.19-22.

as God is."³ Living from the ground of our heart, where God is and we are, in the oneness of love, infused in oneing wisdom, moment by moment, is the gift he leaves us.

This Spiritual Friend

Cloaked in a cloud of humility, this anonymous author (fl.1380), possibly from England's East Midland area, is thought to be a solitary associated with the Carthusian monks. He is a humble soul who writes letters to someone seeking to learn the art of contemplative prayer. He shares openly of himself, only because God stirred him for many days, "to think this and feel this and say this."⁴ He attends to and follows these stirrings, so much so that he successfully guides his readers towards cultivating and nurturing the same gift of contemplation. Though his most celebrated work is the *Cloud of Unknowing,* if we are to interpret his insights into contemplation, it is important to also consider his *Epistle of Prayer, Epistle of the Discretion of Stirrings* and the *Book of Privy Counselling*. All these letters act as a whole in illuminating the lovely work of contemplation. His translations, *Denis's Hidden Theology, Pursuit of Wisdom* and *Discernment of Spirits* support the letters, giving further access to the theology that informs his opinions. With all this obscurity about the historical details of this seer's life, what is clear is that he is a wise contemplative, who shows us how to integrate the vibrancy and dynamism of the *eros* of healthy masculine energy, as we seek to come to wholeness oned in God.

Though intensely apophatic, perhaps surprisingly, this seer draws on the tradition of desire (*desiderium*).⁵ His writings overflow with an intense longing for God expressed through the highly charged, yet carefully channelled passion of *eros*. As Turner observes in his study of *eros*, this language of desire manifests:

> at a point of intersection between this world and the next, between time and eternity, between light and dark, between anticipation and fulfilment. This meant that the concept of love as a "yearning" or a longing"- as an *amor*

---

³ PC: 139.13-14.
⁴ C: 88.47.7-9.
⁵ The author integrates the Song of Songs, Pseudo-Dionysian desire as the search for goodness and perfection, the Augustinian *felix culpa* that incites a desire to love beyond the confines of sin, and the Gregorian *desiderium* that distinguishes between *caritas* (love of God and neighbour), *amor* (delight in the presence of the Beloved), and *desiderium* (longing for the absent lover). See, Michael Casey. "Spiritual Desire in the Gospel Homilies of Saint Gregory the Great," *Cistercian Studies* Vol.16, 1981, 297-314. He also adopts rich imagery from courtly love literature.

desiderium, or in Greek, *eros* exactly expressed what they wanted by way of a language of love.⁶

Still, as this author's rich vocabulary of inspired passionate words and silences expresses this longing for God, in a way that heightens our longing for union with the Absolute, he takes us further into the longing beyond longing. He awakens a "naked intent," that is so profoundly *kenotic*, it *noughts* us, as it draws us into the cloud of unknowing between us and God, until there is no cloud between. There is only God who is. He teaches the most self-emptying, single-pointed loving, that un-selfs our egoic self, as it centres us in the silent still point of our heart, in our naked-self oned in the naked being of God. He summons us to yield into the oneing and *noughting* and allow the wisdom that emerges to transfigure, to divinise us. All his writings invite his readers into a naked, spacious, formless, abandon, until in silence and stillness, beholding blindly, we are oned to God in love. He invites us to follow him as his eloquent voice arises from the depths of silence, addressing us personally as his spiritual friend in God.

This Chapter

Immersing all we will explore within the context of oneing, in this chapter, we will be guided by the cloud of unknowing seer through his multihued imagery and lively dialogue, into the silence of our heart, into God. After exploring how he speaks about being oned to God through his central metaphor of the cloud of unknowing, we will focus on his invitation to behold blindly and feel nakedly our naked being in the naked being of God. Subsequently, we will ponder his emphasis on naked intent and illume the way of prayer he teaches. Our focus will be on following the stirrings of love, taking a prayer word and piercing through the cloud of unknowing with longing love, into God. We will then see how this simple way of prayer immerses us in oneing wisdom. Finally, we will draw out implications for illuminating contemplation.

Speaking About the Love of God

All the letters that the author writes, like Julian's showings, are a beholding of love that teach us how to be so silent, still, single pointed, so oned in beholding, that there is only one beholding. In sensitising us to the nuances of beholding

---

⁶ Denis Turner, *Eros and Allegory: Medieval Exegesis of the Song of Songs* (Kalamazoo: Cistercian Publications, 1995), 20.

that he portrays as "naked," or "blind beholding," he presents colourful, vivid, earthy metaphors that encourage us in a spiritual exercise that is a cloud of unknowing. "O how wonderful and glorious it is to speak of the love of God, which no one can speak of perfectly, but by impossible examples,"[7] he remarks. Accordingly, this cloud of unknowing is an impossible example, that likens this way of prayer to Moses entering the darkness of the cloud on Mount Sinai. In this holy darkness of the cloud, our seer elaborates, "God shuts down all knowable knowing, in a manner that is fully invisible and intangible. Moses feels the Presence, who is above all things, without any feeling or thinking. ... In this voiding of all knowing, ... he is knitted to God. In knowing nothing, Moses knows above the mind."[8] This strikingly *kenotic* language of unknowing, voiding, invisible, intangible, infuses a sense of transcendence, as Moses feels, without feeling, or thinking, in the voiding of unknowing, in the solitude of his heart-mind, that he is knitted to God. Moses realises that he participates in God. Through this lucid language that voids our mind of imagery, we see how this cloud of unknowing metaphor holds the unspeakable secret that only an empty heart knows, in the intimacy of being oned to God in silence.

Therefore, as this seer whispers of what is unspeakable and describes this voiding that draws us beyond our mind, he takes us into a cloud of unknowing. He does this humbly, always leading the reader into the prayer he is describing. He invites us into an ever-*kenotic noughting* and oneing, so that as Marion and Laird affirm, the words uttered are filled with Logos, filled with love. This seer's heart is so emptied and filled with love, that he surrenders all that he knows into a cloud of unknowing, abandoning his words to the Word. Similarly, he places us in the same abandon, so that the Word speaks in the dark inspired whisperings of the silence of our heart. He enfolds us in a cloud of silence, immerses us in the language of silence, and enables us to become the place of oneing wisdom. In this author's artistic inventiveness, the endlessly revealing cloud of unknowing metaphor evokes layers of meaning. And, although it suggests distance between ourselves and God, primarily, the cloud draws us into itself, to experience how the divine lies hidden within a cloud, in the heart of our hearts. To enter into this fecund, womb-like cloud, we must shift our centre of knowing from our conceptual mind, into our heart and learn how to be at home in the darkness of unknowing, until the darkness illumes the One who indwells our hearts.

---

[7] P: 53.21-24.
[8] HD: 5.15-21; 5.20-24.

Yet, this wise teacher appreciates the confusion that such a metaphor can convey, so he takes great pains to elaborate. He explains how as we release all thoughts and enter into the ground of our heart, we find a darkness, like a cloud of unknowing, that will not let you, "see God clearly by the understanding in your reason, nor feel God in the sweetness of love in your affection."[9] Immersed in darkness, we cannot see, or think, or feel, or know anything consciously. Carefully, ponderously, he then directs, "shape yourself to abide in this darkness as long as you can, crying out to the God you love; for if ever you would feel God, or see God, ... it is necessary to be in this cloud and in this darkness."[10] He encourages us to abide in this darkness, by placing thoughts in a cloud of forgetting, until there is nothing in our mind, only God.[11] Still, he warns not to be too literal:

> Do not think that when I call it a darkness, or a cloud, that it is a cloud congealed with vapours that float in the air, or the darkness in your house at night, when your candle is out. For you imagine this darkness and cloud with the curiosity of your mind. ... For when I say a darkness, I mean a lack of knowing, like everything you do not know, or have forgotten, is dark to you, for you do not see with your spiritual eyes.[12]

Thus, the cloud of unknowing points to the lack of knowing felt by our conceptual mind as we shift our attention from thoughts to our heart-mind, that is the ground of awareness itself. The cloud creates the necessary atmosphere for the awakening of the spiritual eyes of our heart that can behold blindly and nakedly feel the luminous traces of divine presence. Here we participate in the divine presence.

Although, it may feel to our discursive mind that being abandoned in the darkness of unknowing is all there is, as we nurture the art of beholding within the cloud of unknowing, we learn to see in the dark, in a whole new unitive way. This feels like no-thing, that we are no-where, for there is nothing thoughts can grasp. The seer clarifies: "Where then, you say, will I be? Nowhere, by this tale!"[13] With a gentle humour, he replies, "Truly you say this well; for there would I have you."[14] He takes us further, beyond concepts, space and time, as he

---

[9] C: 16.3.20; 17.1-5.
[10] C: 17.3.5-9.
[11] C: 33.9.20-21.
[12] C: 23.9 13-24.
[13] C: 121.68.13.
[14] C: 121.68.14.

responds, "Look carefully that your spiritual work is nowhere bodily, for nowhere bodily is everywhere spiritually."[15] In this liminal darkness of nowhere, we are a naked-self, with no-self, because we have no separate identity from God. God is our only reality. We are oned. This oneness is not mediated through language, or feelings, or sensations because there is no object awareness, or sensory experience happening *to* us. He clarifies:

> it is more felt than seen; for it is fully blind and dark to those who look upon it a while. Never-the-less, if I could say softly, a soul is more blinded in the feeling of it, because of the abundance of spiritual light, than for any darkness, or want of physical light. Who is it that calls it nothing? Surely it is our outer-self and not our inner. Our inner-self calls it All.[16]

This softness touches our deepest longing as we see that this nothing is so resplendent with infinite light that it blinds, as it ones us, infusing the gift of unitive perception. This luminous nothing permeates our heart awareness with the intimacy of the silence beyond silence and our heart knows this is All. The darkness of the cloud of unknowing becomes the luminous womb that holds and enfolds our luminous oneness with the divine. The cloud of unknowing becomes an icon of oneing. Then, as words dissolve into the eternal womb of the cloud, our seer takes us even deeper into this unknowing, to learn the art of beholding blindly and feeling nakedly the touchings of being oned in love in this luminous divine nothing, which we will now ponder in more depth.

Blind Beholding and Naked Feeling

The spiritual light in this cloud of unknowing, that is no-thing and no-where, is so abundant, that it blinds all our ways of feeling, sensing and knowing as it transforms the way in which we see and know, into an intensely simple, single-focused, non-conceptual, unitive awareness. In order to guide us in transitioning into unitive seeing, like Julian, this seer draws on the language of beholding, but his emphasis is on the essential blind nature of beholding, that is intrinsically linked to naked feeling. In elaborating on this blind beholding, "You will see," he says, "that the first, and the point of your beholding is substantially set in the naked sight of a blind feeling of your own being."[17] In other words, when we enter into the ground of our heart, the first thing we behold is our own being. We

---

[15] C: 121.68.14-15.
[16] C: 122. 68.11-15.
[17] PC: 141.11-12.

must become "substantially set," in beholding our being. Mirroring Julian's "set in beholding," to be "substantially set," we must not be scattered, or feel separate to our inner-self. We must be still, stably centred in our substance, essence, or heart-self. This perception of the naked sight and blind feeling of our own being arises in the spiritual senses of our heart. We sense stirrings, or touchings of grace within our affectivity (*affectus*), the aspect of our spirit where we sense the Spirit's loving within us.[18] As the seer affirms, we are, "touched in affection by the sensible presence of God as God is in God's self."[19] These stirrings, or touchings, are the real presence of the Spirit, who desires for us to blindly see and nakedly feel the loveliness of God within our spirit.[20] "Gnaw on the naked blind feeling of your own being,"[21] he directs. This gnawing at the edge of our perception, draws us beyond into the being of God. As Hodgson states, "to simplify the consciousness by a concentration of all the faculties on the feeling of one's being, to return to one's centre, is therefore to return to God."[22] We become silent, still, in the soft sleep of contemplation in the cloud of unknowing. We return to our original oneing affection and realise oneness in being.[23] Ira Progoff says this well:

> In this instant, out of the cloud of unknowing, a new unity comes into being. And when it is truly established, it is not merely a composite of two separate identities such as God and the individual human being, but it is a unity in which the separateness of man is obliterated in God so that oneness is established as an actual fact of existence.[24]

The illusion of separateness dissolves as we behold blindly and nakedly feel the transcendent nature of our naked being, where we are "even, met to God in image and likeness."[25] We behold. We hold God as God holds us, or as Julian would

---

[18] For this author "by love God may be gotten and held, but by thought never." C: 26.6.5. He is resonant with Thomas Gallus, and Hugh of Balma, who place the highest power of the soul, in the *apex affectus, principal affectio*, the highest point of our spirit, or *synderesis*, that is affected by God with love and so united to the Holy Spirit. See, *Carthusian Spirituality: The Writings of Hugh of Balma and Guigo De Ponte*, in Classics of Western Spirituality, trans. Dennis Martin (New York: Paulist Press, 1997), 145.

[19] P: 54.5-9.

[20] Wolfgang Riehle. *The Middle English Mystics*, trans. Bernard Standring (London: Routledge and Kegan Paul, 1981), 104, affirms that in Middle English texts the mystical senses are not simply metaphorical. They convey a spiritually felt sense of the presence of grace, while drawing us beyond the spiritual sense of touch.

[21] PC: 156.5-9.

[22] Hodgson, *Cloud of Unknowing*, lv.

[23] We see this in the throwaway line: "Adam fell from oneing affection." PC: 142.14-15.

[24] *The Cloud of Unknowing,* trans. Ira Progoff (New York: Delta, 1957), 36-37.

[25] C: 4.14-15.

say we are enclosed in God and God is enclosed in us. He encourages: "sleep in the blind beholding of God as God is."[26] In beholding blindly in a meek darkness, we return to our naked being in the naked being of God. We see in naked awareness as God sees. We know in the darkness of unknowing that "God is your being and in God you are who you are, not only by cause and by being, but also God is in you by cause and by being." We are "oned to God who is all."[27]

This wise contemplative explains the progression from blindly feeling our naked-self, to feeling God's naked being, explaining: "I let you climb there by degree. I bid you first to gnaw on the naked blind feeling of your own being, until the time that you were able to have the high spiritual feeling of God's being in this mysterious work. For your intent and your desire is always to feel only God in this work."[28] Ever so gently, as we gnaw, the naked feeling of our being yields into God's being." This "high spiritual feeling," evokes the ineffable, highest shining heights of wisest silence, that infuses into our heart perception. He continues: "I bid you in the beginning, ... to wrap and clothe the feeling of your God in the feeling of yourself. After a while, when you became more skilful in being poor in spirit, naked, spotless and utterly unclothed, you were clothed with the gracious feeling of God."[29] In becoming naked, poor in spirit, God clothes us in the gracious feeling of God's self. We become a lover wrapped and enclosed in God: "This is the condition of perfect lovers, only and utterly to strip themselves of themselves for the thing that they love, not clothed in anything, only in the thing that they love; not only for a time, but endlessly enveloped in a full and final forgetting of themselves."[30]

The recovery of this oneness transforms the whole of who we are. It recreates us. It clothes us in the divine image and likeness. Utterly unclothed of all the illusions of who we are, and who God is, we are enveloped in God: "you see your God and your love, and nakedly feel God by the spiritual oneing of God's love in the *souereyn point* of your spirit, as God is in God's self, but blindly, utterly stripped of yourself and nakedly clothed in God as God is, unclothed and not wrapped in any sensual feelings."[31] Blindly, nakedly centred in the ultimate point of our spirit, we realise we are endlessly clothed in God. Beholding

---

[26] PC: 151.24-25.
[27] PC: 136. 7-15.
[28] PC: 156.5-9.
[29] PC: 156.9-15.
[30] PC: 156.16-20.
[31] PC: 169.17-22.

noughts, unclothes us of all that is alien to our true nature in God. We see that we are a lover who lies in the naked being of God, clothed and enveloped in love. Julian's showing of Christ as our clothing wrapped, enfolded and hanging about us mirrors here. Clothed in God, grace infuses a new awareness of our oneness into consciousness.

And so we may ask, how do we enter this cloud of unknowing? The seer presents Mary Magdalene as a model as she, "hung up her love and her longing in a cloud of unknowing and learned to love what she could not see clearly in this life."[32] And he offers a simple meditation practice, a succinct, threefold flowing movement, to assist us. Beginning with lifting our heart with a meek stirring of love, the contemplative enables us to follow the stirrings of love within our heart, pierce into the cloud of unknowing with a sharp dart of longing love into the centre point of our oneing or indwelling, and awaken unitive, or oneing consciousness. Like Julian's prayer, this spiritual exercise begins in a desire that unclothes us of all conceptual ways of knowing and clothes us in God. This contemplative practice is the lovely work that is most pleasing to God.

Importantly, this lovely work of entering into a cloud of unknowing, beholding blindly and feeling nakedly how we are oned to God, is not a strict meditation technique to be adhered to rigidly. Rather, it is the response of a lover, loving a beloved with a naked intent. The *eros* expressed in this naked desire creates the necessary passion and yearning for God that incites us to reorder our priorities, seek to repattern our way of perception and move beyond subject-object observation, into the unitive consciousness of oneing love. Learning the gift of the discernment of heart stirrings even as we pray, we give of ourselves totally to God. Gallaher explains this radical dynamism of desire at work, suggesting that the *Cloud of Unknowing*:

> offers a method by which the suitably disposed reader may practice an advanced and even austere form of contemplation – the divesting of the mind of all images and concepts through an encounter with a "nothing and a nowhere" that leads to the mysterious and unfathomable being of God Himself. Yet as the account of this exercise unfolds, the genial and hospitable tone of the author humanizes the austerity of the method and persuasively draws the reader into what Evelyn Underhill calls "the loving discernment of Reality".[33]

---

[32] C: 46.16.15-17.
[33] *The Cloud of Unknowing*, TEAMS Middle English Texts, ed. Patrick Gallagher (Kalamazoo: Western Michigan University, 1997), 1.

This loving discernment of Reality is at the heart of all the contemplative writes. And this way of prayer teaches how to behold blindly, feel nakedly and discern the stirrings of love within our heart so that we may pierce into the "*souereynest pointe* of contemplative living."[34] He carefully guides us in moving through the purgative and illuminative way, into contemplative union.

As we have already noted, all the contemplative writes is immersed in desire, so before we focus on each of these three movements of his way of prayer, we will converge on what he means by naked intent.

Naked Intent

"Stand in desire all your life long,"[35] the author says. He reiterates, "the whole life of a good Christian is nothing else but holy desire."[36] "To have a naked intent directed to God, that has no other cause then God's self, is enough,"[37] he affirms. This "naked intent" is naked desire that flows from uncreated divine desire, having no other cause than God's self. Naked intent has its source in the "common intent" of Christ, who desires to knit all humankind to God as effectively as Christ is himself.[38] When we reflect this divine desire, like Christ knitting us to God's self in the passion, we do not care whether we are in pain or in bliss. We feel only that we fulfil God's will that we love God, loving only for God's sake.[39] Naked intent is felt within our *affectus*. Literally, "naked" suggests being uncovered, simple, unadorned, stripped bare, so that as with naked feelings we can be clothed in divine desire. It is an expression of being poor in spirit. "Intent," from Old French "*entent*" and Latin "*intentus*" evokes intending, purpose, inclination.[40] It also intimates a fervent desire to pour out our love, until we are empty, noughted. In this *noughting*, desire becomes hidden, dark, obscure, unknown, and yet this very obscurity infuses the energy of the divine desire, seeking God's self in us, with naked intent. Critically, this intent is never cold or wilful, rather naked intent has a lovely, meek, light quality. This lovely, meek lightness places our centre of awareness in our heart and prepares us to

---

34   C: 2 Prologue.3.
35   C: 15.2.12-13.
36   C: 133.74.2-3.
37   C: 28.7.8-10.
38   PC: 142.20-22.
39   C: 58: 15-18-20; 1-2.
40   *The New Shorter Oxford English Dictionary on Historical Principles,* Vol. 1, ed. Lesley Brown (Oxford: Clarendon Press, 1993), 1389.

draw on a prayer-word to focus our attention and pierce through the cloud of unknowing with a sharp dart of longing love. Naked intent infuses a desire to foster a "naked mind"[41] that can behold blindly and feel nakedly our oneness in God, in love.

Therefore, inspired by naked intent, we will now focus on the threefold flowing movement of this art of prayer. We will explore the nature of heart-stirrings that incite our desire to pray, drawing on a prayer word to centre our gaze, and the *kenotic* movement of piercing through the cloud of unknowing in contemplation into the point of our spirit in God.

The Art of Prayer

Following the Stirrings of Love

When the Spirit stirs our hearts, enkindles our desire and fastens it to a leash of longing,[42] the author suggests, "Lift up your heart to God with a meek stirring of love."[43] This lifting our heart, to the point of unknowing with the one who is beyond all knowledge, is a heartfelt, joyful response to the Spirit's enflaming of our desire, that we nakedly feel as a stirring. He upholds, that stirrings "are caused only by grace that we feel within."[44] And he instructs, "Lean *lystly* into the meek stirring of love in your heart, and follow it forever."[45] Throughout, he draws on multiple descriptors to describe these Spirit stirrings. He mentions "a meek blind stirring of love,"[46] "a devout and pleasing stirring of love,"[47] "a secret love,"[48] "a perfect stirring of love,"[49] "a little blind love,"[50] "a meek blind stirring of love,"[51] "a true stirring,"[52] "a great stirring of love,"[53] "a liking stirring."[54] All these delicately nuanced qualities characterise the subtlety of heart-stirrings that we behold blindly and feel nakedly within our spirit. These stirrings enable us to

---

41   C: 9.34.23.
42   C: 14.1.3-4.
43   C: 16.3.3.
44   DS: 68.18-21.
45   C: 92.14-17.
46   C: 22.4.18.
47   C: 26.6.9-10.
48   C: 34.9.9.
49   C: 52.20.21-22.
50   C: 58.24.8.
51   C: 22.4.18.
52   DS: 68.18.
53   P: 50. 20.
54   PC: 166.14.

hang, "fully in the darkness of the cloud of unknowing, with a loving stirring and a blind beholding, in the naked being of God, only."[55] He counsels, "Direct all your beholding into this meek stirring of love in your will."[56] In other words, we feel nakedly into the stirring, until it lifts us into God. Stirrings draw us into their origins in divine love.

Therefore, although "stirring" is frequently translated as impulses, or as acts of will,[57] the qualifiers meek, devout, pleasing, secret, perfect, blind, true, great and liking, suggest the mystical quality of these heart-stirrings. They are so refined, the impulses of our thinking mind, projections of our psyche, feelings, sensations, or wilful responses, feel boisterous in comparison. In contrast, true stirrings enable us to place all these ways of knowing in a cloud of forgetting, because attending to stirrings, shifts our centre of awareness into the stirrings that are intrinsically unitive.[58] Our seer highlights the transcendent nature of a stirring:

> Although sometimes called stillness, or rest (*stede*), do not think that a stirring is a stillness such as abiding in a place without moving. For, the perfection of this work is so pure and spiritual, so in itself, it cannot be described as either 'stirring' or 'stillness'. Some might call it a 'sudden changing', others a 'still (*steedely*) stirring'. It is beyond time, place and bodily awareness. ... This work is so pure and spiritual, that ... it is beyond either stirring, or stillness.[59]

Dark, yet luminous, beyond stillness, or movement, a stirring is so of the Spirit it is sensed only by the eye of our heart blindly. Stirrings are more like what Robert Sardello identifies as, "*empathetic resonances.*"[60] Empathetic emphasises the shared naked feeling of the resonance within our spirit that naturally resounds from within our oneness with the Spirit's stirring. Hence, stirrings are even more numinous than the resonance of presence, the current of silence, shimmering of stillness, or the flow of love in Love. Moreover, the seer's careful instruction to lean *lystly* into stirrings, directs us to lean, to press into, gnaw into stirrings, focusing all our attention within the stirring. The Middle English "*lystly*," accentuates how we must draw on our desire to lean deftly, with a soft yet eager longing that is open and receptively listening with our whole being. Leaning

---

[55] C: 32.8.5-8.
[56] C: 93. 50.11-12.
[57] For example, see Progoff, *Cloud of Unknowing*.
[58] C: 22.4.11.
[59] C: 110.59.19-22; 111.59.1-4.
[60] Robert Sardello, *Silence: The Mystery of Wholeness* (Berkeley: Goldstone, 2006), 13.

lystly is an actively-passive, heart-listening. It is an effortless reclining into the stirrings, until they draw us into God.[61] Stirrings is an important word for this contemplative, as he remarks that the whole of the work of the *Cloud of Unknowing* is a stirring.[62] Carmen Acevedo Butcher suggests that stirrings is his favourite word.[63] He affirms: "Trust steadfastly. It is only God who stirs our will and our desire, fully by God's self, without cause, without or within."[64] "It is marvellous the number of stirrings that may be in a soul that is disposed to this work."[65] A stirring will naturally centre us in our heart, in God.

Take "o" word

In following the stirring of love, to be oned to God in our heart's depths, it can be helpful to have a tool to assist us focus with single pointed attention within the depths of our heart. So, the seer encourages us to be like a sculptor and use a prayer-word to void away all that hides the image of God hidden within the centre of our being.[66] Our guide advises, "take a little word of "o" syllable."[67] He suggests a word like God, or Love. The shorter the word, the better because this work is so single pointed, so swift in shifting our centre of attention into the present moment of being in the naked being of God, it is shorter than an atom.[68] We then wrap our desire in the word and fasten it within our heart. *"To fasten,"* is to attach, to join, or bind with a knot, to hold secure. It also conveys imprinting with a kiss. Thus, as we fasten our desire wrapped in this word to our heart, our heart becomes an envelope hiding our desire. This hiding of desire in a word is important. He explains: "this hiding will bring you out of the boisterousness of bodily feeling, into the pure depths of spiritual feeling, and forevermore knit the spiritual knot of burning love between you and your God, in spiritual oneness and according of will."[69] Enfolding desire in a prayer-word, enables us to focus our whole attention on the naked feeling of being knit in a knot of enflaming love, knitting, oneing and according our will. We return to the original love-knot

---

[61] See, *New Shorter Oxford English Dictionary*, 1602. Also, *Cloud of Unknowing*, n.14/11, 183.
[62] C: 110.59.16
[63] *The Cloud of Unknowing with the Book of Privy Counsel*, trans. Carmen Acevedo Butcher (Boulder: Shambala Press, 2009), 236.
[64] C: 70.23-24; 71:1.
[65] C: 22.4.8-10.
[66] HD: 5.33-34; 6:1-17.
[67] C: 28.7.16.
[68] C: 17.15-17.
[69] C: 88.74.14-18.

that we explored with Julian, as the Spirit knits us into the knot of the enflaming love of transforming union.

Practically, we recite the prayer-word silently, whenever a thought arises, so that our mind remains naked. At first, the word acts like a shield or spear, treading down thought in a cloud of forgetting, and beating on the cloud of unknowing that is between us and God. These vigorous movements accent how, when we first begin to meditate routinely, we must be proactive, often harnessing the power of the word, until we become more single-focused within our heart. Distractions can be oppressive, even overwhelming. Our beholding can feel boisterous, because we are distracted and scattered by noisy, competing desires. Our unconscious can begin to unload with unresolved grief from the wounds of life, our fear of intimacy, or unhealthy psychological patterns. All these wounds need to be processed in the luminosity of the cross with compassion, as we will see in the following chapters.

Additionally, we can be brutally impatient with ourselves, in our failure to achieve a quiet disposition, or bored and tempted to give up the practice. Our author encourages perseverance for gradually, the faithful reciting of the prayer-word enables, "a full yielding into God of all that we are, by God and in God, so that we are fully meek in the *noughting* of ourselves and the high alling of God in perfect love."[70] The word facilitates the *noughting* of ourselves and the alling of God. Eventually, as we innately follow Love's stirrings, we realise we are not the one who activates the prayer word. It is the Spirit who releases the word into our spirit, hollowing and enabling us to meet all conceptualisations with the loving stillness of blind beholding. Over time, the word becomes so organically part of the ground of our heart, that it naturally activates within us, beyond our awareness. Eventually, the word is simply silence, for we are oned to God.

Piercing into the Cloud of Unknowing

Increasingly, as drawing on the prayer-word becomes more natural, reciting the word enables us to momentarily recollect and pierce through discursive consciousness, into the *souereynest pointe* of our spirit. This *souereynest pointe* is the ultimate, inner most transcendent point of our heart, the point where we are knit in knot of burning love in God. Critically, in the single-pointed blind

---

[70] PC: 139:14-15.

beholding, where "the point and prick of our beholding,"[71] is set in God, the eye of our heart is not focusing *on* this point. Rather, this is a non-conceptual beholding where our whole being is so en-static, still, within our naked-self, we are *in* God. "The spiritual worker should forever-more be *in* the highest and most *souereynest pointe* of the spirit,"[72] he affirms. Thus, in reciting the prayer-word, we are like a cupid shooting a fast, sharp dart of longing-love, into the unfathomableness of the cloud of unknowing, into God, until there is no dart of longing-love, only God. His frequent reference to a sharp dart of longing-love, conveys a sense of the power of the healthy masculine *eros*, hidden within our heart's depths, to pierce through and centre us in love, so quickly, there is not time for our conceptual mind to activate. His language is forceful: "Smite upon the thick cloud of unknowing with a sharp dart of longing love."[73] "Beat evermore on this cloud of unknowing … with a sharp dart of longing love."[74] He confirms, "a blind shot with a sharp dart of longing love will never fail to prick the point which is God."[75] Love pierces into God.

This pricking into God wounds God, who says: "'You have wounded my heart, my beloved, my spouse, you have wounded my heart with one of your eyes.'"[76] A silent, still, single-focused loving gaze wounds, ravishes God's heart, as God receives us into God's self. The seer stresses how this ever-loving single pointed gaze can: "'find, feel and touch God, even in God's self.'"[77] Echoing, "the prayer of the humble pierces the clouds, where God dwells" (Eccles 35:17), our contemplative asks why this short prayer of one syllable pierces God? He responds with St Paul's timeless words: "Surely, because it is prayed with a full spirit, in the height and depth, length and breadth of the spirit."[78] Drawing on the prayer-word with a full spirit is key, for it is essential that we behold blindly with no cognitive, self-reflexive awareness, or activated knowing. As the prayer-word facilitates our whole being becoming silent, still, absorbed, within this *souereynest pointe*, love knits and ones us, in the knot of burning love, in an alling. Infused in a meek darkness, we indwell within the divine self-knowing. We know darkly, in Love's unknowing, within the height and depth, length and

---

[71] PC: 1.11. Note the resonance with the *apex affectus*.
[72] C: 74.37.12-13.
[73] C: 26.6.11-12.
[74] C: 38.12.12-13.
[75] DS: 72.10-14.
[76] DS: 72.12-19.
[77] DS: 72.22-23.
[78] C: 75.38.6-9.

breadth of our spirit that is in God. He explains that God's endlessness is the length, God's love the breadth, God's might the height, and God's wisdom the depth of our spirit.[79] In Martin Laird's perceptive words, we perceive how: "the very attention that gazes into the vastness is itself this vastness, luminous depth gazing into luminous depth. You are the vastness into which you gaze."[80] The inner eye which beholds the height and depth, length and breadth of the divine, is itself this vastness. In crying the prayer-word and centring into these depthless depths, we enter into the eternal present moment, into the point of boundless love, where there is no isolated, separate beholder, only the oneness of love. God is and we simply are. We are utterly ourselves within the depthless, endlessness of oneing love, in contemplation.

Thus, the cloud of unknowing, becomes the cloud of oneing, of alling, where like Moses on Mt Sinai, we are noughted and oned, until we realise that the cloud that we thought separated us from God, is the divine presence. Our contemplative affirms:

> you see your God and your love, and nakedly feel God through the spiritual oneing of God's love in the *souereyn pointe* of your spirit, as God is in God's self, but blindly, utterly stripped of yourself and nakedly clothed in God, as God is, unclothed and not wrapped in any sensual feelings. ... God is perceived and felt in God's self as God is.[81]

In this present moment loving, in the ultimate point of our spirit, utterly noughted of all cognition, blinded and clothed in God, God is perceived and felt in God's self, as God is. We behold that we can no more be separated from God than God can be separated from God's self.[82] Like Julian seeing God in a point, in this point of our spirit in God, in this spiritual oneing of love, we perceive the oneing of love, through being the oneing of love. We live within the flow of the vibrant dynamism of this ever-penetrating, ever-expanding, enveloping, *noughting*, oneing and alling that fills us to overflowing with oneing wisdom.

---

[79] C: 75.38.14-19.
[80] Martin Laird, *Into the Silent Land: A Guide to the Christian Practice of Contemplation* (London: Oxford University Press, 2006), 66.
[81] PC: 169.17-24.
[82] PC: 170. 1-3.

Oneing Wisdom

This way of prayer transforms our being and seeing, as we learn to blindly behold and nakedly feel God within the love-making of the *souereynest* pointe of our spirit. Interestingly, the seer invites us *"to know knittingly"* in a manner that is marvellous,[83] this blissful being of ourselves in God in this point. This *"knowing knittingly,"* is a knowing that infuses from being knit within the spiritual knot of burning love within us. It is the contemplation that arises from participating in this Love's enflaming, that although invisible and incomprehensible to our discursive mind, is the most inebriating wine to our spiritual senses. "Your spiritual affection is so filled with the fullness of love," he notes, "you live virtuously with a pure spirit, in God, your ground. And your grape-stocks rebound full of wine."[84] This rich image of our spiritual affection filled with the fullness of divine love, being like the most opulent wine, celebrates how we are filled with the inebriating joy "of the spiritual wisdom of true contemplation and a savouring of the Godhead."[85] In loving contemplation, we taste the wine of divine love and are filled to overflowing with oneing wisdom. Here, we see how the power of the *eros* of healthy masculine that can pierce through the cloud of unknowing, into the receptivity of the heart of God, releases oneing wisdom. Our seer encourages us, "graciously rest in the lovely oneness of God, where the sleep is soft."[86] We become softly, stably oned, in God our ground.

This lovely work of prayer is simple and direct. It creates a silent, still, tranquil heart that is naturally, "silently speaking and speakingly silent."[87] A silent, centred eye of the heart, imparts a silent way of being, whether we are in silence, sound, or even noise. Thus, the cloud of unknowing becomes the shining darkness of wisest silence, that infuses shining divine wisdom into our darkest darkness, suffusing the illuminating clarity of unknowing, into our hearts. As we conclude these reflections, this beautiful contemplative's prayer, expressed in his interpolation of Pseudo-Dionysius, draws us into the Silence of silence, to behold blindly and feel nakedly, how we indwell the source of unbegotten and everlasting oneing wisdom. His luminous words draw us above our mind in

---

[83] PC: 144.9.
[84] PC: 144.17-20.
[85] PC: 144.25-26.
[86] PC: 148.1.
[87] DS: 72.1.

affection to illume like a shining beam of God-like darkness,[88] as they enfold us into the point of our oneing affection:

> I beseech you, draw us up, according and molding us
> into the most resplendent point of unknowing (*souereyn-unknown*),
> into the highest shining height, (*souereyn-shinyng*)
> of your dark inspired words (*derke inspirid spekynges*),
> where the pure things of divinity are covered and hidden,
> under the highest shining (*souereyn-shinyng*) darkness of wisest silence.
> May the luminous clarity hidden within your brilliant darkness,
> shine brightly, (*souereyn-clearest souereynly for to shine*)
> though in a manner that is always invisible and untouchable,
> fully fulfilling (*souereynli-fulfillyng*) with dazzling clarity,
> all those who no longer have the eyes of their minds.
> And, since all these things are beyond the reach of the mind,
> if I may, I desire to acquire them for myself with this prayer.[89]

Notice the beautiful shining glow of the repetition of *souereyn* (most resplendent) contemplation. In this cloud of unknowing what is *souereynly-unknown, souereynly shines,* with a *souereyn-clarity, souereynli-fulfillyng* us. In the shining darkness of wisest silence, our hearts glow with the radiance of divine transcendence, as this flood of luxurious images carry us across the boundaries of language, to enter brilliant, transcending, illuminating, darkness. Beyond our minds, where words dissolve into luminous silence, into the dark inspired whisperings of love, we discover divine wisdom. Here darkness is not dark. It radiates and illuminates with a translucent clarity as the wisdom of silence, bursts forth from the length and breadth, height and depths of our naked-self in the naked being of God. When our hearts overflow with such an abundance of wisdom, the gift of seeing from our oneness in God emerges. In this oneing, we perceive holographically, that all is in All, (Col 3:11) in an endless alling. And so this seer says: "I greatly commend this *lysti* (desirous) *slei3t* (wise) work, which is the radiant wisdom of the Godhead, graciously pouring into humanity's soul, knitting it and oneing it to God's self in spiritual wisdom and prudence of spirit."[90] Through this loving work of prayer wisdom pours into our soul.

---

[88] HD: 3.17.
[89] HD: 2.17-27.
[90] PC: 145.3-6.

Illuminating Contemplation

In contemplation we are naked in the naked being of God, oned to God, the *Cloud of Unknowing* seer affirms. His reflections on the transformation of consciousness that takes place in contemplation, raise important questions about how we might support the maturing of oneing consciousness in this time of evolutionary growth towards the transformation of consciousness into God. Irrevocably, we know that unless we evolve in our capacity to see from within the graced awareness that we are one and in a relationship of oneing, of alling in the All, humanity will not survive. We are at an unprecedented phase of necessary spiritual evolution. We must take the next step in the evolution of consciousness. And as more qualitative research into the neurological effects of meditation on the formation of new neural pathways and the awakening of centres of the brain takes place, this Christian author has a significant contribution to make. As we have seen, this perceptive seer offers us a way of gradually shifting our centre of awareness from seeing by cognitively distinguishing subject as separate to object, to unitive heart beholding. The way in which he specifically encourages a transformation in our ways of knowing so that we may be oned to God in contemplation and live stably in this oneness, infused in oneing wisdom, rewires our brain as unitive consciousness awakens. As this unitive vision continues to elucidate and amplify the centrality of contemplation in this evolutionary growth, I will highlight four significant insights that illuminate contemplation.

First, this seer immerses us in contemplation which for him is a cloud of unknowing. While we know well the cloud of unknowing between us and God, this is not the fullness of revelation. This is especially poignant today, for culturally we have lost any sense of our heart one in the divine heart. Yet, this perceptive soul reassures, that the cloud that at first seems to hide the divine presence, becomes the nothing, the no-place, the cloud of divine presence within ourselves. The cloud becomes the womb of divine love, the divine knowledge that we indwell, the source of oneing wisdom that is a naturally, unitive, heart-perception. We might call this a naked consciousness, or naked awareness, that infuses a sense of oneness that is an unbounded, blind awareness. This shift in consciousness is not so much about what we see, in the meek darkness of the cloud, but where we see from. We see from being knit, oned and accorded to God. In this knitting, oneing, according, we behold blindly and receive infused divine love-knowledge, beyond the conceptual mind. So, this author creates a mystical epistemology of knowing through the unknowing of loving, that enables a fertile dialectic between the cloud of unknowing that is between us and God and the cloud of unknowing that is God and reveals to us how our naked being is in naked Godhead.

Second, like Julian, for the author of the Cloud, contemplation ones the soul to God. However, this seer's metaphysics of oneing has an even stronger *kenotic* quality than we see in Julian's turning into the Christ who is the ground. Like the work of an artist sculpting away all that hides our centre in God, this way of prayer involves a voiding, a *noughting*, an emptying, so that in ontological poverty, we become nothing but a pure outpouring of love. To our conceptual mind this seems like nothing, while our heart knows this is all. What is so important in all his texts is that this *kenosis* is a *kenosis* of desire, of the hidden *eros* of naked intent. Therefore, the work of prayer begins with the kindling of desire, and the passionate enflaming of *eros* that we bury within the ground of our heart, so its energy may empower the activation of the prayer-word organically. Uniquely, this seer encourages such an intense naked intent, a desire beyond desire, that he invites us to risk all that we are, in love, to this lovely work of prayer.

Thus, his way of entering into this cloud of unknowing is not "a letting go" which can feel dismissive, or even violent. Nor is it a denial of our body, feelings or emotions. Rather, it is a total self-giving in love, enfolding all that we are, ever deeper into the endlessness of love. Our motivation has its source in divine desire and our work is inspired by divine desire, so that our prayer is an act of unconditional surrender in love. Language like "piercing through the cloud of unknowing with a sharp dart of longing love," emphasises the laser-like momentary point where all conceptual focusing dissolves into naked being, in the eternal now of Love's oneness that is timeless, spaceless, everywhere and nowhere. This *souereyn,* pointless point, this void of Love's oneing, this spiritual knot of burning love, marks the transition point into the heart-mind's unitive vision within the Godhead. The seer's insistence that just one glance of the eye of our heart touches, ravishes, wounds God, emphasises how radical this single pointed pure loving is, as we release into the Spirit knitting and oneing us to God in spirit and love. Accordingly, contemplation becomes a radical act, a real choice for life in God.

Third, this way of prayer creates what Teilhard de Chardin calls, "a long-trained mind, that has received the grace, that enables us to cherish our passivities."[91] The nurturing of a refined mind that is silent, still and yet *lystful*, delicately, responsive, is essential for us to evolve into a stable unitive consciousness that is informed by divine perception. However, if we become strained, too fixated on keeping rigid rules, or the correct technique, prayer can become tedious and laborious. The essential outpouring of love in the *kenosis* of surrender can be lost, and the prayer become a method, rather than a way of making love in open receptivity to divine desire. We can feel we are thrust into a never-ending search for an unobtainable, oppressive ideal of what union with God should be like. In these purgative times, this seasoned guide comes into his own, as he highlights essentials, foreshadows pitfalls, and prefigures invitations for yielding into greater depth as our prayer becomes naturally more unitive.

As Davies and Turner affirm, circles of dialectical affirmation and negation arise in the passage from sense to contemplation, as "the movement of negation as 'forgetting', is held in tension with a movement of affirmation or 'spiritual practices', and each informs the other."[92] This seer choreographs a spiralling dance between technique and ontology, as the practice creates the necessary spaciousness that opens us to the gift of contemplation, that ones us to God. This dynamic negating and affirming, emptying and filling, that spirals us into the point of pure awareness, shifts our centre of consciousness from the cognitively dominated thinking, to the natural knitting, oneing and according of blind beholding within the *souereyn* point of the mind of our heart in God. Perceptively, he sensitises the eye of our heart to the most finely nuanced, immanent, transcendent stirrings of the Spirit within our heart and shows us how to discern, lean *lystly* into and follow these Spirit stirrings, until they draw us into God.

Fourth, grace is so active in this loving work of prayer that we become infused in luminous oneing wisdom. We become enlightened, as this endlessly unitive oneing of wisdom transforms our consciousness and we see from naked being. In a beautiful reflection in his *Hagia Sophia*, Thomas Merton celebrates the enlightenment that Wisdom so generously and abundantly infuses:

---

[91] Pierre Teilhard de Chardin, *Writings in a Time of War,* trans. René Hague (New York: Harper and Row, 1968), 128.
[92] *Silence and the Word: Negative Theology and Incarnation*, eds, Oliver Davies and Denys Turner (Cambridge: Cambridge University Press, 2002), 3.

> The stars rejoice in their setting, and in the rising of the Sun. The heavenly lights rejoice in the going forth of one man to make a new world in the morning, because he has come out of the confused primordial dark night into consciousness. He has expressed the clear silence of Sophia in his own heart. He has become eternal.[93]

Our seer desires that we may be the one person who can make the world new in the morning because we are permeated in the luminosity of Wisdom. As one person at home in our eternal nature, we know we are all people, the earth, the universe, all, in the Alling. This contemplative immerses us into the primordial darkness of unknowing, into the emptiness of naked blind beholding, into the consciousness of naked being, into the eternal, into the translucent shining darkness of wisest silence. He shows us how to become the oneing and be an expression of oneing Wisdom. He places us within the love of God penetrating, pouring out from this naked ground into our hearts and into the world. This wise contemplative teaches us to trust the darkness as the dwelling place of God that fills us with luminous oneing wisdom.

Let us conclude this reflection by inclining into the stirrings of love within our own heart before we join Meister Eckhart in the next chapter.

---

[93] See, Christopher Pramuk, *At Play in Creation: Merton's Awakening to the Feminine Divine* (Collegeville: Liturgical Press, 2015), 58.

Praying Contemplatively

*Incline lystly
to this meek stirring of love in your heart
and follow it forever.
It will be your guide in this life
and bring you to bliss in the next.*[94]

Embracing Stillness

I come Beloved,
leaning into you and following
your stirring of love in my heart.
Awaken the eye of my heart
and teach me how to behold blindly, to feel nakedly,
to wait expectantly, as silence infuses my being
in your presence.
I gaze into the still, deep-less depth of my centre
Trusting the darkness that illumes your light.
May I behold our oneness and rest in your oneing love. Amen

---

[94] C: 92.48:14-17.

Ruminating on Scripture

Deep calls to deep.
Psalm 42:7.

The Music of Silence

Clouds of unknowing wrap my wandering mind in infinitely luminous silence.

Contemplatio

I invite you to find a quiet place and become aware of the ground of desire you stand within, sensitizing to the stirrings of divine desire flowing through you. Recall how our Beloved says to us "you wound my heart, my Beloved, you wound my heart with one glance of your eye." The loving gaze of your eye beholding blindly delights the Beloved. Become attentive to the magnetic pull of this *eros* of desire in the depth of your heart, drawing you into naked being, into the naked being of God where you are oned in God, in Love.

Feel the desire in your heart opening from the ground within your heart's depths, alluring you, sensitizing the eye of your heart to awaken and see with a blind beholding, *lystly* being present in the present moment, in a luminous darkness.

If you have a prayer-word, become aware of the word fastened, enfleshed in your heart, or choose a word that you can draw on when needed.

Gently, as silence enfolds you in love, begin to centre by focusing your inner gaze in the inner depths of your heart, simply being drawn by the stirring of the Sprit within your heart into present moment oneness. If you feel the energy of your wandering thoughts, or feelings seeking to distract you, draw on the prayer-word and gently respond to the thought with the word, while continuing to pierce through into the darkness of the cloud of unknowing with your blind eye of love. Remain centring in the loving resonances that are infusing into your heart awareness.

As you centre and feel drawn more deeply, yield into the vastness of Love's beholding in the meek darkness. Nakedly feel yourself present in the oneness of Love. Gaze, behold from the ineffable luminous vastness, simply being in love.

Remain in this naked silence for as long as Love guides you.

When Love draws you to finish, as our seer so often says, thank God heartily.

Blessing

We behold blindly and see that all is Love.

III

The Birth of the Word

Meister Eckhart

When all things lay in the midst of silence
In the middle of night
Your secret word leapt down from the heavens.
Wisdom 18:14

And so, if God is to speak His Word in the soul,
she must be at rest and at peace, and then He will speak His Word,
and Himself, in the soul - no image, but Himself![1]

Lying in a hospital bed shocked and dazed after surgery, words from the Book of Wisdom kept flowing through me: "In the midst of silence a word was spoken" (Wis 18:14). Though vulnerable and in pain, I knew these words were being uttered from the vast silence in the ground of my heart that is the home of the eternal Word who became flesh. There was no physical silence in the room. My body ached; medical noise surrounded me. And yet, in the deepest truth of who I was, I felt an unfathomable, intimate, and expanding Silence, a presence infusing me within and beyond my body. I knew the eternal Word was being spoken in the depths of my heart – my deepest reality was in the ground of eternal Love. I was being called to live this time of suffering in solidarity with

---

[1] *The Complete Mystical Works of Meister Eckhart*, trans. and ed. Maurice O'C Walshe (New York: Crossroad, 2009). Hereafter, MW. Sermon and page number are given. MW: 1.33-34.

all those who suffer, to meet them in their suffering. Through my oneness in the Word spoken within me in Love, I was actively participating in crucified love, making love a stronger energetic field in our world.

Centring in my heart, some years later, this same silence allures me into her luminous shining point. Later, I seek words to give glimpses into the layers of my prayer:

> Immersed in a silvery darkness, I turn into, re-turn to the abyss of silent love, into the pure silence that always was, that always is and always will be. I feel the silence that envelops everything, the silence of the absolute, the silence of the ground of all being, the silence of consciousness endlessly rising, the silence that is my being, one in the silence of cosmic being. This is the silence of solitude, enfolding and unfolding, in the abyss of my womb.
>
> Yielding into the enveloping, I sense emptiness, bareness, hollowness, as well as wholeness, oneness, fullness. Gently abiding, I become the emptiness, the silence holding eternal pregnant Love. Boundless, spacious, enfolding, enclosing, unfolding, birthing. One in the ground, enfolded into the silent middle, I listen and hear the heartbeat of this foetus of silence, pregnant with creativity. Love infuses, births in my essence, the Word – Wisdom, Christ – Christa illumined within me. Ripples of infinite fertility flood into my being – from the divine Silence, into Word enfleshed. Here in my heart-womb, I live in this continual birthing.

This sense of the silence of the ground of my heart-womb holding a foetus of Love, pregnant with divine life is the gift of being human that belongs to us all. Both personally and communionally, we hold within us, the eternal conception of the Word spoken into creation and into the womb of Mary of Nazareth. And we hold within us the birth of the one named Jesus, who becomes the Christ within our own heart and within the heart of the cosmos. Moreover, this infinite fertility is organic, natural, evolving as now, we are called to be conscious that we are ever pregnant with an ever-pregnant God. We are a *Theotokos,* or God-bearer. Organically and transcendently, we hold within us the spark of the original divine birthing of light, the conceiving of the Holy Spirit and giving birth to the Word, giving birth to Wisdom, and the ongoing speaking the Word in our world through our lives. We participate within the Infinite, incarnating itself in the finite, evolving, "through a series of self-creating emergent levels to the point at which the Incarnating Infinite can awaken within the activities of the

Finite and know itself."[2] In my journey of ongoing birthing, the voice I have found most helpful in recognising this circle of giving birth to the Word, as we become the Word, who in turn gives birth back into the Godhead, where the Infinite can awaken within the finite and know itself, is the German mystic Meister Eckhart. Now we will join Eckhart, as we continue into the depths of this infinite birthing within the ground of the womb of our heart where Love can awaken within us and know itself as Love.

Meister Eckhart – Pregnant with God

There is a powerful dream recorded in Eckhart's sermon on Paul's blinding, (Acts 9:8) where Eckhart describes a man, probably himself, who had a waking dream. He dreamt "that he became pregnant with Nothing like a woman with child, and in that Nothing God was born."[3] Eckhart goes on to explore the depthless fertility of this nothing, enabling us to see how this nothing is the divine nothing, the one who is beyond all names, all images, all things, who is no-thing. This naming and un-naming of the divine foetus as "Nothing," immerses us into the apophatic, as it spills our minds out beyond all conceptual frames of reference and stretches us into unitive consciousness. Here, our minds expand beyond time and place, beyond subject and object, beyond emptiness and fullness, beyond nothing and everything, so that this foetus may reveal itself as itself, beyond "what is" and "what is not." Then, in the transparency of the negation of negation, the nothing becomes something, as in that Nothing God is born. In this birth of God, consciousness is transformed as "in the nothing we see, only God." Still, the dialectic between nothing and all things continues, as Eckhart notes how all creatures seem like nothing in the Nothing-ness of the divine. All creatures are nothing because they are filled with God who is nothing. Reciprocally, creatures are filled with God and God is filled with creatures in this Nothing. Eckhart draws together the negation and affirmation of our being pregnant with Nothing and makes his point that God is the essence that contains all essences. Pregnant with Nothing, we carry the foetus, the divine essence within the depths of our heart-womb. We are reminded of the Cloud author who says, while our outer-self calls this nothing, our inner-self knows this is all.

---

[2] Beatrice Bruteau, *God's Ecstasy: The Creation of a Self-Creating World* (New York: Crossroad Publishing, 2016), 163.
[3] MW: 19.140.

This man, who is pregnant with Nothing, Eckhart von Hochheim, commonly known as Meister Eckhart, (1260-1328), is a Dominican preacher, who has the gift of words. In contrast to the hidden identity of Julian and the *Cloud of Unknowing* author, Eckhart is a more public figure. He is a renowned theologian, an academic writer, who gives us glimpses into his heart through his passionate sermons. He speaks, not only to the academy, but to everyday parishioners, Dominican sisters and Beguines seeking to enter into the depths of contemplative prayer. Though he was a more public and political figure, travelling the roads on foot preaching, administrating, and being concerned about practical affairs, like Julian and the *Cloud of Unknowing* author, he has a natural mystical sensitivity and capacity to write eloquently about contemplation from his own deep prayer. Eckhart integrates the rich heritage of Dominican philosophy, the ponderings of Augustine, with the eloquence of German mysticism. As an academic, he composed a large corpus of scholarly Latin works, and as priest-spiritual companion he wrote directions for his novices and instructions on discernment, consolations and suffering.

It is his numerous sermons however, spoken within the context of the liturgy and then recorded in his vernacular German by one of his listeners, probably a Dominican sister, that we will concentrate on in this chapter. Frequently, in these sermons Eckhart says, "Now listen carefully,"[4] as he invites us to be like the psalmist who cries: "I will be silent and hear what God speaks in me. He speaks peace to his people … to all those who have turned again toward their hearts."[5] Eckhart continues to explain how turning into our hearts, draws us into our centre, where the ray of divine light, fires and enflames us in love. This enflaming of the word occurs in "that place" within, that is: "so pure and transcendent and lofty that all lights are darkness and nothing compared with this light."[6] Eckhart invites us to centre in and listen from within the silence of the pure transcendent illuminating light in "that place." Here, we "hear without any sound and see without matter."[7] In this listening we are illumed by and transfigured in Light.

---

[4] MW: 14.116, e.g. 3:52, 9:87.
[5] MW: 30.184-185. (Ps. 84: 9).
[6] MW: 30.185.
[7] MW: 76.385.

This Chapter

This chapter will focus on how we may continue to strengthen the transformation of consciousness from predominantly conceptual knowing, into a new state of awareness that can lead us back to the divine ground within, where our self-knowing becomes God's self-knowing. After being immersed in the midst of silence, we will focus on what Eckhart means by oneness and ponder his mysticism of the ground (*grunt*). We will see how the *kenosis* of detaching, turning, releasing enables us to create a bare mind, preparing us for contemplation in the ground. Especially, we will explore the role of the intellect in this transformation of consciousness that takes place in our soul's ground as the spark of the divine awakens within us and we give birth to the Word in our soul. Finally, we will explicate how Eckhart's vision of our oneness in the ground, illuminates contemplation today.

In the Midst of Silence

Silence resounds throughout all Eckhart's sermons. He immerses us in a silence that has its own melody, its own voice, a silence that whispers personally and intimately to us in the ground of our heart. In his acclaimed sermon on Wisdom 18, silence becomes foundational. We can picture him in the silence of the chapel at Erfurt, standing at the pulpit, surrounded by the beauty of elegant windows and soaring arches, as he proclaims: "'When all things lay in the midst of silence, …there descended …into me … a secret word.' This is a sermon about the Word."[8] Speaking from the ground of Silence, Eckhart invites us to recollect and turn inward into the midst of silence, in the stillness of silent desert of our heart, where from the womb of divine silence, God speaks. In response, we conceive and give birth to the Word. Furthermore, in a Latin sermon reflecting on the nature of image, he evokes an image of everything creatable, arising from the uncreated, bubbling, boiling depthless-ness of the Silence of God beyond God. He describes Silence, "swelling up from itself in itself and then inwardly boiling without any boiling over."[9] Eckhart chooses the feminine term boiling (*bullitio*) to describe this inner boiling within infinite Silence, stressing the enstatic quality

---

[8] MW: 1.29.
[9] McGinn's translation, in Bernard McGinn, *The Mystical Thought of Meister Eckhart: The Man from Whom God Hid Nothing* (New York: Crossroad, 2001), 72.

of the simmering stillness. This within-ness is infinitely bountiful, bubbling within itself with an abundance of fecundity.

Eckhart further explores the nature of this boiling encircling flow in his sermon on "I am who I am" (Ex 3:14). Vividly, he describes, "the reflexive turning back of His [the Godhead] into itself and upon itself ... dwelling and remaining fixed in itself." This, Eckhart suggests, indicates: "a boiling or giving birth into itself—glowing into itself, and melting and boiling in and into itself, light that totally forces its whole being in light and into light and that is everywhere turned back and reflected upon itself."[10] This *perichoresis* of the reflexive whirling of the divine into itself, boiling, vaporising and giving birth to itself, then shows how the Godhead expressing itself as Trinity, overflows and becomes creation. This ecstatic boiling over (*ebullitio*) of the divine gives birth to us. It is fascinating how Eckhart's language, chosen well before quantum physics, evokes the infinite silence that is the ground of the universe. Like the inner boiling of the Trinity, in the early phases of the universe, foaming empty space boils and froths, seething and bubbling as light glows and rudimentary particles stir and unite. In the boiling, clumps of energy form, fluctuating between particle and field, as they oscillate, and form the universe. Eckhart's vivid affirmation of divine Silence boiling, glowing and melting into itself, giving birth to itself, invites us to express this same reflexive turning into our-self and beholding within, into the ground of Silence within our own heart, where we give birth to the Word. Here, we contemplate the delicate infusing currents and feel the intense subtlety of Silence boiling and vaporising, until we are the Silence itself.

This exquisite imagery of divine Silence boiling within itself, reflexively turning back upon itself, giving birth to itself as a Trinity, and then boiling over as creation, places all that Eckhart will say within "a metaphysics of flow."[11] Becoming attentive to this flow that is the ontological ground of all being, present within the ground of our own being, (which we develop throughout the book), is foundational for contemplation. Eckhart points to how the inner boiling within divine Silence is the source of the boiling over, or overflow of the divine being, that is creation. This enstatic inner boiling is so translucently within the divine, with such magnetism that in contemplation it draws us reflexively into its silent ground, into the source of the boiling. In turning into our heart, and re-turning to the silent ground, we responsively participate in the flow. In becoming conscious

---

[10] Ibid., 73.
[11] Ibid., 71-113.

of this boiling within, boiling and over-flowing without, we choose the ever-*kenotic* response of detaching and emptying ourselves into the dynamism of the boiling. Eckhart invites us to discover the "silent middle" of this boiling, centre in the centre of the intimacy of the ground of Silence, in the ground of our own heart, where we give birth to the Word. Intuitively, we realise how this ever-fertile divine Silence has its own melody, its own voice, its own intimate caress as it speaks the eternal Word, personally in the ground of our heart and cosmically in boundless begetting. Silence creates the sacred spaciousness that extends from the depthless ground of our soul, boundlessly out into the cosmos. Hence, we will now explore more fully how silence reveals the intense infinity and simplicity of divine oneness and our oneness in the One, in the ground.

One in the Ground

This enstatic boiling (*bullitio*) that swells up from itself in itself, inwardly boiling and the ecstatic boiling over (*ebullitio*) that overflows and becomes creation, shows how for Eckhart, foundationally all creation is one within this flowing dynamism of Trinitarian relating. Eckhart's development of his intense mysticism of the ground (*grunt*) shows how we are one in this oneness ontologically and existentially, as we shall now see.

One

Eckhart's address on "God is Love," (1Jn 4:7) gives a powerful example of the foundational nature of our oneness in divine love, as he stresses how God is so loveable that all creatures seek to love this love-ableness, whether we know it or not, or wish to, or not. God is love so fully, and God is so loveable, he affirms, that everything that can love must love God. Hence, God drives everything that is capable of loving out of plurality, into God's own lovable oneness.[12] Eckhart creates a mantra throughout the homily that rings in the silence, "anyone who dwells in love dwells in God and God dwells in them."[13] And he expounds: "If then I am in God, then where God is, I am…Where I am there God is: that is the bare truth, and it is as truly true as God is God."[14] The bare truth is that we are one in a dynamic mutual indwelling loving. Discovering this bare truth is the one thing necessary. Moreover, Eckhart cries the immortal prayer of Jesus, "Father

---

[12] MW: 5.62.
[13] MW: 5.63.
[14] Ibid.

make them one, as I and thou are one" (Jn 17:21).[15] Embedded in this passionate cry is an invitation to nurture the intimacy that is between Jesus and his Father His persuasive language draws us into this intense relationality, calling for a profound self-*kenosis*:

> where two are to become one, one of them must lose its being…and if God and your soul are to become one, your soul must lose her being and her life. As far as anything remained, they would indeed be united, but for them to become one, the one must lose its identity and the other must keep its identity: then they are one. Now the Holy Ghost says, "let them be one as we are one. I pray Thee, make them one in us."[16]

If we are to be one we must lose our being, empty self of self, and become a naked-self. We become nothing, pregnant with nothing. Notice the distinction Eckhart makes between being united and being one. If we are united there is something left over, separate from God, while in being one, our whole identity is one with the divine. Eckhart encourages us to lose our being, and become divinized, truly one. Furthermore, he expands on what he means by being one in his sermon, "One God and Father of all" (Eph 4:6), declaring:

> One is something purer than goodness or truth, … one is the negation of the negation … One is the negation of negation and the denial of denial. What does *one* mean? One means that to which nothing is added. The soul receives the Godhead as it is purified in itself, with nothing added, with nothing thought. One is a negation of negation.[17]

Becoming detached and empty, free of all things, all thought, in this delightfully intense negation of negation until we receive pure Godhead and are one, is at the heart of all Eckhart teaches. Reiner Schürmann affirms, "All these negations constitute a true henology of the *grunt*."[18] Choosing this extreme *kenosis*, this negation of negation, this *noughting* of *noughting*, this denial of denial, returns us to the purity, the translucency of being one in the ground. Here, Eckhart's henology, or discourse on the oneness of the *grunt*, overflows with apophatic paradox, as the reverberation of the negation of negation, places us in the unimaginably intense unity of oneing.

---

[15] MW: 5.64.
[16] Ibid.
[17] MW: 97.467.
[18] Reiner Schürmann, *Wandering Joy: Meister Eckhart's Mystical Philosophy* (Great Barrington: Lindisfarne Books, 2001), 45.

Eckhart opens a space within us so that we may seek oneness, and in contemplation become so empty, free, no-thing, that we awaken in the ground of God's pure unity, and realise indistinct identity in the "simple One." Discovering this oneness gives us the ontological stability of participating in the One, in the ground. At the same time, in what Schürmann describes as a wandering identity, we continually release into the *noughting* of *noughting*, in being one with God. Schürmann affirms we must truly engage with this deontology of risk:

> to become free as I was when I was not, … means to regain the original identity with the self, in the ground of the mind to which God gives himself in his being. Identity is gained only this way; identity with God is wandering. The deontology of risk and the way of detachment teach the wandering identity.[19]

This wandering identity, where we simply let ourselves be who we truly are in the Godhead, simply wandering joyfully, is a oneing identity. McGinn affirms Eckhart's intention, that: "the semantic field of ground-language is always geared to one goal: achieving indistinct identity of God and human in … the "simple One" (*einvaltigez ein*)."[20] For Eckhart, we will wander and "never find rest until all becomes one in God. God is one: that is the soul's blessedness, her adornment and her rest."[21] Eckhart desires for us to release into and live this oneness joyfully.

The Ground (Grunt)

Ultimately, this oneing identity is most powerfully expressed in Eckhart's use of the *grunt* (ground) motif. "God's ground and the soul's ground are one ground,"[22] he says continuously. The ground marks the placeless place of this shared dynamic oneing identity, where, "God enters the soul with His all."[23] Like the cloud of unknowing metaphor, the ground metaphor, vibrantly takes us into the experience it describes. In Eckhart's creative hands the ground becomes the depthless, breadth-less foundation of all we might seek to utter about our oneness with God, holding within it our innate union in Christ, in the Trinity, in pure Godhead, to the point where all dualisms dissolve. Ground is an ever fertile, primordial word, that filled with the soft music of infinity, whispers something

---

[19] Ibid., 46.
[20] McGinn, *Mystical Thought*, 47.
[21] MW: 97.469.
[22] MW: 51.273.
[23] MW: 1.31.

about everything.[24] If we try to describe this ground, or define it, or trace out its boundaries, we become lost in the infinite, because "ground," whispers of the Absolute.[25] McGinn upholds that *grunt* is a dynamic, master metaphor. "*Grunt*, therefore, should be understood not as a state or condition but the *activity* of grounding – the event or action of being in a fused relation."[26] *Grunt* is in fact the activity of grounding.

Thus, Eckhart's mysticism of the ground evokes the depthless depths of the Godhead, pure love, the uncreated silent middle, the silent desert, or essence of our soul, and the dynamism of our oneness and endless oneing in this ground, while always plunging us deeper into ever revealing mystery of participating in the groundless ground grounding. This suggests that in the ground of our soul, we are ever unitive, ever oneing, evolving. When we enter into our soul's ground and our intellect yields into translucent oneness in the spaciousness of this silent desert, all distinctions, all dualisms, all subject-object categories dissolve. A oneing consciousness awakens. Importantly, in the awakening of this ground-awareness all subject-object dualisms dissolve. The vibrancy of the vibrations between loving and knowing, giving and receiving, fuse into a simple oneness.

In speaking of this wisdom way of unitive knowing, Eckhart affirms: "The more someone knows the root and the kernel and the ground of the Godhead as one, the more he knows all things."[27] Eckhart seeks for us to attain this oneness and come to know the pure awareness which God is. Here, Eckhart's image of our ground as like a citadel, or castle, heightens, for this fortress is so elevated that nothing can gaze into it, neither our intellect, or even the Father, Son or Holy Spirit as distinct persons. It is only God who is: "one and simple, [who] can enter that One that I here call the citadel of the soul, but in no other mode can He get in: only thus does He enter and dwell therein. In this part the soul is the same as God and not otherwise."[28] This unity that is the ground, is so one and simple, so enstatic that nothing but essential oneness can enter. Eckhart counsels, "Understand: all your perfection and all your bliss depends on your traversing

---

[24] Karl Rahner, *The Content of Faith: The Best of Karl Rahner's Theological Writings,* ed. Karl Lehmann and Albert Raffelt and trans. Harvey Egan (New York: Crossroad, 1993), 161.
[25] McGinn, *Mystical Thought*, 39, notes the semantic richness of *grunt* used concretely to describe the physical ground of earth, the bottom, or lowest side. Etymologically *grunt* is related to *abgrunt* (abyss). Abstractly, *grunt* indicates origin, cause, beginning, or rationale, as well as the inmost, hidden, essence of something.
[26] Ibid., 48.
[27] Ibid., 49.
[28] MW: 8.81.

and transcending all creatureliness, all being and getting into the ground that is groundless."[29] Being in and seeing from within the consciousness of this groundless ground grounding is the transformation that Eckhart encourages. He inspires us to "delve deeper ever seeking,"[30] simple oneness in this ground. Upholding this essential unity, he affirms:

> there is no greater union than that of the three Persons being one God. Next to this, … there is no greater union than that of God and the soul. When the soul receives a kiss from the Godhead, then she stands in absolute perfection and bliss: then she is embraced by unity. In the first touch with which God touched the soul and continues to touch her as uncreated and uncreatable, there, through God's touch, the soul is as noble as God … is. God touches the soul like Himself.[31]

In the ground we receive the kiss from the Godhead, as God touches our soul like God's self, embracing us in unity. Let us now explore how we can detachedly, turn and release into the ground, respond to this divine kiss in contemplation and awaken the oneing consciousness of the ground.

Detaching – Turning – Releasing – Breaking Through

Eckhart affirms that this way of detaching or releasing (*gelassenheit*) that he advocates is not about taking us out of life, by cultivating an outer desert away from life, but immersing us more deeply in our origins in the ground in the midst of life. Persuasively, he advocates a radical way of seeking God alone, in our daily living, by cultivating an inner desert in our mind. He teaches us how to nurture an emptiness, a bareness, a poverty of being that enables us to be pregnant with nothing. Like the *Cloud* author, he advocates a dynamic *noughting* of *noughting* in a radical releasing, until we become free enough to live from the ground of our soul without a why.[32] Eckhart encourages us to turn within the ground of our soul, releasing, breaking through (*durchbruch*), bursting forth, returning to our ground where we are pervaded with God's presence, transformed into the divine image, made essential by God. In other words, through a nomadic releasing, we become so inwardly free, detached, so pure a reflection of the divine image within us "that God's presence shines … without any effort."[33] In

---

[29] MW: 80.400.
[30] MW: 66.338.
[31] Ibid.
[32] E.g. MW: 16.125.
[33] MW: *Talks of Instruction*, 492.

order that we may be present within this shining presence, Eckhart encourages us to release all outer and inner attachments and void our mind from images, as we turn, release and break through into the divine essence, into oneness, where our consciousness transforms.

Eckhart clarifies how this true possession of God:

> depends on ... an inner mental turning and striving toward God – but not in a continuous and equal thinking of Him. ... A man should not have, or be satisfied with, an imagined God, for then, when the idea vanishes, God vanishes! Rather, one should have an essential God, who far transcends the thought of man and all creatures. Such a God never vanishes unless a man wilfully turns away from Him.[34]

Importantly though, this turning and striving must have a gently detached quality, of continuously releasing our mind beyond any conceptualizing. Eckhart seeks for us to have God essentially, divinely, transcendently by being so empty, voided, detached, free of images, we are filled with God. Anyone who has God essentially, Eckhart affirms:

> takes Him divinely, and for him God shines forth in all things, for all things taste divinely to him, and God's image appears to him from out of all things. God flashes forth in him always, in him there is detachment and turning away, and he bears the imprint of his beloved, present God.[35]

Emptiness becomes fullness, darkness illuminates as filled with divine luminosity we see all things illumed in divine presence. Detaching, turning and releasing become a re-turning and breaking through into the ground, into the fullness of luminous presence. Detaching and breaking through all things until we are pervaded in presence is at the heart of Eckhart's way of prayer.

However, because this gentle, wayless way of essentially being infused in presence is so simple, we find the risk involved in this radical poverty of detachment challenging. As we detach and release all that we are, all our ways of thinking and seeing, choose to empty self of self and lose ourselves in the ground, we risk losing ourselves, and even God, in this radical surrender. Here Eckhart encourages us, affirming how this detaching-turning-releasing into the ground takes us into the silence of unknowing where the voice of love speaks, "'I will lead the noble soul into a wilderness, and there I will speak into her

---

[34] Ibid, 491.
[35] Ibid.

heart,' (Hos 2:14), one with One, one from One, one in One, and a single One eternally."[36] Eckhart inspires us to risk this radical detachment and turn into the ground of our soul in the midst of our heart, in contemplation, where in the indwelling, God touches our uncreated soul, "with His simple essence without the intervention of any image."[37] In order to be in the touch of God's simple essence, pervaded one with One, one from One, one in One, he invites us to cultivate what he calls a bare mind.

A Bare Mind

Eckhart asks rhetorically, "What is a bare mind?" He affirms: "A bare mind is one which is worried by nothing and is tied to nothing, which has not bound its best part to any mode, does not seek its own in anything, that is fully immersed in God's dearest will and gone out of its own."[38] A bare mind is poor in spirit, detached from all things, wanting nothing and desiring nothing, until there is nothing but God. To cultivate this bareness, he affirms, we should:

> pray so intently, as if we would have all members and all powers turned to it – eyes, ears, mouth, heart, and all the senses; and we should never stop until we find ourselves about to be united with Him whom we have in mind and are praying to: that is – God.[39]

In cultivating a bare mind, we detach from all images as we turn our senses and will into the ground, releasing beyond all conceptual, discursive, or spiritual knowing, until we breakthrough and return to the pure simplicity of naked awareness, to the virginity of our bare mind, in God.[40] In this bareness we see as God sees and can say, "the eye with which I see God is the same eye with which God sees me: my eye and God's eye are one eye, one seeing, one knowing and one love."[41] A bare mind sees, knows and loves as God sees, knows and loves. Notice how the fostering of this bare mind, by turning our will fully into God's will, is reminiscent of Julian's prayer, where we turn our will into Christ, our ground. However, for Eckhart, although the union of wills is essential in this

---

[36] MW: *The Nobleman*, 564. See, Hos 2:14.
[37] MW: 1.32.
[38] MW: *Talks of Instruction*, 487.
[39] Ibid.
[40] A "virgin" is empty, void of alien images, as we were when we were not. MW: 8.77.
[41] MW: 57.298.

return,[42] he develops the role of the intellect far more than Julian or the *Cloud of Unknowing* author do, creating a lovely dance between loving and knowing.

Hence, his insights into the intellect are helpful for us, as we seek to eliminate the dualism between affect and intellect, heart and head, soul and body in this evolution of unitive consciousness.[43] His stress on how the intellect detaches from understanding, in order to comprehend in bare awareness, to know through unknowing in contemplation, and yet receive the illuminating spark of the divine self-knowing and give birth to the Word in our soul is invaluable, as we seek this transformation in consciousness. Accordingly, we will now focus on what Eckhart means by intellect.

The Intellect

For Eckhart, the intellect (*intellectus*) is a power of the soul, that is so pure it comprehends the bare divine presence immediately, and in the inflowing it receives divine nature.[44] Crucially, the intellect is not the thinking, discursive mind, rather it is pure in itself, immediate, free to receive the divine inflow. Thus, we could say that the intellect is our soul-mind, or consciousness, that can observe thoughts and the movements of our heart, and reflexively knows that it knows. As the awareing of the intellect becomes more intensely reflexive, more naked and bare, there is a flow from actively seeking union with God, to a more passive simple abiding, to our potential infusion in divine presence.[45] When the intellect is stably established in God, Eckhart says, "it is transported by the Holy Ghost into the image and united therewith. And with the image and with the Holy Ghost it is carried through and inborne into the ground. There, where the Son is in-formed, the soul too will be in-formed."[46] Thus, the Spirit unites with our intellect, and enables us to be inborn in the Word, in-formed within the foetus of the Word in the ground.

---

[42] The will for Eckhart, like the *Cloud of Unknowing* author is ever turned to face God in the divine will drawing divine love into itself. Thus, God is drawn by the soul, and the soul is drawn by God. This is called divine love. See, MW: 52.277.

[43] Charlotte Radler, "In love I am more God": The Centrality of Love in Meister Eckhart's Mysticism," *Digital Commons @ Loyola Marymount University and Loyola Law School*, digitalcommons.imu.edu, suggests that for Eckhart, there is always a dynamic flow between love, being and the intellect.

[44] MW: 51.272.

[45] The active intellect is ever ready to act, while the passive intellect yields into God, until God is the one active within us. The potential intellect identifies the potential knowledge that is to come through God's action within us. See, MW: 3.46-47.

[46] MW: 54.286.

We might ask along with Eckhart: "How can it be that detachment of the understanding comprehends all things within itself without form or image, without turning outward or transforming itself?"[47] His response is succinct: "I say it comes from simplicity, for the more pure and simple a man is of himself in himself, the more simply he will understand all multiplicity in himself, while himself remaining immutable."[48] It is only a simple intellect that can understand our oneness and our uniqueness in multiplicity in God. In a way we could say that detaching, releasing in the *noughting* of *noughting*, has its own intelligence that carries us in love into this exquisite simplicity. Paradoxically, when we abandon all multiplicity, we return in simplicity and find all things in the now of unity.[49] This intuitive comprehension that is essentially unitive, arises the more we are truly in ourselves, present from within the divine image within us.

Eckhart's reflection on the transformation of St Paul into the image of God (2 Cor 3:18) is helpful here. First Paul becomes detached, then free of images, until finally he has bare understanding. As Paul's mind becomes bare: "the clear light of the Godhead pierced his soul, then from the bright rose of his spirit there was drawn out the loving flow of divine contemplation."[50] This loving flow of contemplation happened, Eckhart clarifies: "only on account of the translucency of his soul, through which love flowed by the generating power of the Godhead."[51] He nuances: "The soul knows from without: God understands within Himself by Himself, for He is the source of all things."[52] In other words, the flood of luminous divine presence that flows through the generating power of the Godhead, pours into the translucent intellect of Paul's soul and eventually into his bodily awareness. The bare understanding that arises has its source in God, in the image of God within Paul. God understands from within God's self. There is a sense of the self-presence of God to God's self in Paul, unmediated by any feelings or images that gradually flows into his conscious awareness. Again, with apophatic paradox, Eckhart draws on the primordial metaphor of the spark (*viinkelin*) to describe the enlightenment that takes place in the intellect of our soul in this loving flow of divine contemplation.

---

[47] MW: 51.272.
[48] Ibid.
[49] MW: 51.271.
[50] MW: 54.288.
[51] Ibid.
[52] Ibid.

The Spark of the Intellect

Eckhart affirms: "The soul has something in her, a spark of intellect, that never dies; and in this spark, as at the apex of the mind we place the 'image' of the soul."[53] This spark of the divine nature within us, Eckhart also describes as the citadel, guardian, silent middle, or point we have explored with Julian and the *Cloud* author. It is timeless, without place, without Here and Now. This spark marks the point that is eternally aflame with divine light begetting light within our bare mind.[54] Flowing from the Holy Spirit and yet remaining in the Spirit, in this spark: "God is fiery, aglow with all His riches, with all His sweetness and all His bliss."[55] This spark radiates from the most intimate point of enstatic within-ness, or what Eckhart calls simple in-standing, in-sitting, indwelling within the divine self.[56] This is the profound within-ness, of the boiling of the Trinity, glowing into itself as, "light that totally forces its whole being in light and into light."[57] And we recall how this boiling light expresses itself as creation. Thus, this spark illumes the point where light pours into light, where awareness is identical with indwelling in this infinite boiling of Trinitarian loving. Our consciousness arises from within this luminous intimacy.

Eckhart's words incite our awareness of this spark of illuminating bare understanding, as he draws us into the rhythm of detaching and turning into the centre of our soul. He affirms that when one, "turns away from self and from all created things, then... (one) will attain to oneness and blessedness in his soul's spark, which time and place never touched. This spark... wants nothing but God, naked, just as He is."[58] Moreover, this spark is not satisfied with knowing even about the three divine persons, rather:

> it wants to get into its simple ground, into the silent desert into which no distinction ever peeped, of Father, Son or Holy Ghost. In the inmost part, where none is at home, there that light finds satisfaction, and there it is more one than it is in itself: for this ground is an impartible stillness, motionless in itself, and

---

[53] MW: 7.73.
[54] Eckhart's identifying the spark with the intellect, has some resonance with the Orthodox tradition's sense of *nous,* though I am not suggesting a direct source here. Also, in keeping with his Dominican brother Aquinas, Eckhart sometimes identifies the spark with the *synteresis (synderesis),* as conscience, "binding and turning away from." (MW: 32a.193), emphasising that the spark of our innate attraction to good incites us to turn away for evil.
[55] MW: 8.79-80.
[56] MW: 24b.163.
[57] McGinn's translation, See, McGinn, *Mystical Thought,* 73.
[58] MW: 60.310.

by this immobility all things are moved, and all those receive life that live of themselves, being endowed with reason.[59]

This awakened spark of our intellect takes us into the simple oneness, into the ground of the silent desert of our heart, where no one is at home. There is no God and us. There is only the simple one of the ground, the pure stillness from which all motion arises. This simmering stillness, this motionless motion, in turn, infuses into our reason noetically. This reason endowed by this spark of consciousness is, for Eckhart, the reason of an enlightened intellect, or soul-mind, that is single minded, that sees from within the unity of being one in the Oneness of the divine. Most amazingly, echoing the tradition of the mystical marriage, the spark is the husband, our bare intellect in God, who makes love with our soul. In the love-making we conceive and give birth to the Word in our soul.

Giving Birth to the Word in Our Soul

Elaborating on the story of the widow (2 Kgs: 4:1), Eckhart portrays the widow as the soul, asking God to find her a husband, who is, "the spark of intellect, … the head of the soul, … is none other than a tiny spark of the divine nature, a divine light, a ray."[60] Eckhart explains how this spark of divine light awakens when we turn into the centre of our soul where, "the intellect penetrates right up into the essence … it takes Him in Himself, sinks into the essence and takes God as He is pure essence."[61] Here, "the divine light is without interruption, working within, even though she does not know it, because she is not at home. When the spark of intellect is taken barely in God, then the 'husband' is alive."[62] The husband can make love with his wife and in the nakedness of making love take God bare. "Then the birth takes place, then the Son is born,"[63] And importantly, "This birth does not take place once a year or once a month or once a day, but all the time, that is, above time in the expanse where there is no here or now, nor nature nor thought."[64] Conception takes place within the spark when we are at home, and are a "virgin wife." In other words, we are so detached, we have a bare, empty, virginal mind. Unencumbered by anything, husband (our bare

---

[59] MW: 60.311.
[60] MW: 31.187.
[61] MW: 31.188.
[62] Ibid.
[63] Ibid.
[64] Ibid.

intellect) and wife (our bare soul) can make love, conceive and give birth to the Word.

In another flamboyant reference, Eckhart envisages this virginal, luminous apex of our mind as the mouth of our soul, where the Father speaks and places the divine Word within our soul's mouth. This means, Eckart affirms, that God touches our mouth, speaks to us through, "the kiss of the soul, where mouth has come to mouth," bearing the Word in our soul, speaking the Word in our soul.[65] This kiss where mouth touches mouth is so intimate, close, passionate, as God kisses our soul with God's self. And yet, always taking us beyond, into bare awareness, Eckhart's imagery soars beyond language as when in another sermon he clarifies, "sometimes I have called it the guardian of the spirit, sometimes I have called it a light of the spirit, sometimes I have said that it is a little spark. But now I say that it is neither this nor that; and yet it is a something that is more exalted over 'this' and 'that' than are the heavens above the earth."[66] This blazing, embryonic spark identifies the intense unity that is aglow with divine fertility. Eckhart reminds us that the divine now says to us, "Behold, I have today chosen you. ... In a 'today' God promises to choose us, where nothing is, where yet in eternity there is a 'today.'"[67] In this pure presence of today, in this naked moment, we are a vast, depthless, space-less womb-soul, pregnant and waiting to give birth to the Word.

"Where is He who is born?" Eckhart asks as his response calls us to present moment bare awareness in the eternity of today. "This eternal birth occurs in the soul precisely as it does in eternity, no more and no less," he says, "for it is one birth, and this birth occurs in the essence of the ground of the soul."[68] The birth is taking place in our soul now. Critically, this gift is ours both personally and communally as: "God speaks in my spirit and your spirit and every spirit equally in the same Word."[69] In this spirit, we are all, natural daughters and sons of God, just like the Word itself is. Yet this birth is not simply within us, for as we give birth to the Word, reciprocally, the Word is born back into the Godhead. This suggests that just as God is endlessly conceiving, becoming pregnant and giving birth to the Word in us, we also are endlessly conceiving, becoming pregnant and giving birth to the Word within the divine womb. Eckhart qualifies: "If a

---

[65] MW: 22.154. For Eckhart, the mouth is the highest sense of the soul.
[66] MW: 8.80.
[67] MW: 22.154.
[68] MW: 2.39.
[69] MW: 89.438.

soul stands in this present Now, the Father bears in His only-begotten Son, and in that same birth the soul is born back into God. It is one birth: as often as she is born back into God, the Father begets His only-begotten Son in her."[70] This is a circular, ever flowing, dynamically fertile begetting of union, within union, within union, an extreme encircling enstasy, where in the love making and conception within the Godhead, a pregnant God gives birth to the Word within our souls. As in the love making, we conceive the Word within our hearts, and become pregnant within this divine unity, reciprocally giving birth in the depthless-ness of Trinitarian self-sharing.

The image is so inclusively maternal that in another sermon Eckhart asks and responds:

> Where does the Father-nature have a maternal name? Where it does maternal work. Where the personal nature keeps to the unity of its nature and combines with it, there Fatherhood has a maternal name and is doing mother's work, for it is properly a mother's work to conceive. But there, where the eternal Word arises, in the essential mind, there Motherhood has a paternal name and performs paternal work.[71]

As we become one in this mutual giving birth to each other, the stereotyping of father with the mind, and mother with unity, rightly dissolves. Eckhart's stress on the maternal work of keeping the unity of our nature is important, as he accents the ever-unitive nature of the divine. This suggests that our heart-mind that is the image of the divine is essentially unitive: it has both paternal and maternal qualities. Critically, nourishing this endlessly conceiving unity is essential. For Eckhart, this unity enables us to truly be both Father and Mother, the one birthing and the one birthed, as this unity, "is the distinction, and the distinction is the unity. The greater the distinction, the greater the unity, for that is distinction without distinction. If there were a thousand Persons, there would still not be more than one unity."[72] It is this ever-fertile birthing unity that we must turn into. To do this, Eckhart affirms, we must be a virgin-wife.

In a powerful sermon situated in the home of Martha and Mary (Lk 10:38), Eckhart describes the virgin wife who gives birth to the Word. He explains that a virgin-wife:

---

[70] MW: 66.336.
[71] MW: 90.442.
[72] MW: 66.338.

> is free and unfettered by attachment; she is always as near to God as to herself. She brings forth many and big fruits, for they are neither more nor less than God Himself. ... Numberless indeed are her labors begotten of the most noble ground or, to speak more truly, of the very ground where the Father ever begets His eternal Word: – it is thence she becomes fruitful and shares in the procreation.[73]

This is where we must be: in the virginal ground where a pregnant God begets the eternal birth. Eckhart goes on to say that Jesus, the begotten one born from the divine womb, is the light and splendour of the eternal heart who illumes the divine heart. "This same Jesus is made one with her and she with him;" Eckhart continues, "she is radiant and shining with him in one single unity, as one pure brilliant light in the paternal heart."[74] This luminous unity, within the mind of our soul, where the spark of our awareness is within the divine being:

> touches neither time nor flesh, flowing from the spirit, remaining in the spirit, altogether spiritual. In this power, God is ever verdant and flowering in all the joy and all the glory that He is in Himself. There is such heartfelt delight, such inconceivably deep joy as none can fully tell of, for in this power the eternal Father is ever begetting His eternal Son without pause, in such wise that this power jointly begets the Father's Son and itself, this self-same Son, in the sole power of the Father.[75]

This endless birthing brings delight and verdant, heart-felt joy that pulsates with naked desire to continuously give birth. Eckhart asks what we all seek to know: "'Where do you know this from, and in what way?'"[76] His response returns us to simplicity: "'Just pay attention.'"[77] This birth is always happening, always luminous, always fresh, always new. Paying attention in the naked moment now is what is essential. In this moment, a wonderful reciprocal movement is taking place. In the silent womb of all being, the Father/Mother is speaking the Word from the eternal Silence, giving birth to the Word in us, and in the same birth, we are endlessly being inborn as we give birth to the Word back into God, as God through the Word in one birth. In this flow, the infinite awakens within the finite and knows itself, and the finite awakens in the infinite and recognises its

---

[73] MW: 8.78-79.
[74] Ibid.
[75] Ibid.
[76] MW: 2.40.
[77] Ibid.

divine nature. This cycle just keeps unfolding. Our role is to cultivate presence in bare awareness.

Illuminating Contemplation

Contemplation is to be simply one, simple as God is simple, continuously giving birth to the Word in the ground of our soul. Eckhart affirms the naturalness of contemplation and importantly, he upholds that we pour out for love, the graces we receive in contemplation, and make it fruitful in works.[78] Living daily life fully, while remaining in a state of contemplation, in every moment, is the gift Eckhart leaves us. Thus, Eckhart helps us further illuminate the tradition of contemplation as *theōria,* that is, contemplation as gazing, beholding, *theo*-rising, in the sense of God-rising, divinising our perception as we become one with the simple One. He explicates how contemplation is not the abstract thinking of producing dogma, imagining, or talking about God. Rather, in Eckhart's words, "when God contemplates a creature He gives it being: when a creature contemplates God, it derives its being from Him."[79] Eckhart seeks the transformation of our consciousness so that grounded in God in essence, we derive our being from God and realise that we are already pervaded in presence. Grounded in the ground in contemplation we behold and truly see.

"'And behold': *ecce.*"[80] Eckhart affirms, "*Ecce*, this little word contains within itself all that belongs to the Word, and nothing can be added to it. The Word, that is God, God is a Word, God's Son is a Word."[81] Thus, in this essential beholding, the being and holding is a detaching, turning, releasing, until there is no-thing, no reflexivity, no subject-object, only the Word birthing in us and through us. Gently, gradually as we turn into our silent middle, our "face is so fully turned toward this birth that, no matter what you see or hear, you can get nothing but this birth from all things. All things become simply God to you, for in all things you notice only God."[82] This is the consciousness that Eckhart awakens in us. As this unitive vision elucidates and amplifies the centrality of contemplation in our evolutionary growth, I will highlight four significant insights that illuminate contemplation today.

---

[78] MW: 3.48.
[79] MW: 66.338.
[80] MW: 20.145.
[81] Ibid.
[82] MW: 4.59.

First, Eckhart's invitation to discover our oneness in God, who is the nameless Oneness, whose property is oneness,[83] transforms our whole sense of ontological identity, grounding us in the ground. He reinforces our metaphysics of oneing, as his every word infuses the negation of negation that opens into an endless dynamic oneing in the simple One. Eckhart shows us how, as Beatrice Bruteau says, at the heart of mystic discovery, "we are all one, and that One is unconditioned, unlimited, and undefined."[84] Eckhart affirms how the impassioned cry of Jesus, that we be one, is in fact our reality. We are one. Moreover, Eckhart clarifies that being one is far more than being united. Being one demands the whole of who we are participating in our essential oneness in the divine to the extent that our consciousness is transformed into a oneing consciousness. Eckhart invites contemplatives today to be recollected and turned within the ground of the heart and to live deeply from this indefinable oneing reality, where the divine is fully present, conceiving and birthing in us now.

Second, Eckhart's words continuously draw us into the ever-unitive point of simple oneness, showing us how simple oneness itself dismantles the head-heart, affection-reason, mystical-logical dichotomies that plague our evolutionary growth. These dichotomies make us resistant to the necessary transitions into the transformation of consciousness in the ground of our mind. Like Julian and the *Cloud* seer, Eckhart encourages us to foster a bare mind, by turning our will and all the powers of our soul into the centre of our heart. Nonetheless, he also invites us to pay special attention to the intellect *(intellectus)*. His rich vocabulary assists us to nurture the wisdom of Love's knowing and the role of the affection *(affectus)* and integrate this with our soul intelligence.

Attentively, Eckhart invites us to become sensitive to the intellect's active, passive and potential qualities. He illuminates the luminous unity of the spark of pure awareness, where in the infinite emptying and filling, we release into the divine, knowing the divine self in us. In the silent stillness of contemplation, as the spark of ground awareness illumes, we realise that the spark that beholds is the one beheld. Hence, the task for contemplatives today is to integrate both *affectus* and *intellectus*. When both *affectus* and *intellectus* detach, release and repose in the ground, divine light infuses and the enlightened spark illuminates our bare mind as the Word is born in us. This way of prayer is so simple. We

---

[83] MW: 97.469.
[84] Beatrice Bruteau, *Radical Optimism: Practical Spirituality in an Uncertain World* (Boulder: Sentient Publications, 2002), 64.

delicately, gently, yield into the ground, where permeated in presence, we behold through the luminous grounding oneness of all creation, in the now of unity. Eckhart teaches us to trust the revelation received from this translucent spark of oneing consciousness.

Third, Eckhart's teaches us about the depths and beauty of detaching that is the loving work of contemplation. His wonderful question resounds: "How can it be that detachment of the understanding comprehend all things within itself?" His question invites a desire to continuously empty self of self, in a negation of negation, a *noughting* of *noughting*, and to immerse ourselves in the *gnosis* of detachment that illuminates. For Eckhart, detachment is not harsh or wilful, or a denial of the beauty of creation, but rather a detaching that infuses an exquisite *kenosis* that is like the inflowing and outflowing, infusing boiling of the Trinity. In detaching from understanding, we release beyond any form of cognitive, or discursive knowing, so that in the translucency of a bare-mind-ground-awareness, our awareness is the ground of consciousness itself. Paradoxically, the worry of detaching and the risk of losing all dissolves. We become detached from detachment, abandoning ourselves fully to the divine. Hence, detaching becomes a natural love-making, conceiving and birthing the Word in the silent middle of our soul. In this silent, still point, luminous oneing floods our soul as this spark of enlightenment informs our whole being. We are pervaded in presence, a presence that is stable, constant, enduring.

Fourth, ultimately detaching and birthing are a single movement which we could call contemplation. The birth that takes place in the spark of our soul and reciprocally in the depths of God is a microcosm of the macrocosm, suggesting that our own flow in this birthing process affects the whole evolutionary movement. We could ask another dimension of Eckhart's question: How do we know we are participating in this birth when we have detachment of understanding? Eckhart's response is always to invite greater simplicity until our mind is so bare, so translucent, we are emptied and infilled with God. Every particle of our being becomes involved in this birth, in a stillness that is unspeakably fertile, in a pure presence, where love is all there is. Eckhart takes us into the silent middle where in the point of our conception in the divine, the Word is being birthed in us and awakens the most intimate sense of our shared identity in mystical union. He places us in the fluidity of contemplation, as the Father, who has the Mothering qualities of unity and conception, gives birth to the Word in us. The Word is spoken darkly, silently. We understand with detachment of understanding. Responsively, in the unity of this eternal birth, we reciprocally are inborn into the Father/Mother as we then give birth to the Word in the divine. This circular, ever flowing, dynamically fertile begetting of union, within union, within union, this extreme enstasy that becomes ecstasy is ever dynamic, ever creative. And Eckhart places us right in the middle of this constant overflow of the life of God in creation.

In the midst of silence a Word was spoken. God contemplates and births creation. We contemplate, derive our being from the Word and give birth to the Word. And so we pray with Eckhart: "That we may here so seek this peace and inward silence, that the eternal Word may be spoken in us and understood, and that we may become one…, may the Father help us, and that Word and the Spirit of both. Amen."[85] I invite you to contemplate in silence with Eckhart, before we focus on oneing in suffering, by turning to Mechthild in the next chapter.

---

[85] MW: 3.54.

Praying Contemplatively

*"Truly thou art a hidden God" (Isa 45:15),
in the ground of the soul where God's ground
and the soul's ground are one ground.*[86]

Embracing Stillness

O Silent Love,
Still and calm my mind, void and hollow my being,
soften and enfold my body,
as I turn into the deep silence of the ground of my heart
into the abyss of your eternal Silence.
In the midst of silence, you speak your Word.
I am all yours, silent, still, serene. Amen.

Ruminating on Scripture

The fruit of your womb will be blessed.

Deuteronomy 28:4.

---

[86] MW: 51.273.

The Music of Silence

Sheer silence infuses endlessly.

Contemplatio

"In the midst of silence a word was spoken." Eckhart's words ring in the silence as he invites you to surround ourselves in the silence of whispering stillness and to enter into the inner depths of the ground of our heart, into the silent desert where your ground is God's ground and God's ground is your ground. I invite you to calm your body, rest your senses, and turn your mind into the depths of your heart. Quietly breathe, calming your mind, as it releases into non-conceptual darkness, into bare, naked being. If you find yourself returning to conceptual knowing, simply, gently release into the meek darkness.

Without returning to conceptual thought, darkly intuit the eye of the intellect of your inner heart and release your heart's intellect into the dark silence. Gently centre into the midst of the silence, into the depthless silent middle and lean into the ground of the boiling, bubbling love of the Trinity – into the opening and receiving, the receiving and opening, in an infused turning. One breath, breathing. One love, loving. One ground, grounding. One primordial silence. Eckhart reminds us that God does not come to us in concepts, or in images, because God comes as God's self.[87]

When you feel ready, soften, gentle and become aware of a quality of whispering stillness – feel how you are the whispering stillness that becomes more intense, more expansive as you breathe in each inhalation and breathe out each exhalation. Be present within the vibration of the whispering. Listen as it resonates within the fibres of your flesh, extends deep into your soul and then out into the cosmos. At first the whispering may feel quite fluid, but gradually as you continue to release into the

---

[87] MW: 1.34.

stillness, the stillness becomes misty, softening into the sheer whisper of silence.

One in the One, in the holy spacious ground that is the vibrant oneing place of the ground of the Trinity, feel yourself within the infinitely fertile, fecund, munificent energy. In this luminous ground of the divine womb, God is endlessly pregnant. God births the Word in your soul, and in the encircling, enfolding intimacy you, in response, birth the Word in the divine womb.

Allow as much silent time as you need to bathe in this beauty in bare repose.

With deep gratitude, receive and be the birthing. Notice how the gift of oneness beyond conscious awareness seeps into the day and enables you to turn to the world to see the birth of the Word in all things. Be conscious of how you participate in the divine depths in everything around you.

Blessing

O Silence of my soul
Depthless love in the centre of my heart
I see your presence wherever I gaze,
You are the deep ground of all being
In you, I dwell, endlessly.
Amen.

II

Suffering in Oneing

IV

Flowing Sinking Enjoying

Mechthild of Magdeburg

All I have is yours, and all you have is mine.
John 17:10

The Beloved's eyes in mine
The Beloved's heart in mine
The Beloved's soul in mine
Uninhibited and unabashed [1]

Golden light streamed through a stained-glass window onto the sanctuary of the Gertrude chapel at Closter Helfta. The Cistercian eloquence and simplicity of this sacred space wrapped me in stillness as I entered into this silent place of prayer. I felt cherished, enfolded into intimacy as I gazed. I became aware of golden light that was shining from a side window. Eloquently simple lines danced, flowing gracefully, revealing two lovers in the embrace of each other. The lover's translucence to each other and in each other called me closer. In the midst of the flowing light, I saw they shared one heart. In coming now to the dilemma of suffering and the effect contemplation has on our experience of suffering, we will gaze at suffering with Mechthild and see how all of life, well-being and woe are held within the one divine heart. As I compose this chapter with this insightful Beguine, Mechthild of Magdeburg, I feel myself holding so

---

[1] Translations are from *Mechthild von Magdeburg Flowing Light of Divinity,* trans. Christiane Mesch Galvani (New York: Garland Publishing, 1991), unless noted. Book and paragraph numbers are given. FL 2:4.

much pain and suffering of others. I feel an interlacing of wounds, threads of suffering where darkness, absence, despair, chaos and black holes of uncertainty, threaten to overwhelm. Part of me wants to resist all this pain. Yet deeper, my heart knows to sink deeply into its very centre and there I will find love most present.

The pattern of woven suffering is already within me, etched into my heart and so I enter carrying the pain I have been asked to hold. I hold so many personal memories of pain, misunderstandings, abandonment, but the memory that is most present is of my mother on the last day of her breathing her last breath into God. Cradled by her family, we all took our turn to be with her, loving her, as the divine Beloved drew her last breath into the divine breath. I recall the Beloved's words to Mechthild: "I will draw in My breath, and you will follow Me, like a magnet."[2] My beautiful mother was certainly drawn and now breathes with and in the divine breath in dawn light. Only eighteen months after this, I sat with my father, slowly breathing his last breath into the divine. Over sixteen days and nights, we were together in the silence of love, as his suffering transfigured and he gradually became radiant as the Trinity filled his being with light.

My heart overflows with tears, as I weave all this within, into the darkness of the ground of my heart, into the centre, beyond, beyond. From the depthless abyss of the ground, in the intimacy of the inner wine cellar, flowing light streams out, pouring forth floods of compassion. This luminous compassion seeps through every wound, until tenderly, each wound is illumed by joy. Here in the ground of my heart, Love dissolves pain and transfigures it into joy. Mechthild speaks from this *eros* of desire within human suffering, that is the divine *eros*.[3] Encouraging similar detachment to Eckhart's self-emptying and the *Cloud* seer's naked intent, Mechthild shows us how to be poor, naked and meet our Beloved in naked-love in solace or heart-ache, and drink both the red wine of suffering

---

[2]   FL: 5.32.
[3]   I draw on the term *"eros"*, as it emphasises the powerful energy within ecstatic longing. See, Douglas Christie, *The Blue Sapphire of the Mind. Notes for a Contemplative Ecology* (New York: Oxford University Press, 2013), 243. Plato's *Symposium*, describes how erotic desire must be purified for us to receive the full revelation of beauty. Influenced by this Anders Nygren in *Agape and Eros* (London: SPCK, 1953), presents a dichotomy between selfless Christian *"agape"* that facilitates ascent to God and selfish Greek *"eros"* that fosters descent from God. This dichotomy only maintains dualisms. Most of the mystics in this book inter-relate the loving of *"agape"* and *"eros"*, in a way that dissolves the dualisms of ascent/descent, transcendent/bodily *eros*. See, Sarah Coakley, *God, Sexuality, and the Self: An Essay 'On the Trinity'* (Cambridge: Cambridge University Press, Kindle Edition, 2013), 8.

and the white wine of consultation unmingled.[4] From the depths of her own suffering, Mechthild helps us courageously embrace suffering by sinking into and passing through suffering into the ground of love. While we seek to eliminate suffering, and never to be the cause of inflicting suffering, Mechthild shows us how to live the necessary dyings gracefully as our self in God expands. The question we now face, Ilia Delio suggests is not: "Why does God allow suffering to happen to good people but why do we abandon God in the face of suffering?"[5] Mechthild takes us into existential fear, abandonment, and perceived absence of God, until like the crucified Christ crying, "It is finished," we pass through into pure love.

Mechthild – Spouse of Light

Mechthild of Magdeburg (1207-1282/1294) is a beguine who poured out her life in love to the poor and the sick. She is an artist, a poet, a musician, a spouse deeply in love with her God, who composes in the genre of bridal mysticism (*Brautmystik*).[6] God inspires her to write and invites her to call her book *Das Fließende Licht der Gottheit, The Flowing Light of Divinity,* or, *Lux Divinitas,* in the Latin translation made by her Dominican confessor, Heinrich von Haille.[7] *Flowing Light* has seven books,[8] the sacred number for wholeness. She emphasises that she receives the gift of *Flowing Light* in three ways:

> First with great tenderness,
> Then with great secrecy (*sublime intimacy*),
> Then with great pain (*suffering*) ....
> But it is the nature of love to flow first out of sweetness before becoming rich with knowledge and, thirdly, generous in rejection (*intense suffering*).[9]

---

[4] FL: 3.3.
[5] Ilia Delio, *The Unbearable Wholeness of Being: God, Evolution and the Power of Love* (New York: Orbis Books, 2013), 83.
[6] Beguines lived a simple life in ordinary homes, helping the poor and focusing on a life of prayer. While Mechthild lived most of her life as a Beguine in Magdeburg, she spent her last years in the Cistercian Abbey at Helfta.
[7] This is the title God chooses for her. Mechthild's book is the first full-length spiritual/theological work in German. Beginning in 1250, her first five books were completed around 1260. Ten years later, she added a sixth book, and around 1272 went to join the Cistercians at Helfta, where her seventh book was composed when Mechthild was going blind.
[8] Mechthild resists composing but her beloved replies: "My love, do not upset yourself too much; Truth cannot be burned by anyone." FL: 2.26.
[9] FL: 6.20. Note Tobin translations in brackets. See, *Mechthild of Magdeburg: The Flowing Light of the Godhead,* ed. Frank Tobin (New York: Paulist, 1998), 6.20.

Mechthild lives in the tenderness of flowing love, in the intimacy of ecstatic mystical union. She emulates how imitating the flow of the joy of the Trinity pouring into creation and emulating the flow of the Christ pouring himself into human suffering go together. Distinctively and with creative flair, Mechthild shows us how to flow, or sink into pain, into the depths of humility and what feels like infinite distance from God, until this *kenotic* loving in suffering becomes the most intimate form of love-making and union with God. In a time of so much suffering and estrangement she models for us how to enter the depths of suffering and discover Love's flowing light transforming suffering into joy.

Mechthild writes in colourful, sensual, lyrical, language drawing on a plethora of genres, such as poetry, prose, and visions.[10] Her scenes are colourfully visual, as she paints lyrical, vivid, erotic scenes that attract, or repel our gaze. Especially, she awakens the enlightened eyes of our soul,[11] that behold through the fiery light of the Spirit penetrating our vision like a beautiful ray of sun.[12] She sensitises us to listen deeply to the silence of the harp of the Spirit resounding in love. Sensually sensitive, Mechthild also stimulates our mystical sense perceptions of touch, taste, and smell, without locking us into subject-object sensual awareness. Rather, she enables us to awaken "*sensualized transcendence*,"[13] to taste and digest love, inhale the aroma of the presence, and enjoy mystical sexual intimacy. She sensitises us to the naked-feeling of the kiss of silence and the touchings of union within our heart, in the depthless-ness of eternal, overflowing love.

Mechthild arouses our desire, as she empties us of all sensual desire, drawing us into a desireless abandon until we are immersed in the most distilled sensuality of the love-making of blessed quiet, and awaken in luminous flowing light. She teaches us how to consent, ever more deeply, in times of consolation, or desolation, and to surrender ever more fully into this endless flowing light. Many of her scenes are locutions, or mystical conversations with Christ, Lady Love (*Minne*), Lady Contemplation, or Lady Pain. These conversations are passionate, illuminating an intense intimacy. Simultaneously, she embeds her locutions with theological wisdom that illuminates the human-divine relationship. Her

---

[10] For an overview of literary expressions, see Frank Tobin, *Mechthild von Magdeburg A Medieval Mystic in Modern Eyes* (Columbia: Camden House, 1995).
[11] FL: 2.2.
[12] FL: 5.1.
[13] Bernard McGinn, "Late Medieval Mystics" in *The Spiritual Senses: Perceiving God in Western Christianity,* eds. Paul Gavrilyuk, and Sarah Coakley (Cambridge: Cambridge University Press, 2012), 204, affirms Margot Schmidt's helpful phrase, "*sensualized transcendence.*"

glistening words flow from the divine mouth, into her heart, into her light filled language, onto the parchment of her book,[14] singing of the bliss, intimacy and brightness of love, until her words flow into our hearts and into silence. And so as we ponder her text, I invite you to allow Mechthild to place you within the luminosity of the radiant streams of the flowing light of divine Love, within the abyss of your soul.[15] From her first book until her last, the divine romance ensues through burning love and cooling absence, until Mechthild becomes a fully grown woman, one in God. Mechthild invites us to follow her in this exquisite oneness in flowing light calling us: "Dear friend in God, this path in love I have written for you. It is God who must place it into your heart. Amen."[16]

This Chapter

In harmony with Mechthild's rhythm, in this chapter, we meet Mechthild within the flowing light of divinity, wooed and loved by her Beloved in the communion of blessed quiet. We will explore the *kenotic* quality of this divine flowing light that is the energy field in which all creation has its being, before turning to the intensely *kenotic,* self-emptying quality that she describes as sinking. Highlighting the threefold, "yearning, sinking, flowing" movement of this *kenosis*, we will follow Mechthild as she hangs on the cross, dies into the abyss of suffering and abandonment, and enters the love-making of emptiness. We will then see how this *kenotic* way frees her to live the diminishment of her last years desiring, soaring and playing in the delight of Trinitarian loving. Finally, we will draw out how this *kenotic* way of being illuminates contemplation today.

Communion in Blessed Quiet

Mechthild's first book places us in the sublime intimacy of the blessed quiet of our inner heart as a young Mechthild encounters her Beloved Christ in mystical union. Setting her encounter in a lush forest, in the misty light of the early morning dew, Mechthild awakens our mystical ear to her passionate exchange with her Beloved Christ. The evocative conversation tells of the phases we initially pass through in the *brautmystik* tradition of mystical union. A youthful Christ pines:

---

[14] FL: 2.6. We recall, in Eckhart, the mouth is God's essence.
[15] FL: 2.3.
[16] FL: 1.44.

> I hear a voice
> Which partly sounds of love.
> I wooed her many a day,
> Now that the voice does not reach me
> I am aroused,
> I must go to see her."[17]

Christ's heart-felt words ring throughout the entire book as the spouse ceaselessly pursues Mechthild, desiring to marry her and consummate their wedding. Filled with this same insatiable longing, in response, Mechthild wraps herself in a mantle of gentle humility and prepares for their wedding. Her words resonate in the morphogenic field of contemplation as she portrays herself as Beloved spouse. After exploring seven stages of love, the inter-relationship between sorrow and love, and the fear of the senses that the blazing love of the Trinity will blind them, Mechthild consoles her senses:

> Fish will not drown in water,
> Birds will not sink in air, gold will not spoil in fire,
> For it is there it obtains its true and brilliant color.[18]

Though her senses are still not bound in repose, Mechthild, goes: "to the fairest in the secret chambers of the innocent Divinity: there she finds Love's bed and Love's dress prepared for God and man …. our Lord says: "'Stay Lady Soul.'"[19] As Mechthild finds Love's bed, her senses attempt to control what is happening, so she asks the haunting question we all face when we are drawn to surrender beyond all conscious perception into love. "Beloved, what will become of me?" In response Mechthild is caressed in words that encourage her to trust the fathomless desire and endless generosity of the divine Lover. The Beloved responds:

> Lady soul, you are so much part of my nature that nothing can come between you and Me. … You must shed both your fear and your shame, as well as all outward virtues. Instead, you shall want to experience eternally those virtues which you bear within yourself by nature. That is your noble longing and your fathomless desire which I shall fill eternally with My endless generosity.[20]

---

17 Ibid.
18 Ibid.
19 Ibid.
20 Ibid.

The Beloved's words are tender, encouraging, reminding us that we are always cloaked in the Beloved's nature. We always participate in all that the Beloved is and does. This awareness, that we are so eternally part of the divine nature that nothing can come between us, is foundational in Mechthild. There is no need to be clothed in fear and shame because all is held within the flowing light of divine love. The Beloved invites Mechthild to remove the cloak of her external self, become naked, and clothed in Christ. She is to be her naked-self, simply open and receptive. Mechthild leaves us in silence as words dissolve into flowing light:

> "Lord now I am a naked soul,
> And You, in Yourself, a beautifully adorned God.
> Our communion
> is eternal life without death."
> Then ensued a blessed quiet,
> According to both their wishes.
> He gives Himself to her and she to Him,
> And only she knows what happens to her at this moment.[21]

In the oneness of blessed quiet the beloveds give each other to the other. Mechthild infuses us in the translucency of the blessed quiet where we abandon all language into silence, inviting us to share in the intimacy of this blessed quiet, this exquisite quivering stillness. The two Beloveds one, in the kiss of oneing love. Notably, Mechthild's allusion to sexual intimacy in describing this ecstatic union in blessed quiet, affirms the holiness of sexual union and its aptness for evoking mystical union with Christ. In this ecstasy of love-making, Mechthild's self-image changes forever.

Significantly, Mechthild affirms how, though the present moment unitive-awareness of the intimacy of the two lovers fades into ordinary awareness: "they must leave each other undivided."[22] She is so one with Christ she feels his divinity in her limbs,[23] and yet she is differentiated, beautifully herself, oned and whole in Christ. Seeing with the enlightened eyes of her soul in contemplation how she and Christ remain undivided, transforms her sense of self. Mechthild sings:

---

21 Ibid.
22 Ibid.
23 FL: 2.22.

> Your blood and mine are one, untainted;
> You voice and mine are one undivided;
> Your robe and mine are one immaculate;
> Your mouth and mine are one unkissed.[24]

Mechthild encourages us to live this essential oneness with our divine Lover, to see as Love sees, to love as Love loves, to live within the oneness of undivided love in the ground of our heart confidently, boldly. In her final book, she confirms how in childhood she was the playmate of the Holy Spirit, in youth, the bride of Christ's humanity, while in in old age, she becomes the housekeeper of divinity.[25]

Flowing Light

This intimate spousal union with the Christ infuses Mechthild in flowing light as she sees her relationship with Christ as an expression of the flowing light of the Godhead. In her understanding humanity has always been in a spousal relationship of self-giving love with Christ in the flowing love of the Trinity. This relational intimacy is expressed in the finite when the Trinity, overwhelmed with joy, creates. We can hear joy resounding as Mechthild acclaims: "In the cry of joy in the Trinity ... since God no longer wished to be by Himself, He created the souls and bestowed on them great love."[26] Mechthild's sense of our original creation in joy places Trinitarian joy as the source of who we are: an expression of Trinitarian joy. Vitally, this *jubilus,* creatively holds within it the suffering of the Trinity's longing that initiates the creative process, the pattern of *kenosis*, or self-emptying ecstasy of the love of the Trinity, as well as the passion of divine *eros* expressed in the jubilation of Love. It holds the original dance of the light of love into creation (Gen 1:3) and the enjoyable consummation of Love entering into a mystical marriage with us because Love does not wish to remain alone.

As some translations stress, God could not contain God's self, hold God's self within, or remain in God's self alone.[27] Mechthild senses the fertility of this

---

[24] FL: 2.25.
[25] FL: 7.3. Though Mechthild describes "a woman", this is also Mechthild.
[26] FL: 1.22
[27] See, *Flowing Light of the Godhead*, ed. Tobin, FL: 1.22; Bernard McGinn, *The Flowering of Mysticism* (New York: Crossroad, 1998), 233; *The Revelations of Mechthild of*

fecund love, which is expansively cosmic and yet intimately *Minne*. Associated with romantic courtly love, *Minne* is divine love that is an affectionate, feminine, tender love.[28] This cosmic, joyous love that is *Minne*, cannot remain self-contained, it must mingle with us. Mechthild asks: "Of what are you made soul, that you ... mingle with the Holy Trinity and yet remain in yourself?" Mingled suggests being mixed within, blended, fused within the Trinity, emphasising a unity that makes us one and yet differentiates by making us whole in ourselves. Mechthild sees that she was, "created in the same condition as Love."[29]

In affirming our shared identity with Christ, Mechthild adapts the creation myth (Gen 2:22), suggesting that we are born from the bodily rib of Christ. Filled with wonder at the extent of this shared identity, Mechthild acclaims: "Lord heavenly Father you are my heart! Lord, Jesus Christ, you are my body, Lord Holy Spirit you are my breath! Lord, Holy Trinity, you alone are my refuge and my eternal rest."[30] Mechthild awakens us to our divine identity in the heart of God and the body of Christ. If we sense our distancing from the flow, Christ as ever-returning abundance, pursues us with floods of mercy, enabling us to return to the flow. Mechthild affirms our innate desire to live from this flow:

> The wonderous union of the Holy Trinity,
> Immaculate, from which all has flowed,
> Which was, is now and ever shall be...
> I must return there...[31]

It is impossible for the Trinity not to flow out, create and fill us with love, but it does not finish there. As embodied lovers, we have this same flowing light of love that is *Minne*, which fills us with an insatiable yearning to love beyond the consolation of this youthful desire to be one with Christ. As Mechthild becomes a fully grown spouse, she knows that in returning to this wonderous Trinitarian union, she must surrender beyond consolation, and become one with the crucified Christ in pouring out love and sinking into the depths of suffering and

---

Magdeburg, or The Flowing Light of the Godhead, ed. Lucy Menzies (Mansfield: Martino, 2012), FL: 1.22.

[28] Bernard McGinn, "Late Medieval Mystics" in *The Spiritual Senses: Perceiving God in Western Christianity,* ed. Paul Gavrilyuk, and Sarah Coakley (Cambridge: Cambridge University Press, 2012), 201, suggests *Minne* is polyvalent. *Minne* is love that is God, love as a cosmic force, love as a personification and love as human emotion.

[29] FL: 1.22.
[30] FL: 5.6.
[31] FL: 7:25.

estrangement from God. Mechthild sinks beyond all conceivable closeness until she is indwelling in the same abandon as the crucified Christ.

Sinking

The intensely *kenotic* movement of "sinking" (*versenken*), means literally to sink, descend, fall, flow down, drop into, diminish, decrease, dissolve. But there are important nuances in the way Mechthild describes this intensely *kenotic* power in our soul that is an ecstatic expression of divine desire, enabling us to pour out self in love. Imitating the flowing light of the Godhead pouring into creation and Christ pouring out his life in love on the cross, sinking takes us to the humus of suffering, as it continuously opens us into the ground of love.[32] While both love and humility are essential in this movement, it is important for contemplatives to realise that this *kenosis* of sinking humble-loving is an intrinsically Trinitarian flow of "rising yearning, sinking humility and flowing love."[33] This threefold yearning-sinking-flowing movement that we adopt in prayer, has its source in the Trinitarian out-pouring as love, "wanders through the senses, storms up to the soul with all the virtues … climbs eagerly towards God, flowing towards the wonder that comes to meet her." The yearning-sinking-flowing of sinking humble loving, "chases her upward towards Heaven and draws her down to the abyss."[34]

This is an intensely synthesising, binding, expanding, oneing movement. The soul, bound to humble love yearns and sinks into the abyss of abandonment, which paradoxically consummates in the flowing Light of the Godhead. In sinking, we are like a pilgrim, who having climbed a mountain, descends to the other side. Like the sun sinking into the night, "the soul is so irradiated by the heat of long love" that she becomes "weak from the embraces of the Holy Trinity" and sinks and cools.[35] Mechthild enables us to see how, as the soul sinks, "God fills [(us])… with one mind."[36] In this sinking we become one with the mind of the Christ as our hearts, minds and bodies imitate his humble out-pouring of love into suffering. In Mechthild's understanding paradoxically, any

---

[32] Ulrike Wiethaus, *Ecstatic Transformation: Transpersonal Psychology in the Work of Mechthild of Magdeburg* (Syracuse University Press, 1996), 42, adopts "sinking-love", while Tobin, *Flowing Light*, 18, emphasises sinking-humility.
[33] FL: 7.34.
[34] FL: 5.4.
[35] Ibid.
[36] Ibid.

ascent to God, must be a descent into the dark loving and intense suffering expressed in the *kenosis* of the cross.

Yearning – Sinking – Flowing on the Cross

Sinking has a powerful energy that describes how love necessarily takes us into the darkest cavities of death. While we can resist this *kenotic* movement and become caught in a repetitive cycle of suffering, when we choose to sink into the midst of suffering, we discover the most intensely unitive love only found in the depths of suffering. Choosing this way of sinking into what is dying within us, draws us into the rhythm of the paschal mystery, into the mystical death and union in resurrected life. What is striking in Mechthild's choice to be one with the crucified Christ, is that Mechthild becomes so one with the wounded Christ, that we see only Mechthild on the cross. There is a profound sense of Christ – masculine and Christa – feminine, being one in this deep dying. In choosing this *kenotic* way of loving, Mechthild places us personally, all humankind, and creation with her. As her sensual words resound in the darkness in her heart rendering poem, we feel ourselves, how this deep dying into the abyss of absence, becomes the way of finding God in a living love. Identifying herself as the Loving Soul, she cries:

> She carries her cross on a sweet path
> As she truly surrenders herself to God in all her sufferings.
> Her head is struck with a reed
> When her great holiness is likened to a fool.
> She is nailed firmly to the cross with a hammer of passionate love
> So that no one can remove her
> She suffers great thirst…
> Her body is killed in a living love,
> And her spirit is raised up above all sensations.
> After this death she descends into Hell
> Powerfully, she consoles all mourning souls
> With her prayers of God's goodness…
> She is stabbed in the side with a sweet spear
> By one blinded to innocent love
> And out or her flows many holy teachings.[37]

---

[37] FL: 3.10. My translation.

Notice how, in the darkness of intense pain of crucifixion, there is a powerful yearning movement of surrendering into God in all Mechthild's suffering. As she thirsts, her body dries and dies in a living love. It is essential to see how although Mechthild is suffering immensely, this is not desolation. She is not lost in her own pain, totally devastated, or inconsolable. Rather, she honours her pain. Her desire is to enter into the depths of this pain so fully in Christ, that she can also console all mourning souls with what she knows of God's goodness. There is a sense of oneness in suffering, of compassion, as Mechthild sinks so deeply into suffering, she goes into the depths of hell, into the Sheol of human misery, and comforts all those in hell. In contemporary terms, Mechthild is tending her own pain and choosing to sink into the shadow of the collective psyche and all that is alienated to divine love, bringing love where love feels most absent. She knows the interconnection between personal healing and communal healing.

In this mystical dying, as Mechthild's body sinks so low, her spirit soars so high. Mirroring the Christ whose lanced wounded side opened into his heart, his inner being, Mechthild then presents us with a portrait of her side pierced open. Surprisingly, instead of blood and water flowing out, from her open wound flow many holy teachings. For Mechthild, in the movement of yielding and opening into love in living her crucifixion, divine wisdom flows from the depths of her wound. We see how present *Minne*-Love is in the depths of our suffering, teaching us about Love. Mechthild is unique in the way she identifies the presence of the Trinity in this dying as what begins in the depths of suffering in the pain of the human condition, transforms into a mystical marriage in the Trinity. Her surrender into the darkness and the unknowing of this deep dying, into the darkest abyss where love feels most absent, becomes saturated in air and light. Mechthild draws us into this luminous transformation in the most sublime love. Still exposed:

> She hangs on the cross of sublime love,
> in the pure air of the Holy Spirit,
> in the eternal sun of the living Godhead
> until she is completely dry.
> In a holy death, she is taken down from the cross
> and says: "My God, Love, receive my spirit. It is finished."[38]

---

[38]   Ibid.

In her shared identity with the *kenotic* pouring out of the love of the crucified One, we see Mechthild flows into the lowest point of the humus of her pain and even the affliction of hell, until all the moisture streams from her body and she is left dry. She is left suspended in a dry barren nothingness, until what at first feels so far from the intimacy she has known, becomes the most sublime love-making of dying into Love. In this mystical dying, Mechthild breathes her last, into the pure air of the Spirit and yields into the darkness that covers the eternal light of Divinity. Quoting John's passion narrative (Jn 19:30), where the crucified one gives over his Spirit into God, Mechthild describes how one with her Lover, she gives over her spirit. Spirit unites with spirit. Mechthild is drawn into illuminating light.

The poem continues describing Mechthild being laid in the grave of deep humility, until she rises joyfully on Easter day having enjoyed "the sweet lamentation with her Beloved in the nuptial bed."[39] Here we see how critical the time of being in the earthiness of the grave of deep humility is as Mechthild lies in the humble, empty, poverty of waiting. Only sheer silence can enshroud this humble waiting that becomes the marriage bed of ecstatic union. This takes us back to the blessed quiet of the bed of love Mechthild enjoyed when she was younger,[40] but now the desire expressed between the lovers is a "sweet lamentation." This desire that knows the depths of suffering can now live in the fullness of resurrection, in the joy of the flowing light of divinity.

The scene closes with an important note: "Such a passion must be suffered by every soul truly penetrated by the love of God."[41] Mechthild shows us how to live our crucifixions in a way that our suffering becomes the point where we experience the deepest intimacy of the kiss of Love. She reminds us, deep dying is necessary to living. And she gives us a powerful vision of how we may also come to embody that our suffering is the Beloved's suffering, and our suffering is the suffering of the world. Whenever we feel we are left exposed, hanging on the cross, we are the Christ-Christa, one in this one dying, that draws us into the air of the Spirit and the light of eternal Love. When we feel this annihilation, that who we used to be has died and we are waiting in the starkness of the grave of humility, Mechthild reminds us that this poverty of humility is the marriage bed. It creates the necessary spaciousness for the love-making of blessed silence. In a

---

[39] Ibid.
[40] FL: 1.44.
[41] FL: 3.10.

following scene, Mechthild's vision becomes more luminous, as her Beloved gives her a light in a lantern, so that all those who behold the light will be illumed in a special ray of understanding. Mechthild wonders who the lantern will be. Her Beloved responds, "'I am the light and your breast is the lantern.'"[42] This is what Mechthild calls us to be, as we enter into our necessary dyings, a lantern whose heart is shining with the light of the risen Christ.

Yearning – Sinking – Flowing into Absence

As we take this lantern now into the deep suffering of our world, illumed by the paschal mystery of dying and rising, we will follow Mechthild into a dramatic conversation. Mechthild presents us with a confronting example of how this energy exchange within this yearning-sinking-flowing, mirrors the way of the cross and so invites us into a deeper expression of *"the willed vulnerability,"*[43] that Sarah Coakley affirms is at the heart of contemplation. Coakley stresses how, "the contemplative steps wilfully into an act of reflexive divine love that is always going on, always begging Christomorphic shape. This engenders divine power not as 'force' but as Christo-form 'authority'."[44] Mechthild models for us how to step wilfully and abandon ourselves to reflexive divine love. As this reflexivity of love flowing into love becomes, simply one love, we become this Christomorphic shape. Mechthild embodies this *kenosis* so fully that we see Mechthild crucified with Christ, so one with Christ in her self-emptying in sinking love, Mechthild becomes Christ. She becomes Christo-Christa as Christ and Mechthild, masculine and feminine are one in the crucifixion. Becoming the outpouring of love of the crucified lover, necessarily takes Mechthild into the infinite ache of alienation, where only naked desire can flow in the opaque darkness. This desire creates more desire. Her yearning only increases her yearning. Her desire is so Christ-like, that Mechthild surrenders into infinite alienation from God within creation and falls among "ill-fated and cast-away souls."[45] This is the Christomorphic shape Mechthild invites us to become.

Stable enough in herself in her Lover, within the enclosed sanctuary of the Trinity,[46] to feel the infinite ache of the communal absence of God, Mechthild

---

[42] FL: 3.12.
[43] Sarah Coakley, *God, Sexuality, and the Self: An Essay 'On the Trinity'* (Cambridge: Cambridge University Press, Kindle Edition, 2013), 343.
[44] Ibid.
[45] FL: 4.10.
[46] Ibid.

has freely chosen to sink into this dark abyss. The translations constant alienation,[47] estrangement,[48] or forsakenness,[49] emphasise an overwhelming sense of absence, or abandonment. Yet, Mechthild evokes how in this absence, God is strangely with her.[50] In other words, this acute abandonment has a melancholic intimacy. Mechthild says she desires this absence more than the Beloved's presence. It is important to qualify that Mechthild is not choosing to suffer for suffering's sake, or deliberately abandoning her Lover. She is choosing to love beyond the limits of consolation, for love of her Beloved, so that alienation, estrangement, forsakenness, absence, abandonment, enigmatically become intimate words, that take her into a holy apophatic abyss. Poignantly, Mechthild surrenders until she, "no longer knew God's intimacy and blessed love went on its way."[51] Mechthild enters into the unconscious depths of the absence of God, daringly choosing to love beyond egoic control, beyond self-gratification. She loves only for Love's sake.

As Mechthild's confrontation with her limits and the intensity of feeling the absence of her Lover heightens, and threatens to overwhelm her, questions and doubts personify and haunt her. Still, humbly faithful to simply loving for Love's sake, she sinks beyond all comfort, feeling, imagery, belief and boundaries of her conscious awareness. In this dark emptiness, Trinitarian consciousness awakens. Mechthild mystically hears from deep within her suffering, the tender voice of the Trinity: "Remember what you experienced and saw when there was nothing between you and Me." Christ consoles: "Think of what your body has suffered because of My pain," while the Holy Spirit continues: "Think of what you have written."[52] In this encounter, Mechthild offers us a threefold pattern of response to moments of darkness and perceived absence of God. Rather than resisting feelings and becoming caught in a net of confusion, she invites us, to sink beyond discursive memory, until our soul-memory awakens from the point where we are written into the book of the Godhead.[53] Affirmed in her identity as lover, Mechthild cries: "Welcome blessed alienation."[54] Alienation becomes her

---

[47] Galvani translation.
[48] *Flowing Light*, (Tobin) and McGinn, *Flowering of Mysticism*, 241.
[49] Menzies, *Revelations of Mechthild of Magdeburg*.
[50] McGinn, Flowering of Mysticism, 241.
[51] FL: 4.10.
[52] FL: 4.12.
[53] FL: 3.2.
[54] FL: 4.12.

lady in waiting. Mechthild desires such a deep transformation "in the palate of her soul,"[55] that she is prepared to wait in alienation, as long as needed.

Then, mirroring her descent into hell, she sinks further into a searing communal darkness, where people ask her to be a messenger to God for them.[56] This suggests that Mechthild is within the depths of communal pain, in the collective shadow of trauma and suffering of humankind, as she was in hell on the cross. With authority, she responds, "Lady Pain, I now command you to release me, for now you are the highest thing within me."[57] When pain is at its highest, inflicting its most intense suffering, so that there is nothing but an abyss of the absence, Lady Pain rises from her body, like a dark cloud and drifts to God. We see here how, as Mechthild honors her feelings of alienation and sinks into the core of her isolation, the power of fear that had such a hold on her dissipates and leaves her with nothing but absence. In this searing absence, there is nothing but God. She knows irrevocably, with her whole being, how in the midst of the most searing absence, abandonment, separation, or estrangement from God, there is divine Love. Divine Love cannot abandon us, because the flowing light of love is the source of all being. In the depths of this earthy grave of pain, Mechthild meets her Beloved in heaven.

The drama continues, as Christ then welcomes Lady Pain. Although Lady Pain clothed the body of Jesus on earth, the risen Christ now says to her, "However much I loved you, you cannot enter here."[58] In other words, although the crucified Jesus shared this pain, is clothed in human pain, pain does not have its source in the infinity of flowing light. Pain is an expression of the incompleteness of the finite. God can enter pain, be clothed in pain, but pain cannot enter God, or clothe the Godhead. Consoled, Mechthild removes her cloak of pain and comes to Christ as her naked-self, as a naked bride. Christ comforts that he will embrace Mechthild, take her into himself and unite with her in his heart.[59] They become naked lovers clothed in each other. The blessed silence of the oneness of love illumes. Mechthild's earlier awareness of Christ clothing himself with her soul, making Mechthild his closest dress resonates.[60] Now reciprocally, Mechthild clothes her Beloved with her naked-self, in the ever enfolding,

---

[55] Ibid.
[56] Ibid.
[57] Ibid.
[58] Ibid.
[59] FL: 4.12.
[60] FL: 2.5.

encircling, embrace of being in one another.[61] Thus we see how the beautiful expansion of ecstatic union that began in the loving of the marriage bed, and extended into dying on the cross, waiting in the tomb and the ecstasy of rising in resurrection light, now extends into suffering and estrangement. Absence becomes ecstatic, drawing Mechthild into the divine heart. This enlightening scene reveals how, when we enter into the depths of the most charring pain of infinite separation, in the absence, the Beloved embraces and draws us into ecstatic union within the divine heart. In this *kenosis* of sinking-love, Mechthild breaks through all dualistic egoic limits and understandings of what love should be, becomes free of dependency on any one way of experiencing mystical union, and enters into a unified consciousness with her Beloved. Mechthild acknowledges the gift Lady Pain has given her remarking: "The closer I come to you, the more wondrously God falls on me."[62] In falling into the depth of unfathomable pain, she sinks beyond all limits, into Love. Mechthild's poetry resounds like a mantra:

> the further I sink,
> the more sweetly I drink.[63]

The further Mechthild sinks beyond all separateness, the more the abundance of Love overflows, enfolds, encloses and fills her awareness with Love. Mechthild inspires us to hold sorrow and woe gently, and to see that we hold two golden cups both filled with living wine. One holds the red wine of pain, while the other the white wine of comfort. We can drink of them both and discover how they are both the wine of love.[64] The further we sink the more sweetly we drink of the wine of the flowing light of divinity and discover the true nature of joy. Ecstatic joy does not bypass suffering. On the contrary, it is when we sink into the very depths of the wrenching pain of the absence of God that we discover the Trinity at its most intimate. We return to our source that is flowing light and once again, we become filled with divine desire, with *eros*, that is so transcendently sensually divine and human.

However, what is important in Mechthild's choice to sink, is that she is a mature woman, who knows she is unconditionally loved by God.[65] It would be a

---

[61] Ibid.
[62] FL: 4.12.
[63] Ibid.
[64] FL: 2.7.
[65] I encourage anyone who feels like Mechthild to follow this path with a spiritual companion.

misreading of Mechthild to interpret her as advocating the annihilation, or death of self by someone who has not a sense of a differentiated self in God, as loved and loveable. This would be psychologically harmful. Rather, when Mechthild sinks into darkness, in sinking-humility, though she has a sense of her own incompleteness, and confronts her limits, she also knows herself as eternally participating in the Trinity. She has embraced her identity as the lover of Christ and knows that her Lover is lovesick for her, as she is for him.[66] Most importantly, Mechthild has lived the journey of the cross, knows the barren emptiness of the grave and become one with her Lover in the love-making of resurrection. She also knows the deep truth that whenever she has gone towards her Beloved with a blossoming desire, his promise resounds within her, "I must touch you with my divine nature as My own queen."[67] Her union with Christ has given her an identity that is one with Christ and beautifully differentiated. She is naturally herself. Discerningly, Mechthild, as spouse of Christ, is choosing to seek a pure love, that is unattached to either pleasure, or suffering. She yearns-sinks-flows towards her Lover, even to the depths of suffering the loss of her Beloved. She is prepared to enter into the darkest night of spirit (which we will explore with John of the Cross) until her oneness with her Beloved comes to fruition in the love-making of emptiness.

Desiring – Soaring – Enjoying

Sinking imparts a fresh intimacy, opening Mechthild into an expansive, *kenotic*, encompassing flow that deepens her Trinitarian consciousness. Sinking unleashes a new dynamic passion for the divine *eros* of flowing light that frees her to lift her spirit, soar and praise God, with all her heart in all things and gladly give thanks for all of life's experiences. Through patiently giving herself to love in poverty, disgrace, loneliness, suffering, spiritual aridity and many more isolating feelings, the *eros* that lies dormant in suffering awakens her from the illusion of separation, transforming her, so that she can love purely. Suffering in love becomes joy. In the depths of the ecstasis of sinking, *eros* releases in her, and becomes the ascensional force that Teilhard describes, freeing her to sing, shine and soar like a bird as she lives life more blissfully. In a vivid poem, Mechthild wonders how her way of choosing to live her suffering effects the Trinity and hears in the depths of her heart, the chorus of the Trinity:

---

[66] FL: 1.4.
[67] FL: 3.15.

> It comes to the divine palace
> Of my Holy Trinity.
> Where it does such wonders
> That it flows through my three persons.
> It moves and excites and makes playful with love
> My entire Trinity.[68]

Yet, there is more, as the divine lovers invite Mechthild into the meeting point between this world and heaven to join with them in this playful loving in complete intimacy. The Son pleads with Mechthild to:

> … lie in the divine arms
> Reposefully and bare,
> That I must play with her…
> And she shall forevermore
> Soar and play with body and soul
> In My Holy Trinity.
> Sated and quenched like a fish in the sea.

What a beautiful way to enter into the liminal space of the bare point of now, nakedly reposing in the embrace of love. Here in this bareness, time and eternity converge as divine *eros* pours out. Desire meets desire in the harmony of body and soul, in bare repose, as joy resounds. The haunting existential question: "why all this suffering?" dissolves, as Ilia's question of "why we abandon God in the midst of suffering?" is highlighted. When Mechthild chooses to sink beyond the consolation of the presence God, into the darkness of absence, she was not egotistically abandoning God. Rather, she humbly chooses to share in the *kenosis* of her Beloved, loving beyond her known limits. Mechthild is filled with consolation as her Beloved asks:

> Where then is all the sorrow
> Which she has suffered through and for me?
> I will compensate her sweetly.[69]

With her whole being immersed in desire, Mechthild sees how suffering in and through Christ, as a naked lover, has prepared her to live in the point between heaven and earth, to play, body and soul, in the Trinity. Importantly, although Mechthild has displayed some ambiguity about the body, she now appreciates

---

[68] FL: 5:25.
[69] Ibid.

that it is body *and* soul, in its unity, that is satiated by naked love. The ecstatic union of being in the embrace of one another, is not dis-embodiment, but an enfleshing of our soul, blessing our sexuality. It is the wholeness of our soul and body in harmony that comes into this naked embrace of transcendent, playful fluidity. This vision brings lightness of heart to Mechthild, as sorrow dissolves into the *eros* of Trinitarian playfulness and she tastes the sweetness.

The intensity of divine *eros* dissolving the effects of our perceived estrangement from the flowing light of the Trinity continues to expand in Mechthild's sixth book, as she tastes the sweetness of Love's naked embrace and the fruition of being in naked repose magnifies. Her words softly tone from her infusing heart as her Beloved:

> begins to shine lovingly on the soul as she overflows with heart felt love. ... He begins to teach her His will and she begins to taste His sweetness as He begins to greet her with His Divinity so that the power of the Holy Trinity infuses her soul and her body and she receives true wisdom. ... He begins to woo her until she grows weak. ... He becomes lovesick and tempers His love, for He knows her limits better than she does herself. She begins to yearn to place her trust in Him, and He gives her full knowledge, and she begins happily to enjoy His love through her flesh.[70]

In the same yielding of rising-sinking-flowing, Mechthild invites us to release into the ecstasy of infusing light. Here we taste the sweetness of this wine of love filling our being, infusing our flesh, making us whole. She leaves us with a sense of how in this love-making, the ecstatic, transcendent, intimacy of being in one another, is not just spiritualised, in order to have full knowledge it must have a bodily dimension that naturally flows into our sexuality. The inner kiss of her Beloved communing within unites spiritual and bodily sensual knowing, initiating a bodily infusion of wisdom. Johnette Putnam reminds us, that as this transformation of energies takes place in the inner marriage, there is an integration of the intra contra-sexual dimension of our self. This wholeness fosters the gradual transcendence of self as an isolated individual, into a true personhood in universal love.[71] As on the cross, Mechthild again undermines gender stereotypes, as she reveals how we are transformed into universal

---

[70] FL: 6.1.
[71] Johnette Putnam OSB, "Mechthild of Magdeburg, Poet and Mystic," in *Medieval Women Monastics Wisdom's Wellsprings*, eds. Miriam Schmitt and Linda Kulzer (Collegeville: Liturgical Press, 1996), 224, 227, points to how Jung used Mechthild as an example of the marriage of the *anima* and *animus* in psychological maturing.

personhood in Christ, in the *eros* of the flowing light of love through ecstatic union. In this union, feminine and masculine love energies naturally infuse. We transfigure beyond gender distinctions into luminous, flowing, Trinitarian intimacy. We become universally human, in the image and likeness of the flowing love of the Trinity. Loved in our embodiment, our Beloved continues to be lovesick for us until we stop resisting this embodiment and sink into love just as generously as Mechthild sinks into pain.

Now living in Helfta, Mechthild becomes a humble beggar woman, frail in her body, suffering the diminishment of ageing, coping without the pain relief we have today.[72] She has lived the fullness of pouring out her life in love. Now it feels like she is sinking even further than before into fragility, this time with little choice, as her body prepares for its final consummation in ecstatic union in eternal light. Here, Mechthild as beggar woman is at her most beautiful, for when she has sunk lowest into the depths of her suffering, been stripped of her autonomy and drunk from the cup of anguish, her heart overflows in gratitude. Her song of gratitude haunts us, as gracefully she thanks her Beloved that she has lost her sight, for now she has wonderous sight. She has lost the power of her hands and her heart, and now is served with the wonderous hands and heart of others.[73] Ecstasy and diminishment comingle, as humbly Mechthild waits lovesick and ready for the greatest wedding, at the longest banquet that her Beloved promised her. Forever a spouse of light, the Beloved's song resounds over all she has shared with the promise:

> And there I will give you a sweet kiss on the mouth,
> So that all my Divinity
> Shall rush through your soul
> And my threefold eyes
> Shall evermore and ceaselessly
> Play in your twofold heart.[74]

This joyful invitation to play within our heart, in the heart of Trinity, in the embrace of the eternal kiss, to feel the rush of flowing light swirling though our being, and see with Trinitarian threefold eyes, affirms all that we are saying about the evolutionary desire of God for us to be one. It energises us to live from the

---

[72] This beggar-woman reflects the servant girl dressed in red-brown rags that Mechthild describes earlier. See, FL: 2.4.
[73] FL: 7.64.
[74] FL: 4.5.

passion of the divine *eros* within us and see through the eyes of the flowing light of the Trinity. This energy field of flowing light that unites body and soul, making our inner and outer world one, belongs to us now, whatever our age, or stage in life. In our youth, in our full grown-ness, in our ageing, we are filled with flowing light in an endless cyclical pouring forth and returning back to the heart of eternal flowing light.

Illuminating Contemplation

Mechthild's contemplation dissolves all distinctions between the ecstatic union of blessed quiet with Christ, in the loving of the marriage bed, the dying on the cross, sinking into suffering and estrangement, and the ecstasy of union in the flowing light of the Trinity. For her, absence and presence both ecstatically draw her into the divine heart that is contemplation. Therefore, Mechthild has an enormous contribution to make to our insights into the transformation of consciousness through contemplation, in times of suffering. She models for us how, through rising yearning, humble sinking, and flowing love, we can surrender into the intimacy of mystical union in the marriage bed of blessed quiet. But importantly, she shows us how sinking into suffering and what feels like an infinite distance from God, can become the ultimate mystical union, when lived within the flowing *kenosis* of Christ crucified. Mechthild awakens us to see how as her soul sinks, and she humbly drinks deeply of pure love, God fills her whole being. Consequently, Mechthild calls the Father her heart, Christ her body and the Holy Spirit, her breath, making the Trinity her refuge and eternal rest. In response, the Trinity affirm her as "a mirror of eternal contemplation."[75] As contemplatives seek to be a mirror of contemplation, amidst such enormous pain and estrangement in the world today, I will highlight four important insights that can support us as we face the perennial question of suffering in the light of contemplation.

First, Mechthild lays the foundations for her theology of suffering by taking us into the energy flow of *Minne*, into a mystical seeing through the light of fiery Spirit flowing through our soul.[76] The growth in consciousness that she explores from sensual knowing, into knowing through desire, into knowing through light, awakens us within the light of love. Encountering *Minne* enables us to embrace and be present within the love of the Trinity transforming suffering into joy. In

---

[75] FL: 5.7.
[76] FL: 5.1.

this light we can "see all around" who is being revealed and what is being said.[77] This seeing from within the light of the Spirit is open, expansive, all seeing, so that the soul's, "eyes are truly open and she professes that God is everything in all things."[78] Accordingly, this awakening of the eye of our soul, illuminated by flowing light, infuses wisdom as it generates a continual centrating, spiralling movement from outer sensing, releasing into inner mystical sensing. We release into the ecstasy of blessed quiet, which in turn binds the outer senses to the inner senses, in the mystical love-making of the kiss of blessed quiet. We remain in the quivering stillness of being one in one another. Mechthild stresses that body and soul must both be involved as our eyes open and we see that God is everything and in all things. Mechthild draws us into the pure silence of ecstatic union, grounding and enabling contemplation to be our natural state.

Second, Mechthild expands on the sensually transcendent dimension of contemplation, encouraging us into the *eros* of spousal intimacy. This demands a complete giving of ourselves to our divine lover in deep interior love-making. Mechthild enables us to reclaim the language of the love-making of sexual union, as sacred language to express divine-human intimacy. Within the circular energy flow of flowing light, Mechthild awakens the love language of our physical senses, and binds them to the transcendence of the mystical senses, taking us beyond the body-soul split, into sensually unitive consciousness. She shows us how to sense from within the luminously transcendent sensuality of the sexual intimacy of ecstatic union in blessed quiet. This mystical love-making of blessed quiet extends from the delight of youth in repose in the bed of love, to the suffering of the cross, the starkness of the grave, and the most apophatic, searing times of absence, to the love-making in the Trinity.

Mechthild sensitises us to the delicate nuances of the wisdom infused, as we become one in the love-making of the inner marriage with our divine Lover, in all seasons of our lives. Especially important for contemplatives today, is the way Mechthild assists us to delight in how our sexuality is a sacred energy that opens into the sensually transcendent, luminous ground of the *eros* of the flowing light of love. This energy of sacred *eros* is a pathway for this universal transformation into light. We are embraced in humanity, infused in divinity, constantly lead by the playful Holy Spirit into the future fullness of a passionate, vivifying, loving divine-human relationship. Mechthild is unique in her capacity

---

[77] FL: 2.19.
[78] Ibid.

to harness the energies of erotic desire and celebrate the fullness of our humanity that includes the holiness of our body and sexuality. This ecstasy of wholistic mutual self-giving breaks open a new awareness of the holiness of our bodies that is critical for today.

Third, Mechthild teaches how to live into the *kenotic* quality of flowing love that is *Minne*, in all of life's circumstances, especially in times of suffering and experiences of the absence of God. In particular, her *kenotic* sinking releases into the oneness of the threefold energy flow of: "rising yearning, sinking humility and flowing love."[79] In Mechthild's theology, sinking becomes an ecstatic expression of desire that takes her into the humus of suffering, as it continuously opens her into the ground of pure loving. Sinking imitates the deep *kenosis* of the pouring out of love of the crucified one that transforms her into the Christomorphic shape of Christa. Hanging on the cross, sinking into the lowest point of suffering with Christ, becomes the most sublime love-making of dying into Love. In this mystical dying, Mechthild breathes her last, into the pure air of the Spirit and yields into the darkness that covers the eternal light of divinity.

As she is laid in the grave of deep humility, the grave transforms into the nuptial bed of ecstatic union, in resurrection.[80] This paschal movement of dying and rising in mystical union, then prepares Mechthild for evermore *kenotic* outpourings of love that are unattached to either consolation, or desolation. Mechthild suffers the loss of all she knew about her Beloved, until this ravishing *kenosis*, draws her into the ecstatic union of the naked lovers clothing each other that enables her to become a bride of the Trinity.[81] Like Eckhart's detachment beyond understanding that comprehends all things within itself, Mechthild helps us face suffering beyond understanding, offering contemplatives today a raw, radical, trustworthy way of *kenosis*. She teaches us how to enter the depths of suffering and estrangement, within a yearning-sinking-flowing movement, so that suffering and absence become the holy *eros* of Christ drawing us into the flowing light of the Trinity.

Fourth, Mechthild creates a metaphysics of oneing as flowing light, that goes to the heart of our identity as a person in God. Thus, she places us, within the luminosity of the radiant streams of luminous divine love. She invites us to come to know more intimately the flowing light within our own soul's ground, that is

---

[79] FL: 7.34.
[80] FL: 3.10.
[81] FL: 2.9; 2.22.

the flowing light that is existence itself. This flowing light is an endless luminous oneing light creating more flow, more oneness, more love. Mechthild teaches us not only how to be in the flowing light of love, but to be this flowing love. When we are in this flow, we soar with ease like a bird through the air and sink into the depths of suffering, always in harmony with the melody of the joy that flows from the lyre of the Holy Spirit. Barbara Fiand reminds us that as we evolve in integrating the whole of who we are, our task is to take in and integrate light, merge with ourselves, and our destiny and positively shape the future of our planet. She reminds us: "As each of us becomes whole, we radiate light, – light from within – unimpeded by our self-imposed emotional and physical blocks. The medicine of the future is light. We are healing ourselves from that which is our essence."[82] Mechthild affirms how there is within us the natural fertility of flowing light, a capacity to give self away, to lose self in another, to unite and awaken within the other. Deep within all created being there is an effortless, inexhaustible sweet flow that endlessly fills the vessel that we are, so that we too become this eternal fountain of outpouring love, pouring love back into the Trinity by giving this light of love to our world. This fecund pouring out of *Minne*-love is particularly poignant in times of intense suffering so that all our diminishments become an exquisite love-making in the enjoyment of the ecstasy of flowing light.

I invite you to conclude this reflection by sinking into this flowing light with Mechthild, before we reflect on the wisdom of Clare of Assisi.

---

[82] Barbara Fiand. *Awe-Filled Wonder: The Interface of Science and Spirituality* (New York, Paulist Press, Kindle Edition, 2008), Loc. 354.

Praying Contemplatively

*Lavish is the overflow of divine love
that ceaselessly pours itself out
so that the empty vessel of ourselves
may be filled and overflow with love.*[83]

Embracing Stillness

Flowing light of Love,
Bathe me in the flowing light of your infusing presence
as I come to this time of contemplation.
You are full and overflowing,
wooing me with your blessed quiet.
As I gently bathe in your tranquil presence,
show me how to see from within our oneness
and recognise myself as I truly am,
flowing in your flowing light, loving with your flowing love.
Amen.

---

[83] FL: 7.55. My translation.

Ruminating on Scripture

You fill us to overflowing with living streams of life.
Psalm 36:9

The Music of Silence

Flowing silence illumes.

Contemplatio

The Beloved says to you, "Come at midday into the shade of the well into the bed of love; there you shall be refreshed by Love."[84] So I invite you to come into the shade of the well, to find a quiet place and become still, silent, rested so that your heart is flowing.

Feel the flow of your heart becoming more and more tranquil, as you hear Mechthild's words: "The closer she becomes the sweeter the kisses on her mouth taste. The more lovingly they gaze at each other, the more reluctantly they depart from each other."[85] Become attentive to this luminous gaze of the Beloved that immerses you in light.

As you breathe, feel the touch of the breath caressing, opening, expanding, softening every particle of your being into the energy flow of flowing light. Feel the gentleness, the warmth, the aroma of luminous presence delicately oneing.

Mechthild whispers in the shimmering silence, "The more she is enveloped, the more quiet she becomes."[86] Feel the flow of the enveloping, enfolding, embracing inviting you into a sinking-love.

---

[84] FL: 1:44.
[85] FL: 1.22.
[86] Ibid.

Release every particle of your being in sinking-love, drawing your breath, you spirit, your mind deeper and deeper into Love's abyss.

If you are grieving or suffering, and a memory or felt sense of pain arises, continue to sink lovingly into the humous of suffering, and beyond, beyond, beyond.

Sense the caress of Love continuing to envelop, enfold, embrace, one you in this sinking, until you are in the silence of the oneing of the making love of blessed quiet, in the kiss of the quivering stillness, one in one another.

Bask in the blessed quiet.

When you feel the Beloved draws this prayer to a close, gently remain one in one another, in the sinking-love of blessed quiet as you move into the rest of the day.

Blessing

Infuse the day in blessed quiet.

V

In the Vulnerable Embrace of Love

Clare of Assisi

*Wisdom is a reflection of the eternal light,
untarnished mirror of God's active power,
image of God's goodness.*
Wisdom 7:26

*I hold this memory in my heart,
and my spirit melts within me.[1]*

Gazing at the iconic painting, *Crucifixion Shoalhaven,* by Arthur Boyd, I see a naked crucified Christa hanging, exposed on a tree-like cross planted in the bed of the Shoalhaven river. The ashen body is sensual, wounded, vulnerable, tortured by the trauma of life's afflictions. Yet there is a dignity, a serenity about the way she receives all that has happened. The cross stands starkly against an Australian desert landscape as the mauve-grey sky, charcoal burnt bush and the shallows of the river mirror the colours of timeless suffering. As I gaze, behold and enter into oneness with the Christa figure, I imbibe the primordial stillness of this moment in time. I feel the deep pain. In my gaze, I see blood flowing in the river, creating a lament from the deep wounding of my own life, the pain of

---

[1] The translations of Clare's Letters to Agnes are my own, taken from the Latin, in Edith Van den Goorbergh and Theodore Zweerman, *Light Shining Through a Veil* (The Netherlands: Peeters, 2000). Hereafter L. Letter number and line numbers are given. L: 4.26. Cf. I remember and my spirit faints, consumes away, humbles (Lam 3:20).

communal vulnerability amidst so much collective trauma, along with the anguish of creation being brought to extinction. Next to this painting hangs an equally exposed, naked Christ, *Crucifixion Rose*. His limp body infuses into the sandier tones of this painting. Arising from the riverbed, it questions whether this archetypal story of human/divine love, vulnerable, tortured, crucified, has anything to say to our contemporary world. The two paintings draw us into the existential suffering held sacred in their embrace, into the liminal space where we encounter the crucified and risen Christ/Christa, or what I will call Christo-Sophia. Christo-Sophia is the one who holds human and divine, Word and Wisdom, masculine and feminine in the fullness of our oneness in God. In this liminal consciousness of Christo-Sophia, we touch the eternal. Critical to the trans-figurative movement of dying and rising, is the integration of the Christa and Christ in the depths of our deepest wounds in the mystical marriage. Both the Christa and the Christ need each other, to tell this story, if they are to take us into the iconographic mystery, into the participatory love-knowledge of the risen Christo-Sophia, who is the Mirror of Eternity. It is this exquisite exchange of love that takes place in the oneing of this mutual embrace of Logos and Wisdom that transfigures us. This is the crucified Lover that Paul recognised as Christ the power and wisdom of God (1 Cor 1:24) and Julian of Norwich acclaims as Christ the deep wisdom of the Trinity our Mother.

These luminous icons of crucified love mirror in my own prayer, as I record in my journal:

> I stand in the waters of the trickling creek where I live and feel welcomed by the spirits of my Aboriginal sisters and brothers. They are here with me inviting me deeper into *dadirri*.[2] The centre of my heart connects with the centre of the earth, the *anima mundi* feels so alive, luminous, vibrant. I have a sense of crucified love, of the land so brutalised, of the pain of our wisdom ancestors, of the pain of the world, and I also feel myself exposed, as naked Christa hanging on the cross, vulnerable. I desire to embrace all that is crucified and feel drawn into the divine embrace. The waters of the creek flow around me, shining radiantly after fresh rains, mirroring love. Recently I felt so exposed, wiped out, belittled. Vulnerable to the competing energies, I fell over, bruised and cracked my ribs. A crack in my identity, an invitation to go deeper, into my naked being in the naked being of my Beloved. Ah, I realise, a wound in my side, opening

---

[2] *Dadirri* is a term that draws us to a deep still heart listening shared by Dr. Miriam-Rose Ungunmerr, an Aboriginal elder from Nauiyu (Daly River).

into my heart. Vulnerable love lies hidden in this deep pain. I feel the falling, the sinking, the dissolving, deep into the being of my crucified lover, the Christ.

The enfolding, flowing, tender infusing of being in one another becomes lighter and lighter, creating translucent points of luminous stillness. My body aching with the pain of the fall, softens and feels drawn into a tender embrace. The enfolding, flowing gently, infusing, absorbs the pain, ones. The timeless luminosity of ever embracing love ripples out with a serene glow of light infusing light. All is the flow of the shining emptiness of the embrace of silent love. In the lovemaking of emptiness, heart centre in heart centre, a new identity is forming of Christ-Christa in our oneing in love. Christo-Sophia rises in my heart. All is one, in the oneing of Love.

Clare, we will see draws us into this icon of suffering, into the depths of our personal and communal wounds so that we may discover the exquisite transformation of our mind, our soul, our being in Christ, who holds all things in oneness as the mirror, or icon of eternity. The role of an icon is to create a sacred space where our gaze can focus, pass into the dark nights of liminal space and then into eternal divine consciousness. Clare draws us into the deep pain and unspeakable trauma of the cross and then shows us how to enter Love's embrace in the depths of the cavernous darkness of our wounds and become one in the mystical marriage. Held in the incandescence of the mirror of eternity, the inner light of our Christ consciousness awakens. Having journeyed with Mechthild, hanging on the cross and sinking into an abyss of absence, we will now join Clare and focus some more on the trauma of human suffering expressed on the cross. We will see how in the midst of suffering, Clare invites us to come into the embrace of the suffering Christ, where, in the depths of suffering in transforming union, we become a luminous mirror of eternity, that organically reflects light from Light.

Clare – Light Mirroring Light

Living earlier than the mystics we have journeyed with so far, Clare of Assisi (1194-1253), was a follower of St Frances and founded the order of Poor Clare, a monastic order for women. She has few recorded words, yet what she does write is so poignant for these times.In lingering now and listening to Clare's voice as she sings of her vulnerable lover, we will become immersed in Clare's wisdom through her four brief letters to Agnes of Prague (1211-1282), and a letter Agnes wrote to Clare. She also composed a letter to Ermentrude of Bruges, and her *Rule and Testament*. Her sisters compiled an exposition of her life, *The*

Golden Legend, after her death. With so few words to ponder, what she says and the silence surrounding her words becomes all the more magnified. Edith Van den Goorbergh and Theodore Zweerman suggest that Clare is an artist who embroiders and creates a design that shows at a glance: "where the connections are, what the heart is and which patterns are arranged around the heart."[3] Ilia Delio affirms this delicate creativity, reminding us that Clare's spirituality does not develop systematically in her letters, but rather shines out like: "a finely stitched pattern on a soft delicate cloth. One has to read her letters slowly and prayerfully as she weaves her ideas into the pattern of Christ."[4] This finely stitched pattern, like petti-point needlework, continually focuses us to see God in the point of the heart of the cross. Clare teaches us how to come into a mutual embrace in vulnerable love and centre in Love's eternal point.

Clare embroiders a tender and loving icon of vulnerable love, endlessly meeting us in the depths of our own, and our communal, vulnerability. Her delicately stitched images, especially her vision of the poor Christ, catch our eye and allure us to gaze, centre in the Christ, imitate the pattern of his *kenotic* outpouring of love, into an ever-emptying abandonment of all things, and pass through into the mirror of eternity. All that she writes comes from this *kenotic* love, as when in the first letter to Agnus, she pours out her love: "with humble prayers from the heart-womb of Christ" (*humilibus precibus in Christi visceribus supplicandam),*"[5] Literally, her words emphasise her humble prayer that arises from the viscera, the liver-heart-stomach, of Christ. Sometimes translated from "the bowels of Christ,"[6] "the mercy of Christ,"[7] or, "the innermost heart of Christ,"[8] Clare is speaking from within the abyss of humility, from within the inner most visceral affection and oneness in the heart-womb of the poor Christ. She invites us too, to empty into the consciousness that awakens in the deep heart-womb of Christ.

Like Mechthild, this abounding intimacy in humility, comes from Clare's pouring out her own heart in love, until her Beloved fills her emptiness with the vulnerable love of mystical love-making, where she gives herself totally to

---

[3] Van den Goorbergh and Zweerman, *Light Shining Through a Veil,* 25.
[4] Ilia Delio, *Clare of Assisi: A Heart Full of Love* (Cincinnati: St Anthony Messenger Press, 1993), xxi.
[5] L: 1.31.
[6] Van den Goorbergh and Zweerman, *Light Shining Through a Veil,* 42.
[7] Regis Armstrong translation, http://www.slr-ofs.org/st-clares-letters-to-st-agnes-of-prague.html
[8] Joan Mueller translation, https://epistolae.ctl.columbia.edu/letter/560.html

Christ. Clare continually stresses the importance of this vulnerability, portraying just how wounded, humble, naturally of the earth this Poor One is, who meets us in the depths of our suffering. Through imitating the same *kenosis* of outpouring love as her spouse, Clare models for us a way of poverty of being. She teaches us to be *kenotic* love. She shows us how to be so filled with the burning longing of the poor Christ, that we too desire to imitate Christ, to pour out our hearts in love and become poor, humble, of the earth, naturally who we are eternally in Christ, who is the one in whom all things were made from nothing.[9] In her understanding vulnerability, humility and poverty are the language of love. These prerequisite virtues open, release and empty us so that we may live fully in the embrace of our lover, in the kiss of our present moment, being in one another.

This Chapter

In this chapter, after giving an overview of Clare's soteriology, we will focus on Clare's luminous vision into the transformation that occurs as we enter into the pathos of crucified love. After exploring the gaze Clare awakens in us as we behold the icon of the cross, we will see how she creates what I will call "the vulnerable embrace with the poor Christ." We will see how we are held in this embrace, in the midst of our wounds, until through the exchange of love in the wound, we enter into the fecundity of our oneing in the wound. Secure in this embrace, we will then see how, in this deep exchange in the wound, within the dark mirror of the cross, grace transfigures us into the resurrected luminosity of the mirror of eternity, personally and communionally. Finally, we will draw out how Clare's vulnerable way illuminates contemplation today.

Clare's Soteriology

Clare immerses us in Love's embrace, dramatically expressed in the crucifixion and offers us a way of entering into experiences of suffering, abandonment and the absence of God that is intensely healing and life enhancing. Tragically, in too many cases, this central symbol of vulnerable love has been distorted into yet another way of blaming and disempowering the most vulnerable in our society. And heartbreakingly, at times, the scandal of the cross is indeed a scandal, for it has become a weapon of abuse itself, with its limited, vitriolic, guilt centred

---

[9] L: 3.7.

theologies that haunt the human psyche, implying distant, punitive, dualistic images of the divine. The cross has been misappropriated into glorifying suffering, justifying power abuse and inflicting sexual atrocities. In the face of all this tragedy, Clare, *Clara*, whose name evokes luminosity, showers us in another light. She presents us with an icon of a poor, humble, vulnerable, crucified lover, who is fleshy, concrete, connected, whose warmth, tenderness and intimate silence is infinite. To be vulnerable (*vulnerabilis)*, from wound (*vulnus*), is to be wounded, open, receptive and capable of suffering. It is to be moved physically, emotionally and spiritually to the depths of the viscera of our heart-womb, to feel compassion and be changed by another's pain. Clare's vulnerable crucified lover is a totally *kenotic* vulnerable beloved, who meets us in our wounds, pours out love ceaselessly, and draws us into resurrected life to be the poor Christ to others. In her gaze, the poor, crucified Lover is God tortured, torn, desolate, abandoned, who dwells in the depths of the unmemorable memory, who is with us in the unspeakable agony of our collective traumas. This is a vulnerable God hidden in the midst of all physical, sexual and emotional abuse, tenderly sharing our suffering, creating a safe enfolding womb of transformation that warmly, gently, kindly, transfigures our suffering in the oneness of Love's embrace.

Clare models how we can only discover the intimacy and transformative power of oneness in love from the depths of our own suffering in love. She invites us beyond oppressive sin focused soteriologies, into the embrace of an exchange of love within our wounds. This exchange leads us into the deepest intimacy of the kiss in the inner wine cellar of our heart and places our mind in the mirror of eternity. In the luminosity of the mirror of eternity we enter into the depths of our own wounds, into the wounds of Christo-Christa, where our oneness in Christo-Sophia lies waiting to be uncovered. In this embrace, Christo-Sophia fills us with all the creativity of the Logos-Word spoken from the womb of the divine. This ever-inclusive embrace draws us into the silent luminosity of Sophia/Wisdom ever responsive healing, making us one. Clare assists us to plunge into what is most fragmented and incomplete and experience the mystical exchange of love, oneing us in the midst of suffering. She draws us to see from within the eternal shining within the very depths of suffering, and then carries us through the transformation of becoming a mirror of eternity, personally and communionally, for each other in our daily lives. We will now reflect on the nuances of her way of seeing, revealed as a fourfold movement of gazing, considering, contemplating and imitating the poor Christ.

Clare's Gaze

While Clare empties us and takes us into the bowels of human/divine suffering, she concurrently fills us with light. Her words emit a radiance as they illuminate the process of darkness and light becoming one in the Christic body. She points to the light hidden in the depths of our wounds and prepares the ground for the awakening of the inner light of our Christ consciousness, that is, the mirror of eternity. Central to this teaching is *intuere* (gaze), an interior sense perception of the gaze that resonates with Julian's beholding, of entering into silence, awakening the soft penetrating gaze of the eye of our heart, meeting the gaze of absolute love and melting into one vulnerable gaze. *Intuere,* stresses the immediate, intuitive perception that arises from entering into the heart-womb of Christ.

Clare's nuances into contemplation finely tune our deep, interior gaze that sees from within the depths of our oneness with the Christ who suffers. This gaze that Clare teaches penetrates deeply into the wound of divine suffering in an unfolding movement of gazing, considering, contemplating, and desiring to imitate the vulnerable, poor Christ (*Intuere, considera, contemplare, desiderans imitari).*[10] With our gaze fixed on the Poor One, and the Poor One's gaze dissolving us, the light of grace arises in our heart awareness in an actively responsive, yet passive receptivity, considering, or meditating, until we repose in the diaphanous awareness of contemplation of being in one another. This organic movement is like focusing our vision so single mindedly into the finest petti-point, that our gaze acts like a shaft of light that pierces through the cloud of unknowing that we previously explored with the *Cloud of Unknowing* author. In drawing into this loving, unitive darkness of contemplation, Clare emphasises that this takes place in the inner heart of Christ, in the locus of the cross, in the centre of the mirror of eternity.[11] From this centre the desire to imitate Christ arises.

Although this desire to imitate the vulnerable poor Christ could look like simply modelling our-selves on his way of loving, for Clare *imitari,* imitating Christ, is to be an icon of Christ, to become Christ. This desire to imitate has an innate centripetal-centrifugal energy that returns us to our origins in Christ. At once, as the energy of desire draws us inward, in an encircling, ever-centring within our

---

[10] L: 2.20.
[11] L: 3.3.

heart's depths, we simultaneously expand into boundless love. The more deeply we gaze within our own heart-womb, into the viscera, the heart-womb of Christ, the more we are transformed into Christ and drawn out into an expansive, outward looking gaze, that can consider and contemplate vulnerable love in the midst of the suffering of God in the most horrific suffering of humankind and creation. Clare's gentle, intuitive way of seeing, that lingers, ponders, reposes within, and desires to imitate the Poor Christ is powerfully recreative, offering a trustworthy pattern for those who feel violated by trauma to follow. In the face of suffering, Clare invites us into the embrace of the Poor Christ.

Held in this embrace we can see how, in the depths of our most vulnerable, raw, heart-wrenching pain, there is the crucified Christ. This ever-trustworthy embrace makes it safe for us to finally feel the pain of our trauma. Here we know that the pain of creation is the pain of God. Clare's language is impassioned, as she takes us deeper into the gaze, into the depths of the heart of the Poor Christ who is pure *kenosis*, absolute Love poured out. She encourages us: "totally love this Poor One who gave himself totally out of love for you."[12] Her repetition of "totally," shines throughout her writings, as this total love is expressed in total vulnerability. Clare takes us into the embrace of this vulnerability.

The Embrace of Vulnerable Love

"Embrace the Poor Christ" (*sed pauperem Christum, amplectere*)[13] Clare counsels. And in her first letter to Agnes, Clare celebrates how Agnes has chosen to embrace this Poor One. Although Clare's choice, "*amplectere*," can suggest to take and hold, clasp, or cling to Christ, for Clare this embrace is totally free, open and vulnerable. This embrace is never sticky, constrictive, or oppressive because it has a profoundly *kenotic* quality. This embrace arises from the love-making of emptiness. Its source is in the hollow of poverty, arising out of the overflowing fecundity and fullness of the pure emptiness of the divine total self-giving, of the deepest possible *kenosis* of love pouring out love. Like Francis of Assisi, she has married Lady Poverty, as she has chosen to give herself completely to her spousal Beloved, the crucified Christ. The fullness of embrace becomes hers, as she yields, heart to heart, centre to centre, loving, touching and receiving Christ so fully, that she is virginal, shining with the luminosity of original divine poverty. Agnes' choice to embrace Christ in mutual poverty, is

---

12   L: 3.15.
13   L: 2.17-18.

critical for Clare, and for Christ. They need each other for the fullness of love to flourish. This love relationship is also critical for us.

In encouraging this embrace, Clare establishes what Miroslav Volf calls: "a phenomenology of embrace."[14] In this embrace, we create a space in ourselves for the other to come in, as we make a movement out of ourselves so as to enter the space created by the other. We wait, as embrace is never an intrusion, or an invasion, or a taking over of another's boundaries. It is a welcoming of another as a unique person. We wait, until the embrace becomes a reciprocal enclosing. The enclosure of embrace then opens into the freedom of the possibility of ongoing embrace. The embrace creates a safe, liminal, in between space, where our dualistic vision of reality can reshape into a oneing consciousness.

With no limits on the anguish and pain Agnes brings to this embrace, Clare encourages her to live in the dynamism of this embrace always, yielding into its ever-enfolding movement that releases into the spaciousness of poverty, into an ever-deepening movement of oneing. In this endless embrace, her poverty opens into the divine poverty, into the fecund emptiness of the heart of the divine. Clare's consoling words to Agnes draw us into the mutuality of this embrace:

> Now this Vulnerable One holds you close in an embrace, (*amplexibus*) adorns your breast with precious stones, and places priceless pearls on your ears. Your spouse encircles you totally in shimmering gems, and places on your head, a golden crown as a sign of your devotion and love.[15]

The vulnerable embrace of total love, transforms all our wounds into precious jewels, drawing us into the embrace of mystical marriage. Singing with all the passion of the *Song of Songs*, Clare opens us into the fragrance of this depthless, interpenetrating, mutuality in the embrace of our Beloved in contemplation. She encourages us to hear the voice of the Beloved urge us to: "run and not grow weary until you bring me into the wine cellar, until your left hand is under my head and your right arm blissfully embraces me; and you kiss me with the most blissful kiss of your mouth."[16] The wine-cellar identifies the depthless underground of the cellar of our soul. It is the *apex affectus*,[17] the deepest part of our inner-heart knowing, the most unitive awareness of our oneness within the kiss of God in mystical love-making.

---

[14] Miroslav Volf, *Exclusion and Embrace: A Theological Exploration of Identity, Otherness and Reconciliation* (Nashville: Abington Press, 1996), 141-147.
[15] L: 1:8-11.
[16] L: 4.32.
[17] As we saw in the *Cloud of Unknowing*.

Clare urges us not to remain isolated and alone, in our vulnerability, but rather, to risk opening into this eternal embrace from the depths of our own wound. In the moment of risking, and sharing our vulnerability, we realise we are already embraced by vulnerable divine love who knows our vulnerability. In this mutual embrace, an exchange takes place as vulnerability, touching vulnerability, evolves into love. Held close, enfolded, encircled in love, our wounds begin to shimmer with the healing light of the divine, transform and shine like jewels. In this embrace we imbibe energetically how the embrace of vulnerable divine love is stitched eternally into the fabric of our existence, enfolding us into the endless flow of Love, making us one and whole. Clare urges us to "taste the hidden sweetness"[18] that arises from the divine embrace that becomes an exchange of wound, of love, of the whole of who we are in Christ.

The Deep Exchange

"This is indeed a wonderful exchange," (*Magnum quippe ac laudabile commercium*),[19] Clare affirms. This exquisite exchange of love that takes place in this mutual embrace is in fact a oneing that transfigures us. Clare's drawing on the term "*commercium*" (commerce), is rich in theological nuance, for in Clare's day *commercium*, was concerned with the exchange of money for goods. Frequently, this idea of a commercial exchange was developed into a punitive theology of reparation, with an emphasis on Christ suffering to pay back our debt to God caused through human sinfulness. Yet, *commercium,* also referred to a mutual agreement between people, an exchange within a community, a personal, or sexual relationship.[20] When Clare draws on the term, she invites Agnes into a *commercium* with the Poor Christ, as in an exchange of love between Lovers. This exchange is like an eternal marriage, where the poverty of Love poured from the heart of Christ and the poverty of Love poured out from the heart of Agnes infinitely infuse one another. Julian's luminous love-knot echoes. Clare reminds us that it is only in the spaciousness of a poor, open, heart, unattached to anything, that we can enter into the hidden depths of the exchange of love as Lover and Beloved.

---

[18]   L: 3.14.
[19]   L: 1.30.
[20]   Van den Goorbergh and Zweerman, *Light Shining Through a Veil,* 46-48.

We first encounter reference to commercium in Clare's first letter, when Agnes exchanges her regal life as a royal, for the poverty of being a Poor Clare. This is a deeply intimate heartfelt exchange where love is exchanged for love. Clare affirms how this is an extremely admirable piece of commerce.[21] In her second letter, when Agnes feels her choice is under threat, Clare invites Agnes to gaze at the Crucified Poor One. Here the exchange takes place in the midst of absolute vulnerability, when the humble, Crucified One empties himself, pours out love, from the deepest abyss of the bowels of his being. In this exchange, Agnes in her suffering comes face to face with Christ in his suffering. Wound is exchanged for wound, as love pours out. Here again, there is a mutual sharing of love in suffering. The commerce, in this sense a *com-mercium*, is a tender exchange of mercy, of compassion pouring from the womb of Christ, into the womb of human misery, infusing the fertility of the intimacy of mutually shared suffering. In the third letter, the predominant exchange takes place as the dark mirror of the cross transforms into the luminous mirror of eternity. In this exchange, Clare invites Agnes to place her mind into this mirror of eternity and her whole being into the divine being. Here the exchange takes place at the point where the opaque darkness of the suffering of God in human anguish transforms our whole being into luminous resurrected being in Christ, in the Trinity. Finally, in her fourth letter, the evocative image of embrace in the wine cellar, holds the exchange of identity that occurs in the exchange of the mutual kiss of mystical marriage. This exchange of identity makes us one with Christ.

Clare invites us to energetically embody this exchange in the humble outpouring of our essence, into point of the mirror of the cross, into the mirror of eternity, into the divine eternal embrace, and live in the poverty of the fullness of our vulnerable God continually pouring out Love from Love. Clare encourages:

> If you suffer with him, you shall reign with him. If you weep with him, you shall rejoice with him. If you die with him on the cross of tribulation you shall possess heavenly mansions in the splendor of the saints and in the book of life your name shall be called glorious among all.[22]

Clare invites Agnes to be one with the Poor Christ, in the midst of her suffering, in a mutual exchange of love between lovers. In this exchange, the poverty of love pours from the heart of Christ and the poverty of love pours out from the heart of Agnes, infinitely infusing one another in an eternal marriage. When we

---

[21] Ibid.
[22] L: 2.21-22.

feel abandoned in suffering, Clare reminds us to come into the embrace of the wounded Christ, who meets us in the hidden depths of the exchange of love.

The Wound of Love

Clare paints a graphic, vivid portrait of the suffering and vulnerability of God in her crucifixion images. And although, the stark detail of the extent of this suffering challenges our capacity to gaze deeply, as she presents the primal *kenosis* of divine love mirrored in the tortured body of the poor Christ hanging on the cross, Clare urges us to risk gazing and remember. Her words fade into a brutal vacuum as the Christ hangs: "vulnerable, despised, beaten, and bruised repeatedly, all over his body, suffering and dying in the midst of all human anguish."[23] As we gaze at the battered body, there is a haunting sense of the powerlessness of vulnerability. Yet, at the same time, we glimpse the amazing creativity of love at work here. Notice the naked defenselessness of Christ in the "midst" of human fragmentation, anguish, affliction, in the middle, in the centre of the fragility of the broken world. When we gaze and penetrate more deeply into the wound we are drawn, beyond subject-object, and we know we are this one wound. All our own personal suffering, all the suffering of creation is within this wounded body. All that is fearful, fragmented, raw is held in love.

Clare expresses the archetypal wail of Lamentations: "O all you who pass by this way, look and see if there is any suffering like my suffering."[24] This is the lament that arises from the depths of human affliction: "Is there any suffering like my suffering?" Regrettably, in many places in our world, this archetypal cry is a cacophony, as this crucifixion takes place day after day. Clare invites us to face this suffering, to gaze into it, to consider, to contemplate and to imitate the response of the poor Christ. And as we gaze and listen, our souls sink, until in the *kenosis* of sinking into the ground of poverty, love infuses the very places that are so desolate, fearful, barren, aloof. Vulnerability meets vulnerability until, as we consider in an opaque darkness, obscurely, beyond consciousness awareness, the ultimate exchange of love takes place in our body, in the body of God. Clare invites us to remember this exchange of love over and over.

---

[23] L: 2.20.
[24] L: 4.26.

In The Embrace of Re-Membering

The wail from Lamentations continues: "I will remember this (embrace this) over and over and my soul melts (sinks) within me (*Memoria memor ero et tabescet in me anima mea*).[25] This way of remembering is an embracing, a holding, a be-holding in the pure vulnerability of the preconscious memory of the divine *kenosis* of love, that we participate within eternally. We remember, embrace this *kenotic* movement so fully, that in the fullness of surrender, our spirit "melts," into the wounded Christ. This also translates as our spirit "faints," emphasising the sense of uncontrollably surrendering all our resistances, yielding, or in Mechtild's language "sinking" within,[26] into the ground of our heart, into the wound of the divine. Essentially, and importantly, in this *kenotic* movement, there is a oneing between Christ's wounds and our wounds that gradually seeps into our consciousness through Christ present to the Christ-self in the wound. This depthless sharing of our wounds, becoming one wound in Christ, at first occurs unconsciously, until the light of the divine present to itself in the wound, seeps into our mystical senses, and finally into conscious awareness.

This coming to consciousness of this shared identity in our woundedness marks a critical turning point. In the intimacy of this one wound, our whole self-identity transforms radically. Here, we both remember and forget. In remembering, we bring into our heart, an awareness of a past experience that has wounded us. We feel the felt sense of the pain, guilt, or shame. We feel how all this pain locked within our wounds, is held within the one divine wound, and discover the love present in the midst of this pain, tending, healing our wound. Grace releases the constrictions of the pain body and transfigures us into the deepest truth of who we really are in love. In this release, a new pattern formed by love can emerge so that we no longer need to live out of the distortions caused by the pain of unhealed wounds. In fact, we can forget. The memory of an isolated wounded-self no longer needs to be our centre of identity. Our identity is mirrored to us as beloved. In some ways we are always a wounded lover. Nonetheless, in this embrace of remembering our woundedness, our locus of identity shifts from our

---

[25] Ibid.
[26] Joan Mueller translation, https://epistolae.ctl.columbia.edu/letter/560.html

wounded insulated self to our self in Christ, and our sharing of the one wound, shifts to the love we dwell within eternally.[27]

Constance Fitzgerald in her seminal paper, "Memory and Prophetic Hope," points to the ambiguity involved in this way of remembering. This can make us feel "suspended in an intellectual impasse," she says, as she identifies the tension:

> I struggle to hold in tension both the power of memory and the importance of history in giving us context, on the one hand, and on the other hand, the need to forget and be open to the radical transformation of the self and the memory. I ask how we can remember and forget at the same time."[28]

When we come into the embrace of the wounded Poor One, by entering into the deep caverns of our own painful memories, into the shadows of our past, into the opaqueness of the atrocities of the unmemorable, unspeakable memories of humankind, into the distortions of our separated identity, we realise that in the deep caverns of all these wounds, lies the presence of vulnerable wounded divine love, sharing in and healing our wound. In the darkest poverty of our wound, we discover love. Our soul, our spirit melts within us. Christ's spirit melts and our spirit melts. This melting of our spirit, this seeping of love, into every particle of our wounded-self, transforms our memory and transfigures us.

The dark mirror of our wounded-self becomes luminous with light as Christo-Sophia emerges. A new pattern arises that transforms our most wounding memories into oneing points of joy. Martin Laird says this so well: "The doorway into the silent land is a wound. Silence lays bare the wound."[29] The silence of contemplation uncovers our wounds, unloads our unconscious, while simultaneously the wounds then open into the ground of silent love, as we discover crucified love, in the depth of our wound. There is a reciprocal energy exchange, a oneing. The wounds that were once obscure and blind become mirrors of light, shining with the warmth and love of the eternal mirror of love.

The icon of the crucified Poor One marks the point of necessary vulnerability, the free choice to suffer, to openly embody all that is unfinished, in order for the

---

[27] This is Augustine's memory understanding and will within our soul. Thus, memory is not past experiences held within our brain, but "soul" memory in God. It is nonlocal because its source is in the Trinity.
[28] Constance Fitzgerald, "From Impasse to Prophetic Hope: Crisis of Memory," *CTSA Proceedings* (Vol. 64, 2009), 26.
[29] Martin Laird, *Into the Silent Land: A Guide to the Christian Practice of Contemplation* (Oxford University Press, 2006), 117.

total exchange of love pouring into love to evolve. The battered body of Christ is the icon that holds all that is violent, life-denying and destructive. This wounded Love knits and weaves together all the oppressive forces that oppose union, into the powerful energy of pure love, into the pattern of Christ, Christo-Sophia, into the light of the Eternal One. The icon holds the great paradox of divine and human oneness in vulnerability that transforms into resurrected being. Clare then takes Agnes into the infinity of such profound intimacy, to see how the icon of crucified love is the icon of everlasting love, which she calls the mirror of eternity.

Mirror of Eternity

While immersing us in the vulnerability of God in the crucified Poor One, simultaneously, Clare takes us into the darkness of contemplation, beyond words and images, to be transformed into luminous resurrected life of the mirror of eternity. Gazing, considering, contemplating reveals how within the mirror shine blessed poverty, holy humility and love beyond words.[30] It reveals the poverty of the life of Christ from being wrapped in swaddling clothes, to enduring suffering, to dying on the tree of the cross.[31] The mirror reveals how the tortured body of Christ becomes Christo-Sophia, radiant luminous love, the pure mind of Christo-clear light. Clare's heart meets our heart, as her words shimmer incandescently. She invites us into this infinite reflection of light reflecting primordial light, into the timelessness of being:

> Place (*pone*) your mind (*mentum*) in the mirror of eternity (*speculo aeternitatis*); place your soul (*animum*) in the splendour of glory (*splendore gloriae*); place your heart (*cor*) in the figure of the divine substance or essence (*divinae substancia*); and, through contemplation, transform your entire being into the image of the Divine One.[32]

The contemplative embrace intensifies in this icon of the Eternal One, as we place our mind, our soul, our heart within the Christo-Sophia light of the mind, soul and heart of this icon of Love. The finite and the infinite kiss and time and eternity coalesce. Our spirit melts and love illuminates the depths of the intimacy of our timelessly being in the embrace of endless oneing. Literally, in Clare's day, a mirror was a highly polished, circular, convex, metal disc that gives a true

---

[30] L: 4.18.
[31] L: 4.23.
[32] L: 3.12-13.

likeness only when we gaze and centre in the middle of the mirror, at the centre point. If the beholding is off-centre, the image is distorted. If the beholding is centred, we see an accurate image, suggesting that when we gaze into Christ from the depths of our centre in Christ, we see ourselves, as we truly are.

Scripturally, the mirror is associated with wisdom and luminosity. Wisdom, we recall is "a reflection of the eternal light, spotless mirror of God's active power, image of divine goodness" (Wis 7:26). With similar nuance, the Crucified One is an: "image (icon or mirror) of the unseen God, the first-born of all creation…who holds all things in unity" (Col 1:15 –17). Moreover, the mirror becomes the predominant image for contemplation in both letters to the Corinthians: "For now we see in a mirror or glass (ἐσόπτρου *esoptrou*), dimly, until we see face to face," or literally, "we know as we have been fully known" (1Cor 13.12). Paul urges us to unveil this natural face, the face of our heart, reminding us that we must have an "unveiled face," be face to face to know as Love knows us. We are being transformed into this "image (εἰκόνα *eikona*) day by day, within ever-increasing glory, which comes from the Christ who is the Spirit" (2 Cor 3.18).

In the tradition of writings about contemplation, the mirror is the *imago dei,* the icon of Christ, or the heart/mind of Christ within us. In the later reflections of Bonaventure, he draws on the mirror imagery to explain how the world is a mirror of the light of the Trinity, with our soul being an image, an icon intensely reflecting divine Light. When we place our active mind within our soul, we see how our soul is a mirror reflecting the generating mind, word and love of the Father, the Word and Holy Spirit. In other words, our soul radiates this mind, intelligence and love of the Trinity. Bonaventure affirms how in this mirror, "as from a candelabrum, the light of truth glows within upon the face of our mind, in which the image of the most blessed Trinity shines in splendor."[33] The mirror highlights illumination, enlightenment from the light, the spark, the ever-reflecting immortal diamond, the illuminated mind, or the centre of our soul that reflects the pure luminosity of the divine consciousness within us. The mirror points to the transition point, where in poverty, we enter into the humility of the

---

[33] See, Zachary Hayes, *Bonaventure Mystical Writings* (Phoenix: Tau Publishing, 1999), 79. Also, "When the soul reflects on itself, it rises through itself as through a mirror to speculation about the Blessed Trinity of Father, Word, and Love; three Persons co-eternal, co-equal, and consubstantial, so that whatever is in any one is in the others, but one is not the other, but all three are one God." Hayes, *Bonaventure,* 82.

crucified Christ who is the spotless mirror, the wisdom of God, into the life of the Trinity.

Clare's threefold repetition of place (*pone*), meaning to "position," "penetrate into," or "locate," our mind, our soul and our heart within the mind, glory and substance of Christ, is a natural flowing movement. Each organic moment invites an exchange of love, a knitting and oneing that is more expansive, more cosmic. She is saying that we must gaze, behold, in such a way that our minds become stably, permanently, enduringly, located, at home, within this mirror, until we are totally poor, empty with the reflective light of abiding in each other becoming more and more oned. This means there is a oneing of mind in mind, heart in heart, body in body, until we are in naked being, with "no-self," only knowing as we are known, seeing as we are seen. We are centred in the centre of the Eternal One, in the ground of consciousness that is essentially present in the oneness of love. This mind (*mentis*) that Clare specifies includes our discursive mind, settled into the gaze of the mind of our soul, until we have a silent, still mind, "the same mind (φρονεῖτε—*phroneite*) as Christ Jesus" (Phil 2:3-5).

Concurrently, this flowing movement of gazing, beholding, softly, almost motionlessly, naturally places our soul, (*animum*) within the numinous, and our heart (*cor*) within the divine being (*substantiae*), or heart. Here, we contemplate "in a mirror dimly," (1 Cor 13:12) in the darkness of vulnerable love. We spontaneously know through love, that risen life also dwells within us. We are in the lovemaking of emptiness, the kiss of silence, the pristine clarity of stillness that eternally ones. Clare appreciates, so profoundly, how we can go within our own heart and discover the intimacy of this timelessness of being. She urges us to return to our origins, to awaken our immortal memory, to transform our entire being, into the image of the Godhead and taste the hidden sweetness of Love. In tasting our Beloved, our outer and inner face fuse, transfiguring us spiritually, physically, organically. Our own icon of reality becomes a mirror of eternity. Our Christic nature evolves.

Raimon Panikkar reminds us that Christ is the icon for the whole of reality and it is our essential task, to complete our own icon of reality.[34] And Shelly Rambo warns how difficult this becomes when we lock trauma away in our unconscious, bandage over unhealed scars and foreclose on practices of attending to our wounds. Enabling this Christic icon to emerge, Rambo bemoans, is even more

---

[34] Raimon Panikkar, *The Fullness of Man* (New York: Orbis Books, 2010), xx.

formidable when people around us mirror back to us bigoted, confining, demeaning, pictures of ourselves.[35] It is our evolutionary task to bring to consciousness the light in which Christ, as the Christ-self manifests within all of us. Panikkar calls this a Christophanic experience. He urges us to open our third eye and see how human beings are a "Christophany," a reflection, an icon, or mirror image, of Christ, with a heart whose inner centre encloses the treasures of divinity and the mysteries of humanity. Here the oneing love of Christo-Sophia evolves within us, in self-transcending Love.

Being a Mirror

Clare urges us to gaze into this mirror every day, to see our face in it, clothed by it, adorned by garlands of its precious virtues, and radiate the beauty of the love we receive.[36] As we enter into our own wounds, come to the Poor Christ, in naked poverty, into the very being of the abyss of human-divine suffering, in the moment of recognition that we are one in suffering, everything changes. Ilia Delia reminds us that embracing this moment of recognition is crucial, because we realise how suffering can be a "stimulating value for transcendence."[37] We can live our suffering as the necessary struggle that we undergo in creative union, as the energy of our essence dormant within us, seeks to fully flower and release our Christic nature, in and through the wound, so that our whole being is transformed into Christ.

The implication is that we are to participate in the same oneness in the Trinity that Christ has and to live from this identity as an icon, a mirror of divine life. In the heart of the mirror of vulnerable Love, love knits the unravelled fibres of our life into a greater unity, creativity and oneness. Importantly, Clare realises that this returning to the ground of our essential oneness in Christ, the timeless mirror of Love, is not simply a personal experience. The imitation of Christ has rich communal implications. In writing guidelines for her sisters, Clare reminds them:

> For the Lord Himself not only has set/placed (*posuit*) us as an example and mirror (*speculum*) for others, but also for our [own] sisters whom the Lord has called to our way of life, so that they in turn will be a mirror and example

---

[35] Shelly Rambo, *Resurrecting Wounds Living in the Afterlife of Trauma* (Waco: Baylor University Press. Kindle Edition, 2017), Loc. 1795.
[36] L: 4.15.
[37] Ilia Delio, *Making All Things New* (New York: Orbis Books, 2016), 95.

> (*speculum et exemplum*) to those living in the world. Since, therefore, the Lord has called us to such great things, that those who are to be models and mirrors for others may behold themselves in us.[38]

Clare is reminding her sisters that contemplation enables them to have their minds, their souls, their hearts, their whole being, so stably oned within this mirror of love so completely that "others may behold themselves in us." This shining like a mirror is like a spiral of mirrors reflecting each other, where the reflection loop becomes so deep, that only one true face, the face of Christ shines forth. We see with the eyes of the Poor Christ. We are literally the "body of Christ." When we live in the poverty of this contemplative way of being, constantly drawn into this exquisite transforming union of being one, wherever we gaze, we see Christ. And whoever gazes at us, sees themselves in Christ, in us. When we bring a contemplative gaze to another, we recognise our Christic nature. We see that as we change, our collective unconscious changes and we discover the wounded Christ in the midst of our collective trauma. We see that mirrored in the depths of each other's hearts is our own Christic nature. We see that our true Self is our Christ Self. We see our oneness in mind, soul and heart in the body of Christ. We see how we participate in Christ's ongoing incarnating presence. A Christic communal consciousness awakens, that we will explore with Teilhard and Beatrice.

Clare enables us to be a communion of light reflecting light, shining as luminous mirrors of Love. Moreover, as we learn to see from within the endless luminosity of light reflecting light, luminous communion conscious emerges. These reflections within reflections, within the one reflection of the Christ, reflect the souls of every human being back to one another, opening us into the amazing potential of communal discernment that arises from the depths of this mirror. Clare draws us into our collective human Christic nature, enabling us to evolve as human beings. At the end of her last letter to Agnes, Clare immerses us in the silence of the timelessness of love reflecting love, as she invites: "be silent, as it is said, and let the tongue of the Spirit speak."[39] Centred in the Mirror of Eternity, gently, softly, lovingly we give ourselves to the Silence in communion consciousness where only love can speak. This icon of vulnerable love shining from the depths of the eternal, continuously draws us into itself and into Love's

---

[38] "*Know Your Vocation,*" Lines 20-22, in *Clare of Assisi Early Documents*. trans. Regis Armstrong (New York: Paulist Press, 1988).
[39] L: 4.36.

oneing, enabling us to be the mirror of Christ in the whole of our body-heart-mind awareness.

Illuminating Contemplation

Clare shows us how to gaze, consider, contemplate and imitate Christ by embracing suffering, with a contemplative, evolutionary heart. She takes us into our own personal, naked vulnerability, into the dying of the crucified, into emptiness, into the transforming light of contemplation, where the radiance of resurrection emerges. In this time of unprecedented suffering, she shows us how suffering, darkness, abandonment, death, are not ends in themselves, but expose the infusing presence of the poor Christ. Clare invites contemplatives today to become icons of contemplation, contemplating each phase of this paschal wounding, dying and rising, and seeing every part of our journey as holy. She shows us how to contemplate the blissful delights in our daily living. She urges us to taste the hidden sweetness, to savor and drink deeply, at the sacred banquet of our own life journey by embracing Christ, with all our heart, in all that we are and do. When our suffering meets the divine suffering, Clare assures us that we are drawn into Christ, into the icon of our deepest most trustworthy truth, into resurrection, into the light of the mirror of eternity. As we hold this memory in our mind, our soul, our heart, our entire being, I will highlight four significant insights that affirm the centrality of contemplation in enabling the mystical marriage to take place in our deep wounding and bring lasting healing.

First, when our heart feels deeply wounded and the tears of blood that flow from the raw exposure of pain feel like they will never stop flowing, Clare draws us into the embrace of the poor, vulnerable Christ, who shares our pain. As we saw in Boyd's vivid crucifixion portraits, and Clare's graphic scriptural images, this pain is tangible. Tacitly, she takes us deep into the wound, into pains depths, without us turning back in on ourselves, or being stuck in the wound. She places us in the flow of grace, awakening the intelligence of the wound, that is the intelligence of divine vulnerability, drawing all suffering into the Christ-self, into the eternal love of the mirror of eternity. In the oneing of this flowing grace, we are enabled to both remember and forget. When we remember with soul memory, we remember from within the spaciousness of eternal love that heals and ones, as we are made whole, in Christo Sophia, in the Trinity. This oneing of all suffering in the luminosity of eternal light frees us, enabling us to repattern our way of seeing and living. Filled with flowing light, we can create new neural pathways and forget unhealthy patterns, as our mind, our heart, our body become one with Christ. Clare shows us how contemplation not only uncovers our wound, but the luminous mirror of the natural face of our soul, that reveals who we are as Christic lovers, Christ in one another.

Second, Clare creates a theology of embrace. She shows us how in the exchange of love in the vulnerability of our shared wounds, the fertility, freedom and creativity of our woundedness in our oneing in shared suffering can continually foster the ever healing, oneing of love. This way of embracing vulnerability reverences our woundedness and our dark nights, enfolding them in the balm of compassion, rather than ignoring, anesthetising, criticising, blaming, or demonising what is vulnerable and fragile within us. In this tender mutual embrace with the divine, our screams can become a lament, our outrage a love-song, our despair hope. Every experience becomes a centre of mystical union, as parts of our self are given back to our self. In a time when an embrace is considered suspiciously, and even potentially life threatening, Clare's phenomenology of a vulnerable embrace, may seem challenging, even subversive. However, Clare reminds us that we indwell each other, within the oneing love of the divine embrace. It is natural for us to live in the vulnerability of a mutual embrace with totally vulnerable love. It is unnatural to pretend we are not wounded and vulnerable, and beyond any need to enter into the vulnerability of embrace. Yet, this is where so many find themselves at present, unable to take this risk of vulnerability. In waiting with the Crucified Poor One, in our wounded suffering, our personal embrace can be for the world.

Third, the evolutionary potential of shared vulnerability is unlimited energy, as Teilhard de Chardin affirms: "Suffering holds hidden within it, in extreme intensity, the ascensional force of the world. The whole point is to set this force free by making it conscious of what it signifies and what it is capable."[40] He affirms how, if all those who suffer, were:

> simultaneously to turn their suffering into a single shared longing ... if they were to unite their suffering so that the pain of the world could become one single grand act of consciousness, of sublimation, of unification, would not this be one of the most exalted forms in which the mysterious work of creation could be manifest to our eyes?[41]

From this point of view then, vulnerability has a healing power transcending contemporary understandings of vulnerability as weakness. Clare enables us to

---

[40] Pierre Teilhard de Chardin, *Hymn of the Universe* (New York, Harper and Roe), 93-94.
[41] Ibid.

enact Teilhard's vision, as we enter into contemplation, and consciously experience our suffering as an act of longing. In the longing, we draw all those who suffer with us into the exchange of mercy, into the mystical marriage, until suffering transfigures into joy, in the infinite intimacy of eternal love. In the vulnerability of our heartache for so much agony within creation, we meet the desire of our vulnerable God. Suffering is transformed into a powerful centrifugal force for more love, into compassion, mercy, and peace. This *kenosis* of yielding into Love's enfolding movement and releasing into the spaciousness our own poverty, into the divine poverty, into the fecund emptiness of the divine heart, into the love making of emptiness, transforms our whole identity personally and communally into Christ.

Fourth, in the face of the distortion in communal foresight, caused by centuries of inherited collective trauma, Clare offers another way of seeing communally today. When our consciousness turns back in on itself, into our heart's ground, into the heart of the poor Christ, into the endless mirroring of divine vulnerability, into the reciprocal reflection of wound in wound, we realise that our wounded heart is reflected in humankind's wounded heart. And reciprocally, all humankind is reflected in our heart. We realise we are a communion of hearts, oned in divine vulnerability. We build a stronger noosphere of heart consciousness that is sensitive and responsive to the world's pain. As we mature in our ability to recognise, how placing our mind in the centre point of love, in the mirror of eternity, places us in the centre of the vulnerability of God, we open ourselves to communal paschal healing, to being drawn communally into a shared dying and rising, in love. What we do personally affects us communally, just as what we do communally affects us personally.

Clare enables us to centre in the One who is our true icon, the sacred mirror of our soul, the only one who reflects our true, naked, heart-self back to our-self. This is the mirror that can transform collective humankind, as we become a translucent, spiral of mirrors of vulnerability reflecting vulnerability, light reflecting light. We become the luminous eternal face of Christ, the light of the world. We learn to see in this contemplative vision through the endless luminosity of light reflecting light. These reflections within reflections, within the one reflection of the Christ, reflect the soul of every human being and the *anima mundi* (the world soul) back to one another, opening us into the amazing potential of communion consciousness that we will explore further with Teilhard and Beatrice. Transforming our whole being into the mirror of eternity has the potential to change the world.

Clare urges us: "Hold what you always hold. Embrace what you always embrace, do what you always do and with swift pace, light step, nimble feet, so that your steps stir no dust. Go forward tranquilly, joyfully and freely, along the path of happiness."[42] The way is the Poor Crucified Christ, vulnerable, wounded, risen eternal light, Light of all lights. This is Christo-Sophia, diaphanous mind of our mind, heart of our hearts, being of our being, the mirror of eternity.

In the next chapter we will join John of the Cross, as he draws us through the dark nights of suffering into the rising dawn.

---

[42] L: 2.11-12.

Praying Contemplatively

Place your mind in the mirror of eternity,
place your soul in the splendor of glory,
place your heart in the body of the divine
and, through contemplation,
transform your entire being into the image of the Divine One
and experience what his friends experience
as you taste the hidden sweetness
that God has kept from the beginning
for those who love God.[43]

Embracing Stillness

Immersed in the pain of the suffering of our world
I arise, tentative,
softly centring,
inner depths quivering.
Poor and vulnerable,
we are one-in-another, infusing
boundlessly.
One eye, one seeing, one being.
Infinite Love pours into

---

[43] L: 3.12-15.

the midst of all suffering.
Crucified love
poured out for all.
In this darkness
in the deep silence
of my heart
I come to silence to gaze, to consider, to contemplate.

Ruminating on Scripture

Although the Beloved's state was divine,
Love did not cling to transcendence.
Love emptied Love's self, poured out Love, became a servant,
and was born as we are; and being as we are,
Love became humble, sensual, finite, of the earth
accepting suffering and death, death on a cross.

From the midst of this deep dying,
Infinite Love raised the Beloved high
and bestowed the name, which is beyond all other names
so that all beings in the heavens,
on earth and in the underworld,
should celebrate the name, Jesus.
And every tongue acclaim
Jesus, the Christ is the Mirror of Eternity,
Omega, radiating
the glory of Infinite Love.

Philippians 2:6-11.[44]

The Music of Silence

Vulnerable silence whispers of the eternal.

---

[44] My translation.

Contemplatio

Clare invites us to gaze, consider, contemplate and imitate the Christ who abides in the depths of our hearts as she says, "there is a treasure beyond compare hidden in creation and in human hearts.[45] So I invite you to find a comfortable sacred place, take some time for silence and enter into the presence of this hidden treasure.

Clare encourages us not to be overwhelmed by suffering, but to gaze with the eye of our heart, and consider how here is our poor, humble crucified God, present in the midst of all suffering. As you settle, draw your awareness into your heart, and gaze softly, with a deep penetrating tender gaze. Gently, become attentive to your sense of vulnerability, the groaning of creation and the suffering within the violent places of the world.

Compassionately centre now into the dark poverty of your own wound, penetrating deeper and deeper, until your spirit melts and your wound is one with Christ's wound. Nakedly feel yourself one with vulnerable crucified love, one in eternal intimacy. Be present within the seeping of love into your wounded-self in this oneing of wounds: — your wound, all humankind's wounds, creations wounds, — one in the oneing in crucified love.

Quietly, continue to gaze more deeply into this wound of love, feel the power of love at your heart-centre drawing you, into the radiant point of pure love. Place, release, centre, your mind, your body, your soul in this point of pure love, in this mirror of eternity. As your mind becomes infused with the mind of the Beloved, delicately intuit, as your heart is in the heart of the Beloved, in the luminous-darkness of the mirror of eternity.

Continue to gently release into the yearning of vulnerable love, into Love's encircling embrace into the centre, into the still point, into contemplatio in the mirror of eternity into Love.

---

[45] L: 3.7.

Softly rest in the silence for as long as you desire.

When you feel the stirring of the Holy Spirit to draw the prayer time to closure, imitate Christ's pouring out of love, shower the radiance of this vulnerable luminous love out to creation.

Blessing

Luminous mirror of poverty, mirror of eternity,
May we see with the tender loving of your gaze
the radiance of your love mirrored in creation.
May your illuminating shafts of light
penetrate and enfold us into your oneing love.
Amen.

VI

At the Time of the Rising Dawn

John of the Cross

Who is she that cometh forth as the morning rising,
fair as the moon, bright as the sun.
Song of Songs 6:19 (Vulgate)

In solitude she lives,
And there in solitude has built her nest;
In solitude he gives
Her guidance, love, and rest,
Wounded like her in solitary quest.[1]

Breathing with the night's darkness, my awareness dilates into a field of love flowing. Gently, lovingly, tenderly, I feel my attention drawn into the inner depths of my heart into the womb of silence singing her love song, caressing my wandering mind that feels heavy, tired, happy to release into love. There is one breath dissolving me into a field of love, dilating, kissing every particle of my being with delicate points of light. Silence, stillness, solitude, my Beloved infusing a fuller tranquility, inviting me into the wisdom of dawn light.

These ponderings recorded in my diary, flow from the womb of silence, resounding with hope, as I enter into the depthless-ness of night's darkness.

---

[1] *Centred on Love: The Poems of St John of the Cross*, trans. Marjorie Flower (Varroville: Carmelite Nuns, 2002). Hereafter, *Dark Night,* N, *Spiritual Canticle*, C. *Living Flame of Love,* F. Verse and page numbers are given. All poems are from this translation, unless noted. C: 35.20.

Later, in reflecting on this silent embrace, where I was caressed by the Beloved in silent music and sounding solitude, the words of John's poem, the *Fount* flowed through my whole being. I hear the primordial silence of this fluid fountain fullness flowing. I feel Light infusing, inviting my eternal memory to illuminate in dawn wisdom. John's radiant words resound:

> How well I know that fountain, filling, running,
> > although it is the night.
> That eternal fountain, hidden away,
> I know its haven and its secrecy
> > although it is the night.
> But not its source because it does not have one,
> which is all sources' source and origin
> > although it is the night.
> No other thing can be so beautiful,
> here the earth and heaven drink their fill
> > although it is the night.[2]

As the rhythm of the flowing water drenches my mind, the eyes of my Beloved sketched deep within this ever-flowing, ever-still, translucent abyss of love, behold in the darkness. The gaze infuses a serenity that softly ripples into every particle of my being, filling, running, flowing – deep peace – deep peace – Love's peace for our world. How well I know this fountain, this flowing love within me and yet this mysterious, ever-hidden, ever-revealing, dark and luminous Source-less source just keeps inviting as:

> This eternal fountain hides and splashes
> within this living bread that is life to us
> > although it is the night. ...
> I am repining for this living fountain.
> Within this bread of life I see it plain
> > although it is the night.[3]

One in this eternal fountain, one heart, one eye, one abyss of wisdom infusing. No self, no other. Nothing. Nada. And yet, repining, I see. – Yes within this bread of life, I see it plain, although it is night. In this time of an intense communal night of sense, when all our old was of seeing and knowing no longer enable us

---

[2] Seamus Heaney translation from *Station Island*, XI. https://thevalueofsparrows.wordpress.com/2018/02/13/poetry-station-island-xi-by-seamus-heaney-john-of-the-cross/
[3] Ibid.

to see and discover the creativity needed for this next evolutionary movement into oneness with God, John of the Cross perceptively shows us how to harness the energies of love and learn to see in the dark from within Love's darkness. He prepares is for the awakening of the living flame of love alive within us and the enlightenment of the dawn of a new era oned to our Wisdom-Word. John saturates us in hope as he shows us the deepest truth of this eternal fountain flowing voluptuously, although it is night.

John of the Cross – Beloved in the Night

In his short life, Juan de Yepes y Alvárez[4] (1542-1591) created some of the most eloquent Spanish poetry and detailed reflections on the rhythms that occur in a soul committed to a contemplative way of life. His most celebrated poems, *Dark Night (Noche Oscura), Spiritual Canticle (Cantico)* and *Living Flame of Love (Llama)* have a detailed theological reflection on the meaning of the imagery he uses. His other poems, *Ballad of the Gospel, Song of the Soul, A Pastoral, After an Ecstasy, Stanzas of the Soul who Suffers with Longing for God, Stanzas Giving a Spiritual Meaning, Other Verses with Divine Meaning, Rivers of Babylon,* some small refrains and *Sayings of Light further* illuminate the great love affair John has with his Beloved, the wounded Christ. With his refined eye, John immerses us in the silence of the soul's depths, pointing to the poverty of language to describe our intimacy with God, repeatedly saying he can say nothing about God, or about union.[5] Still, John paints a beautiful sensual canvas infusing an atmosphere of mystical union that enables us to live from within the fiery creativity of luminous unitive seeing. John's melodious poems and prose arise from the transforming union of his inner heart's depths, and place us in our heart's centre, where we share in communion consciousness our oneness in the Source-less source of the Living Fount of Love.

In her perceptive poem, *The Books of Saint John of the Cross,* Jessica Powers describes John's words as "starry manna," like "starlight that feeds our soul with

---

[4] Juan de Yepes y Alvárez was born in 1542, in Spain. His father died when he was two. His mother then struggled to support her family and placed John in an institution for children of the poor where he attended a Jesuit school. He entered the Carmelite Order at 20 and was given the name Fray Juan de Santo Matía (Fray John of St Matthias). After studying at the University of Salamanca, he was ordained in 1567. Often malnourished and ill, he died in 1591.

[5] All other references to John's commentary are from *The Collected Works of John of the Cross,* trans. Kieran Kavanaugh and Otilio Rodriquez (Washington: ICS, 1991). Hereafter, A is *Ascent of Mount Carmel,* D is *Dark Night,* C is *Spiritual Canticle,* F is *Living Flame of Love.* Chapter and paragraph references are given. C: 26.4.

bread."[6] Resembling points of light radiating from the point of all creative light, John's language shines through the night sky to feed the hungry wandering soul, famished from not being able to find food that will sustain as the spiritual journey unfolds. With her usual ability to pierce into the heart of the matter, Jessica illuminates how, even a crumb of these "immortal delicacies" will infuse us with wisdom that can sustain us as we take the path of contemplation. Jessica concludes:

> and I, so long a fosterling of night,
> here feast upon immeasurably sweetened
> wafers of light.[7]

And so, we who, like Jessica, are fosterlings of night, discover in John's writings immortal food to feast upon, trustworthy wisdom from one who knew the depths of suffering. Betrayed and abandoned by his community, John was faithful to the way of contemplation in the darkest moments of his life. Shining from the midst of darkness, John's mystical words are radiantly colourful, lusciously sensual and magnetically alluring, "a treasure of divine light."[8]

When we feel overwhelmed by darkness, John shows us how to see in the darkness of contemplation, recognise the first glimpses of dawn light, and discover our identity in the Trinity, in an evolving, unceasing birth of beauty. This is the language of a sensitive lover, of a poet, of one who looks for, sees and meets the Beloved in nature and in the human condition in the very depths of vulnerability and darkness. John explains the nature of this contemplation (*la contemplación*) in the night where: "God teaches the soul very quietly and secretly, without its knowing how, without the sound of words, and without the help of any bodily or spiritual faculty, in silence and quietude, in darkness to all sensory and natural things."[9] Quietly and secretly in the darkness of our heart, the inflow of divine Wisdom fills us with a dark loving knowledge of the boundless love of the Trinity. "The language of God has this trait," John affirms: "Since it is very spiritual and intimate to the soul, transcending everything sensory, it immediately silences."[10] Contemplation is ineffable. It is "Ah, ah,

---

[6] *The Selected Poetry of Jessica Powers*, eds. Regina Siegfried and Robert F. Morneau (Washington: ICS Publications, 1999), 132.
[7] Ibid.
[8] 1A: 8.6.
[9] C: 39.12.
[10] 2N: 17.3.

ah!"[11] It is "Pure Spirit to pure spirit."[12] It is like "hiding the soul within itself,"[13] or being engulfed in a "secret abyss."[14] John continually encourages us as night sets in to wait in silence and quietude in "loving and peaceful attentiveness in God."[15]

This Chapter

In the previous two chapters we have seen with Mechthild and Clare how to live into the *kenotic* quality of flowing love, in times of suffering, and discover a luminous sense of ecstatic union with the divine that gifts us with contemplative vision. In this chapter we will focus on how John teaches us to live into the unknowing of the dark nights, learn to see in the darkness, and then negotiate moments of transition into the eternal glow of dawn in transforming union. We will begin in the darkness of the nights of sense and spirit, before we focus on his *Spiritual Canticle* and *Living Flame of Love* to explore how we may prepare to see the luminosity of the rising of dawn, where we enter into the solitude of the serene night of the mystical marriage as our hearts become enflamed. Finally, we will explore how this serene, unitive silence of contemplation, teaches us how to behold in the darkness, birthing a new language of participatory love knowledge that illuminates contemplation today.

One Dark Night

John is most famous for his evocative language of darkness and night, envisaging the inflowing presence of the Beloved within us as one beautiful dark night. In John's artistic hands, "night" becomes "an immortal delicacy," "a wafer of star light" that feeds our starving soul as we wait in the darkness for our consummation in union with the One who is Infinite Night. "Night," becomes an ever-revealing metaphor, erasing boundaries between absence and presence, ascent and descent, dying and birthing. Night is the womb of solitude where Beloved and lover are transformed into each other. "Night" infuses us in eternal wisdom and sustains us as we take the way of the darker nights of contemplation into the tranquility of the rising dawn, into the luminous enflaming love of being

---

[11] 2N: 17.4. See, Jer 1:6.
[12] Ibid.
[13] 2N: 17.6.
[14] 2N: 17.7.
[15] 1N: 10.6.

one. In his *Dark Night* poem, John immerses us in the unquenchable yearning that is always characteristic of the night:

> So dark the night! At rest
> and hushed my house, I went with no one knowing
> upon a lover's quest
> — Ah, the sheer grace! — so blest,
> my eager heart with love aflame and glowing.[16]

This deep darkness of night fills us with an insatiable longing as it immerses us into the obscure way of Love's unknowing. John explains the phases that we go through in these dark nights, that are essentially one night. He clarifies:

> The first the night of the senses, resembles early evening, that time of twilight when things begin to fade from sight. The second night of faith, is completely dark, like midnight. The third the night of union is like the very early dawn just before the break of day.[17]

In this one night, John specifies active and passive phases that unfold organically as the living presence of our espoused one infuses the senses and spirit in our heart.[18] It is important to note, however, that although he outlines the active nights of sense and spirit which become more passive, the boundaries are fluid and repetitive. We experience many nights where sense and spirit are purified. His detailed observation of the characteristics of these sensual spiritual phases are timeless, so we will focus on each in turn.

Nights of Sense

John hauntingly captures the initial sensual transformation that occurs actively and then passively, as we hush, still our house, follow our desire and go in search for our Beloved. In these early days of searching for the Beloved, active, sensual, meditative prayer has dried up. It no longer satisfies because we are being called to contemplation. At this time, although our Beloved is flowing within the depths of our heart and filling us with light, we are unaware of this presence, because our sensual ways of knowing cannot sense the Beloved's presence within our spirit and our spirit has not been sensitised to the Beloved's presence. We feel

---

[16] *Centred on Love,* N:12. This poem was composed between 1577 and 1579, at an unknown location.
[17] Ascent of Mount Carmel, 1A: 2.5.
[18] *The Dark Night* is a prose commentary, written in 1582-85, on the Dark Night poem. It takes up where *The Ascent to Mount Carmel* finishes. It has 2 books. Book 1, 14 chapters and book 2, 25 chapters. John never finishes his commentary.

disorientated, dry, barren, cold, as if we have lost our Beloved and are wandering in a barren desert. Because our tastes are unrefined and we are unaccustomed to the solitude of this dark infusing contemplation, we become restless, unsure, discombobulated. We moan for the way God used to feed us with the consolations of our senses. "The reason for this dryness," John consoles, "is that God transfers his goods and strength from sense to spirit. Since the sensory part of the soul is incapable of the goods of the spirit, it remains dry, deprived and empty."[19]

Unfortunately, John's stress on the darkening of our sensory awareness is often misinterpreted, as separating the sensual and spiritual with a disregard for the sensual. This, however, is not what he means. Rather, John is inviting a deeper spiritual heart-awareness that incorporates the sensual. If we are to awaken this deeper way of seeing, we must tend our sensual-sexual wounds as we have with Clare and find the Beloved deep within them. For it is only when our senses feel filled with love that they are content to rest and let go into our spiritual ways of unknowing. Unhealed sensual awareness disturbs this movement and can keep us locked in this dryness of the night of sense for many years. During this time of the sensual dryness of this transition, it is critical that we stay in this desert wilderness, trusting the dark presence of our Beloved, that feels to us like absence, and remain faithful to this dark way of prayer. And importantly, at another time, we must attend our sensual wounding tenderly. Our Beloved, ever thirsting for our union, intimately, gently and lovingly will continue the work of healing.

Nights of Spirit

As the Beloved heals us and we become more accustomed to this dark contemplation within the depths of the spirit of our heart, the active and passive nights of spirit, set in. In these nights of spirit, our spirit is denuded so that a unitive awareness from the ground of our union in the Beloved in the centre of our heart may awaken. In these spiritual nights the divine Lover continues to infuse our inner being, further cleansing, emptying, annihilating the deep caverns of our memory, intellect and will, of our soul,[20] until we are ready to receive the

---

[19] 1N: 9.4.
[20] The "memory" designates the spiritual power to recall and relive what is past as well as live presently in an anticipated future. The "intellect" is the spiritual power for knowing that has both an active and passive dimension. The active intellect receives information from the senses, while the passive intellect receives knowledge from the substance. See, C: 39.12. The "will" is the movement of love within our spirit that unites with the divine will.

inner-penetrating piercing radiance of divine light in the depths of our centre. John explains how in this time, our memory becomes free of past hurts, our intellect is voided, emptied of the limits of thinking, and our will refined so we may be totally in love and responsive to our Beloved. Thus, these nights of spirit are excruciatingly painful, as our spiritual senses become parched, and we feel we are being annihilated. All our preconceived ideas of self, world and God, dissolve. And the greatest torment is that the Beloved feels so absent that we feel totally abandoned. Here, it is important to remember that, although all our usual ways of knowing dissipate, and our habitual ways of making meaning no longer make sense, in the emptiness of this poverty of spirit, a new intimacy is gestating. We are being wounded in our deepest centre, just as our crucified Beloved is wounded. Though the wounding feels relentless, as we feel wound, upon wound, this is a very poignant phase in our journey that is too often ignored or glossed over with unhelpful platitudes.

It is critical that this phase of perceived abandonment be negotiated, but we need discerning guidance from someone who has already lived this journey. In this pivotal time, we can become locked within this dark torment of meaninglessness and stagnate. Sadly, so many in our culture spend years in this torment because of lack of support, or unconsciously choose to remain in the darkness, because the journey is too demanding of the whole of our love. Perceptively, John models for us how, if we do choose this way of love, seek appropriate spiritual companionship for support, and risk going deeper, blessings abound. At this evolutionary moment, we are being invited to live our crucifixions, by letting go of our old patterns of alienation from each other and the world, releasing the limiting power of thoughts, and the constrictions of a dualistic mind-set. We are being invited to cleanse the caverns of our memory by entering into the pain of our shadows, facing our deepest fears, in the beautiful healing movement of remembering and forgetting that we explored with Clare. We are being invited to love fully, and truly be one with our Beloved Spouse in resurrection light.

Still, these nights of spirit can feel relentless, and they are demanding. Like John's sketch of Christ crucified hanging in mid-air, pouring out blood-tears of love, we can feel we are left naked, exposed, hanging and lifeless.[21] John's language is searing:

---

[21] See, *Collected Works*, cover.

> the soul not only suffers the void and suspension of these natural supports and apprehensions, which is a terrible anguish (like hanging in midair unable to breathe), but it is also purged by this contemplation. As fire consumes the tarnish and rust of metal, this contemplation annihilates, empties and consumes all the affections and imperfect habits the soul contracted throughout life.[22]

Without any consolation of the presence of God, this anguish of hanging in mid-air unable to breath, places us on the cross, as Jesus breathes his last. Together, we share in his existential cry, weeping with our vulnerable Lover, wailing our own scream and the scream of all those who suffer: "My God my God why have you forsaken me?"[23] In the voiding of this existential cry into all that is absurdly nothing, into the lowest depths of affliction, into the emptiness of sense and spirit, the tears of the Beloved, which are the tears of all creation, become jewel tears. This feels like abandonment, absence, an absurd nothingness, an annihilation of spirit. Yet, this exquisite unmaking that takes place in this void of perceived separation from divine love, opens into the infinite intimacy of the exchange of love in our deepest centre. We awaken within the intimacy of *nada*, in the infinitely fertile emptiness of the womb of silent love.

Abandonment becomes the love making of emptiness, opening into an abyss of oneing love. We know through love we are one with God. Our wounds are one, our hearts are one, our whole being is drawn into the intimacy of the divine life. In this cry, the Wounded One, places the most intimate love where God feels most absent. The wounded Christ becomes the archetype for the wound of suffering becoming the wound of love, transforming all suffering into joy. The psalmist's words: "I was annihilated and knew not," (Ps 72.2), become our reality.[24] In this annihilation, in this unknowing, we are "engulfed in the divine and dark spiritual light of contemplation."[25] The more simply divine light touches us, the more all our ways of knowing feel emptied and annihilated, until we are: "transformed into simple and pure Wisdom, the Son of God."[26]

John likens this transformation that takes place, to the effect fire has on a piece of wood. At first, when the wood ignites, the fire burning it makes it black as it dispels all the moisture that will not burn. In the process the wood gives off repugnant fumes, until all its unnatural vapours are eradicated. Increasingly

---

[22] 2N: 6.5.
[23] See, Mt 27:46. 2A: 7.11.
[24] 2N: 8.2.
[25] Ibid
[26] 2A: 15.4.

though, as the wood becomes enkindled, it begins to glow, until suddenly it is fully aflame. Finally, "the fire transforms the wood into itself and makes it as beautiful as it itself."[27] This is the work of the dark nights, to prepare us for a union in love that transform us completely into the beauty of the divine Beloved, into the luminosity of an infused contemplative being and seeing from within one another. Within this awareness, even our most searing moments of existential despair, can open into the most unitive love when lived into discerningly within the pattern of the paschal movement of dying and rising. From this intimate point of our shared wounds, from the transformative centre of the cross, where abandonment becomes the love making of emptiness, we will now focus on how John teaches us to behold in the darkness in his *Spiritual Canticle,* so that we may see the first hints of dawn light inviting us to a new way of unitive love knowledge, or oneing awareness.

Seeing in the Night

John's *Spiritual Canticle* gives helpful details in how to surrender into the movements of heart that occur in these dark nights.[28] It shows us how to yield into the paschal transformation of dying and rising and awaken in the contemplative vision of a resurrected way of being. A pivotal moment occurs when the wounded spouse cries into the darkness: "May my eyes behold you?"[29] May I see you face to face with the eyes of my soul, because you are their light?[30] Her Beloved hears the cry and is so moved by her plea, it wounds the apple of his eye.[31] Traditionally, the eye is considered the window to the soul, revealing the consciousness of a person. "In a real sense the eyes are the other person," Ernest Larkin suggests.[32] For John, the eye is also the intellect, or mind of the heart. Thus, the "apple of the eye" suggests that the pupil of the eye, the inner most depths of the Lover's heart, is wounded by the spouse's longing. Yet the

---

[27] 2N: 10.1.
[28] Based on the Song of Songs, the Canticle was composed when John was imprisoned in Toledo. It begins with the search for the Beloved in the first twelve stanzas, moves into loving union, in stanzas thirteen to twenty-one, until there is a mutual surrender of the two spouses in the mystical marriage in stanzas twenty-two to forty.
[29] C: 10.6.
[30] C: 10.7.
[31] C: 11.1. See, Zech 2:8.
[32] Ernest Larkin, "Contemplation in "The Spiritual Canticle": The program of St John of the Cross," in *Carmel and Contemplation: Transforming Human Consciousness*, eds. Kevin Culligan, OCD and Regis Jordan, OCD (Washington: ICS Publications, 2000), 267.

spouse continues with impassioned yearning: "Show me your face, my Lover."[33] She pleas:

> O crystal spring clear-shining,
> If only, on your silver surface,
> Those eyes for which I am pining –
> Suddenly and quite near! –
> Whose image printed deep within I bear.[34]

As the pining for this imprinted image of the Beloved within to be fully uncovered becomes insatiable, what felt purgative becomes illuminative. The lovers' mutual desire removes veil upon veil of illusions that were hiding the image within, restoring its natural colours and crystal-like glow. In this insatiable longing beyond longing, the Beloved's face, the Beloved's eyes, his gaze of pure crucified love, opens within her heart-consciousness. She knows through love, that the eyes of her heart are the Beloved's eyes. These eyes see with the divine light of Wisdom and know through divine love. This transformation in consciousness, that occurs as we look and see the love in the eyes of the Beloved within our soul, changes our whole perception of reality. We realise that the gaze of the eye of our heart is not separate from our Beloved; it is not possible to view our Lover as someone else. Our Beloved is subject, our deepest I, the ground of our subjectivity.

This shift into the Beloved as subject is what Beatrice Bruteau calls subject-presence.[35] We recognise that imprinted within us is a profound I-I gaze that sees from the luminous trace of the divine light within us. We participate in the radiant light of divine transcendence, just as the divine participates in our finite humanity. We partake of the Beloved and experience the Beloved's eyes within us as subject, in an instantaneously grasped whole that is self-luminous. We see from oneness. When we behold from within this wholeness in our Lover, we are mutually wounded more and more deeply, as one glance of our eye wounds our Beloved.[36] And one glance of our Beloved's eye wounds us, imparting fuller union in what we might call a oneing vision in the ground of our shared identity.

---

[33] *Centred on Love*, C: 11.16.
[34] Ibid.
[35] Beatrice Bruteau, "The One and the Many: Communitarian Nondualism," in *The Other Half of My Soul*, ed. Beatrice Bruteau (Wheaton: Quest Books, 1996), 298.
[36] C: 31.10.

John continues to explore how this image of the Beloved imprinted within our heart, that informs the mind of our heart and our memory, extends into our will, so that we also will as the Beloved wills. He affirms:

> the image of the Beloved is so sketched in the will and drawn so intimately and vividly, that it is true to say that the Beloved lives in the lover and the lover in the Beloved. Love produces such likeness in this transformation of lovers that one can say each is the other and both are one. The reason is that in the union and transformation of love each gives possession of self to the other and each exchanges self for the other.[37]

This exquisite sketch of the Beloved within us enables us to give ourselves in the intimacy of this exchange of love and offer our whole selves to one another. The transformation is so intense each one lives in the other and both are one. We become one in both image and likeness.[38] In this transformation of lovers, what felt dark and oppressive becomes darkly luminous, quiet, peaceful, and tranquil, yet expectant, like the night just before dawn.

The Tranquil Night

Thus, in the dark loving of this transforming being in one another, the Beloved becomes a tranquil night as we rest in his bosom. John elaborates:

> In this tranquility or spiritual sleep in the bosom of the Beloved, the soul possesses and relishes all the tranquility, rest and quietude of the peaceful night; and she receives in God, together with this peace, a fathomless and obscure divine knowledge. As a result she says that her Beloved is a tranquil night for her.[39]

In the tranquil intimacy of sleeping in the heart-womb of the Beloved, we receive fathomless and obscure divine knowledge. The luminosity of this knowing through love is like the first glow of dawn rising over the horizon. John immerses us in a tranquil quietness as his words rise from the light beginning to glow on the horizon:

> it is tranquility and quietude in divine light, in the new knowledge of God, in which the spirit elevated to the divine light is in quiet. She very appropriately calls this divine light the rising dawn, which means the morning. Just as the rise

---

[37] C: 12.7.
[38] Though this image is always within us, in the fall we lost our likeness to the Beloved and the capacity to see as the Beloved sees.
[39] C: 14 & 15.22.

of morning dispels the darkness of night and unveils the light of day, so this spirit quieted and put to rest in God, is elevated from the darkness of natural knowledge to the morning light of the supernatural knowledge of God.[40]

At this time of the rising dawn, our spirit now filled with divine light is quiet, still, tranquil and receives knowledge through love. Thus, we see how the loving work of the dark nights has prepared us to enter into a more stable, tranquil rest. In the intimacy of being in one another our spirit is infused with divine light.

There is a shift in our ways of knowing, from the very obscure dark knowing of the dark night, into the tranquillity and quiet infused by divine light. In this luminous tranquillity, our spirit remains so quiet, so at rest in our Beloved, that we see with dawn lucidity. This is the tranquillity we must cultivate presently, in the evolution of our consciousness, if we are to see the luminous presence of love dawning on the horizon, showing us the way forward in illuminating the sketch, the imprint of the divine within us. We must be open to the radiant dawn light of inflowing Wisdom. John shows us how: "in nocturnal tranquillity and silence and in knowledge of the divine light the soul becomes aware of Wisdom's wonderful harmony and sequence in the variety of creatures and their works."[41] When the eyes of our heart that are the eyes of our Beloved Wisdom open, we see divine Wisdom wherever we gaze.

In the Depths of the Wine Cellar

As we settle into this tranquil night and are held in a habitual embrace, within our Beloved, we come forth: "like the morning rising, beautiful as the moon, resplendent as the sun." We are deeply in repose, "a peaceful and tranquil soul like a continual banquet"[42] Now, as John immerses us in this embracing intimacy, he asks the Holy Spirit to take his pen, as he seeks to shower light on how this embrace prepares us for consummation in spiritual marriage:

> At last the Bride has entered
> the garden of her heart's desire, a place
> wherein to rest, all centred
> on Love, whose arms embrace
> her neck, the while he gazes on her face.[43]

---

[40] C: 14 & 15.23.
[41] C: 14 & 15.25.
[42] C: 22.16. See, Sg 6.10; Prov 15:15.
[43] C: 22. *Centred on Love*, 18.

Having entered the sweet garden of our desire, held in the embrace of our Beloved, wooed by the divine gaze, we are centred in love, in Love's oneing transforming union. We are immersed in the utterly ineffable, intimate union of Spirit making love to spirit, in the love-making of emptiness. Love carries us beyond, into the intimacy of our essential oneing in solitude, in the whisper of sheer silence. The beauty of the love-making of the *Song of Songs* glows through John's words, as he impregnates our awareness with the perfume of the unutterable:

> In the secret cellar deep
> I drank of my true love, then to the plain
> Went forth, as one asleep,
> Knew nothing, joy or pain,
> And of the flock I followed none remain.[44]

This "secret cellar deep,"[45] this depthless abyss of our heart, this groundless ground of the cellar, points to what is most interior, enstatic within us, that is kissed, infused, absorbed into our Beloved. Reciprocally, our Beloved is kissed, infused, emptied into and sealed within us in spiritual marriage. John continues to immerse us the presencing of ineffable beauty, "One can say nothing about it," he whispers:

> just as one can say nothing about God… that resembles him. For in the transformation of the soul in God, it is God who communicates himself with admirable glory; the two become one, as we would say as the window united with the ray of the sunlight, or the coal with the fire, or the starlight with the light of the sun.[46]

In this transformation in the wine cellar, two become one. As we taste the hidden sweetness, and are inebriated in love, John describes how this wine of love is diffused through all the veins of our body, soul, heart, and mind, until we are transformed in God, in this kiss of unutterable oneness. In this kiss, the Beloved teaches us the wisdom and knowledge and love.[47] Our intellect, or heart-mind drinks wisdom and knowledge, our will the sweetness of love, while our memory drinks the refreshment and delight of our eternal union in God. We are, "carried

---

[44] C: 26. *Centred on Love*, 19.
[45] John identifies seven wine cellars, or degrees of love we receive with the seven gifts of the Holy Spirit. C: 26.3.
[46] C: 26.4.
[47] C: 26.6.

away and absorbed in love, entirely transformed in God."[48] We are annihilated in the most affirmative sense of the word, vanishing and dissolving into love. Now mingled with the Beloved, the wine we share is spiced, with our love.[49] This transforming union leaves us in the unknowing of radiant, simple contemplation,[50] in a deep unperturbable repose.

John emphasises the "sweet and secret knowledge" that the Beloved infuses in this simple contemplation. In his *Dark Night* he explains what he means by "secret," stressing that "pure contemplation is indescribable…and on this account called secret."[51] It has the characteristic of "hiding the soul within itself." In other words, we are so enfolded within our-self, we are enclosed in a stable, still, abiding, within our heart. In his *Flame of Love,* John further elaborates on how we must dwell within our heart in secret, because God dwells secretly in our substance.[52] This can feel like being in a "secret abyss," "deep and vast wilderness," or "immense unbounded desert."[53] John affirms, "the more delightful, savourous and loving, the deeper, vaster and more solitary it is."[54] Immersed in wisdom in this inner abyss, we are led to "the heart of the science of love."[55] This sweet, secret, inner wisdom of contemplation, or knowledge through love,[56] awakens unitive or oneing consciousness.

The heart of the science of love is that we see from within our transformed indwelling within each other. In giving ourselves totally in mutual embrace in the wine-cellar, drinking the wine of our Beloved, becoming absorbed in this kiss of the inner marriage, in the pure inner intimacy in the centre and depth of our heart, our vulnerability, our wounds, our poverty, are infused and become the spiced wine of love. We are bathed in the light of divinity and know ourselves as totally cherished. We awaken wounded by the flame of love in the depths of our spirit, as the point of the wound becomes the kiss of infusing consummation. Our unquenchable desire is to remain centred in love, grounded in the wine cellar in all our daily living, in an abiding solitude.

---

[48] C: 26.14.
[49] C: 26.5.
[50] C: 26:17.
[51] 2N: 17.5.
[52] F: 4.14.
[53] See, 2N: 17.6.
[54] Ibid.
[55] Ibid.
[56] C: 27.5.

The Serene Night

Hence, this wound of love that took us to the cross, into the cry of abandonment, into the darkest of sensual and spiritual nights, into the tranquil night, becomes a serene night where we can enjoy the grove of our world and its living beauty. "Serene," stresses the peaceful, calm, clear, deep, abiding stillness, the luminous clarity that arises from our absorption in divine light. In this serene night, a new luminous, clear contemplation dawns, in the darkness, feeling like the day-light of our understanding.[57] Wisdom infuses, as we imbibe the mysteries of our Beloved, that taste like pomegranate.[58] We receive a sense beyond all sensing, of eternal light within our spirit that infuses a beatific clarity, of the divine face within us, endlessly absorbing us into itself so that we reflect the Beloved's face until all we know in this serene loving is the great solitude within our soul. Paradoxically, we are one, and yet uniquely ourselves, as Lover and Beloved in solitary oneness. John's repetition of "solitude," "solitary," emphasising *"solus"* to be alone, stresses how we are alone in this solitude, because we are all-one, in repose in this one love. John's words enfold us in this nest of solitude:

> In solitude she lives,
> And there in solitude has built her nest;
> In solitude he gives
> Her guidance, love, and rest,
> Wounded like her in solitary quest.[59]

Wounded, empty, alone in this solitude, God fills the memory with divine knowledge, as God fills us with God's self. We are in God as God is in us.[60] Delightfully annihilated, we are silent, still, idle, peaceful, serene in a stable transforming union. Here in this nest of solitude in contemplation, our prayer is so naturally unitive, we are so one, we forget the practice of loving attentiveness and simply repose in Love's absorbing Love. We delicately, almost motionlessly respond in loving attentiveness only when we feel ourselves leaving this deeply stable absorption in the divine solitude.[61]

---

[57] C: 39.12. Notice echoes of Eckhart's bare awareness of the eternity of today here.
[58] C: 37.7.
[59] *Centred on Love*, C:35.20.
[60] C: 35.1.
[61] F: 3.34.

John further sensitises us to the whispering, quivering, murmuring, which he identifies as a sounding solitude, that is like silent music.[62] This murmuring solitude is so sublime, it transcends all the harmonies of the universe, as its silent music infuses the tranquil, calm, repose of silence. In the solitude of silent repose, our spirit becomes one with the spirit of God, and all creation in a most resonant way. We hear the silent music as the voice of the Beloved, and the soft breath of the air, sounds like a sweet nightingale, singing its melancholy love song. There is only one sweet song of joy, as in the oneness of our solitude we become enflamed. This living flame of love burns, consuming us totally, but now with no pain.[63] This flame graces us with the serene, luminous, clarity of seeing from oneness.[64]

Seeing Enflamed

The beauty of how profoundly Lover and Beloved are absorbed in each other, in a differentiated unity, magnifies in John's *Living Flame* poem, as John takes us even deeper into this union in the inner depths of our spirit, in our deepest centre. Ever desiring to enable the fullness of this loving of the mystical marriage his poem resounds in the universe:

> Flame, living flame, compelling,
> yet tender past all telling,
> reaching the secret centre of my soul!
> Since now evasion's over
> finish your work, my Lover,
> break the last thread,
> wound me and make me whole![65]

As our Beloved's gaze intensifies and we return this gaze in our look of love, the obscurity of the night where the Beloved feels hidden becomes enflamed. All that we have experienced in encountering our dark God, becomes radiant in love as the flame of love blazes, glows and completes its work so that we may truly be one and see from our oneness. The flame burns so personally, so tenderly, into the most intimate point of our wound that we know irrevocably that as lovers, we share in the one wound. And not only one feeling, but one seeing. We come home to our heart's inner depths which John now clarifies as our "deepest

---

62   C: 14 & 15.26.
63   C: 39.21.
64   C: 39.9.
65   *Centred on Love*, F: 1.22.

centre." He places us in this intimate point where the inner sketched eye of our heart, that is the eye of the Beloved, opens from within the divine sea of flaming light.

John asks: "Who can fittingly speak of this intimate point of the wound, which seems to make its mark in the middle of the heart of the spirit, there where the soul experiences the excellence of the delight?"[66] His radiant words take us into the point that feels like "a tiny mustard seed, very much alive and enkindled, sending into its surroundings a living and enkindled fire of love."[67] Untouched by time and yet within time, this pure enflaming seeding light is the spark we described in Eckhart, the point that is eternally aflame with divine light begetting light. For John, this enflamed seed is where, "the soul beholds itself converted into the immense fire of love that emanates from that enkindled point at the heart of the spirit."[68] This is the point of pure awareness within the heart of our spirit that is aglow with divine wisdom, that beholds from within itself, enflaming our vision. In this fiery seed, we behold from within the intimacy of our oneness in the point.[69]

At the same time, this enstatic point magnifies into a cosmic sense of infinite points of divine light aflame like a sea of living fire. John's words continue to ripple boundlessly into the cosmos as he places us ever more deeply in this infinite ocean of living flame that arises into our awareness from the Light of the presence of our Beloved in us, that is the ground of consciousness itself:

> The fire issuing from the substance and power of that living point, which contains the substance and power of the herb, is felt to be subtly diffused through all the spiritual and substantial veins of the soul in the measure of the soul's power and strength. The soul feels its ardor strengthen and increase and its love become so refined in this ardor that seemingly there flow seas of loving fire within it, reaching to the heights and depths of the earthly and heavenly spheres, imbuing all with love.[70]

When we behold from being centred in this living point, "it seems to it that the entire universe is a sea of love in which it is engulfed, for conscious of the living point or centre of love within itself, it is unable to catch sight of the boundaries

---

66   F: 2.10.
67   Ibid.
68   F: 2.11.
69   Again, this is John's version of the *synderesis*. Notice that it is a point of love.
70   F: 2.10.

of this love."[71] In this single pointed enflamed beholding, our heart knows the deep truth that in the absolute intimacy of this pure point of oneness, we are this vast sea of living flame. Dualisms between earth and heaven, finite and infinite, dissolve as spheres dance. Our seeing is enflamed. In this ground of translucent awareness, we open into the primordial, universal vision of the gaze of our Beloved, Wisdom-Word that embraces darkness and light, absence and presence, subject and object, one and many, time and eternity in a naked now. The veins of our heart-knowing throb with potential as we know through love that we participate in this seed of divine creative possibility, whose roots are expanding and resourcing the future's radiant evolving. A new pattern of our wholeness in our Beloved, Wisdom-Word and a new capacity for communion consciousness in this radiating point that we all participate within emerges.

In this sea of radiant light, the deep caverns of our heart ways of knowing, our memory, intellect and will, become translucent lamps within the divine lamps of fire, glowing with unsullied divine light. The poem continues:

> O lamps of fire bright burning
> with splendid brilliance, turning
> deep caverns of my soul to pools of light!
> Once shadowed dim and unknowing,
> now their strange new found glowing
> gives warmth and radiance for my Love's delight.[72]

Now voided, these deep caverns, our memory, intellect and will,[73] that used to receive divine light as darkness, radiate with divine light, glowing like pools of light. John elucidates: "having become enkindled lamps within the splendours of the divine lamps, they render the Beloved the same light and heat they receive. In the very manner they receive it, they return it to the one who gave it, and with the same exquisite beauty."[74] In this union of light reflecting Light, a new consciousness emerges that perceives through oneness. Our heart memory remembers the original glance of divine love, our intellect, or mind of our heart, shines with divine wisdom, while our will is so united to the divine will that, "the will of the two is one will, and thus God's operation and the souls are one."[75] In the intimacy of love infusing from within our essence in God, we give God to

---

[71] Ibid.
[72] *Centred on Love*, F:3.22-23.
[73] F: 3.18.
[74] F: 3.77.
[75] F: 3.78.

God, from being in God. In this love-making in our deepest centre, of wound in wound, substance in substance, essence in essence, we one.[76] Secretly and silently, we recognise that our Beloved is completely at home within the centre of our heart.

Now conscious that our Beloved is permanently at home, within our heart's depths, the luminous vastness of seeing from within this point of our shared identity continues to expand boundlessly. A whole new Trinitarian awareness rises as Trinitarian communion consciousness. John places us in the fragrance of the breath of the Beloved:

> your fragrant breathing stills me,
> your grace, your glory fills me
> So tenderly your love becomes my own.[77]

Silent, still, serene, idle, in love, grace fills us. John repeatedly affirms how this spirit breath is the same breath that flows between the Father and the Son, drawing us into this same inspiration, ex-spiration of Trinitarian self-giving in love in original divine contemplation. In his *Canticle*, John has already illuminated how in this spiration of the Spirit, God transforms us into God's self. This breath is:

> so sublime, delicate, and deep a delight that a mortal tongue finds it indescribable, nor can the human intellect, as such, in any way grasp it … for the soul united and transformed in God breathes out in God to God the very divine spiration that God – she being transformed in Him – He breathes out in Himself to her.[78]

This all-pervading, animating spiration of love that infuses oneness, breathes in us in such a way that we breathe out, in God to God, with the Spirit's own breath. Influenced by the filioque clause,[79] John stresses the intimacy of the Spirit's breath between the Father and the Son, suggesting that as we breathe in this "between" breath, we have the potential to be "the love between" the divine, human, earth and creatures creating a noosphere of ever connecting spirit breath. We see from within this ever unitive, life enhancing Trinitarian breath.

---

[76] F: 3.79.
[77] *Centred on Love*, F: 4.23.
[78] C: 39.3.
[79] The Latin term *filioque* "from the Son" suggests that the Holy Spirit proceeds from the Father and the Son.

At the end of his *Flame*, John highlights again the power of this animating Spirit within us that awakens a "lofty knowledge of the Godhead." In this sweet breathing the caverns of our heart, now translucent, perceive how:

> God breathes the Holy Spirit in it in the same proportion as the knowledge and understanding of God, absorbing it most profoundly in the Holy Spirit, rousing its love with a divine exquisite quality and delicacy ... the Holy Spirit through this breathing, filled the soul with good and glory in which he enkindled it in love of himself, indescribably an incomprehensible in the depths of God.[80]

The soul breathes in the breath of the Trinity, in a *kenotic* giving of our breath, our life, our-selves, in an infusion of the union of love coming to consciousness, in the unceasing birth of unitive, or oneing awareness. This breath is intimately personal and inclusively communal, as all creation breathes in the one animating inter-connecting breath of Trinitarian loving. In this sweet breathing, every life force participates within and is being transformed into this loving of the Trinity at ever increasing levels of awareness. The beauty of this seeing from oneness shines as we live in the wholeness of being infused with transcendent knowledge. In this flowing breath that creates infinite connection and communion, John draws us from the opaque darkness of night into dawn, into the serene clarity of day light, into the transcendent beauty of divine Love radiating from the depths of all creation.

Illuminating Contemplation

Contemplation, in John, is falling in love and coming into a nocturnal tranquillity and silence, into the embrace of the solitude of the Beloved, into a deeper and fuller absorption of one in the other. John takes us from the depths of the *kenotic* suffering of the cross, into the luminous unitive vision of resurrection. Gracefully, he describes the flow from the active searching incited by an unquenchable desire to find our Beloved who seems absent, into the dark nights of sense, into the loss of meaning and searing nights of spirit, until we come into the embrace of our Beloved in the soft darkness that arises, at the time of the rising dawn. As the night becomes tranquil, and we become lovers filled with each other, we are drawn into an abiding repose in the secret, inner wine-cellar, in the transforming union of the mystical marriage, in a delightful sustaining, serene, solitude. We become enflamed, infinitely absorbed by the living flame

---

[80] F: 4:16.

of love. As the Beloved awakens within us, we intuitively sense that we are participating in the sweet breathing of the love of the Trinity.

Essentially, for John, we are absorbed in pure contemplation, when in the solitude of idle tranquillity, we receive the wisdom and language of God, within the depths of the heart of our spirit that is silent.[81] In contemplation God inebriates us secretly with infused love and wisdom.[82] In John's eloquent words:

> This wisdom is loving, tranquil, solitary, peaceful, mild, and an inebriator of the spirit, by which the soul feels tenderly and gently wounded and carried away, without knowing by whom or from where or how. The reason is that this wisdom is communicated without the soul's own activity. ... And although one is not always so clearly conscious of it, it will in due time shed its light.[83]

In due time contemplation sheds its own light, infusing fathomless and obscure divine knowledge. We become luminous, reflecting light from Light. This prayerful, carefully sketched portrait of the transformation of consciousness that John offers, draws us into a deep solitude where the Spirit infuses us in wisdom and illumes us in light, enabling us to see through the Beloved's eyes imprinted within our heart. Hence, imbibed with this luminous, tranquil wisdom, we will now draw out four quintessential insights that illume contemplation today.

First, John gives us detailed insights into the dark nights of the human condition that we undergo, as the one who is all Light, seeks transforming union with us. He knows the depths of human suffering and the deep *kenosis* that loving demands. By placing us in the opaque darkness of spirit on the cross with our crucified Beloved, John shows us how absence, abandonment, emptiness, annihilation, when lived into with love, become the place of transforming union. Through his dark nights, John takes us beyond the edges of consciousness, and places us on the cross, with crucified love, as our wounded Lover breathes his last. Together, we share in his existential cry, weeping, wailing, screaming with our vulnerable Beloved, one with vulnerable creation. John shows us how, in the voiding of this existential cry into all that is absurdly nothing, in the lowest depths of affliction, in the emptiness of sense and spirit, the tears of the Beloved, which are the tears of all creation, become jewel tears. What feels like abandonment, absence, an absurd nothingness, an annihilation of spirit, opens into a love-making in emptiness.

---

[81] F: 3:36-38.
[82] F: 3:50.
[83] F: 3:38-39.

Then, as his *Living Flame* poem unfolds, John takes us further, showing how this intimate point of our wound, opens into the middle of the heart of our spirit, where our union in the mystical marriage becomes an enflaming centre of love. In the kiss of love, in this point at the centre of our wound, the point feels like a mustard seed that is alive and enkindled. John enables us to truly embrace our wounds as the dwelling place of love and undergo deep and lasting healing. He confirms how the point within us that feels so vulnerable, so unreachable, becomes in fact, a point of the pure light of the original divine gaze within us. In this point of our shared wounding, we see that we are intimately one in an exquisite solitude with our wounded Beloved. At the same time, we magnify into a cosmic sense of infinite points of divine light aflame like a sea of living fire. John's way of seeing the point of our wounding as the point that becomes aflame with love in mystical union, like Mechthild and Clare, empowers us to be truly present to our wounding in a way that brings healing and incites wisdom, enabling the suffering of the universe to become the radiance of love evolving.

Second, although John is often acclaimed for his insights into darkness and night, John is also a great mystic of light, who speaks to our heart in words bathed in a fiery light. As his poems testify, the Beloved is the light that shines in the deepest centre of our heart. Although when we first still of house and turn within to journey to our heart's inner depths, all we encounter in darkness, John gently guides us through the darkness, reminding us, that the brighter the light, the more the owl is blinded. The more we look at the sun, the more the sun darkens our every-day sight.[84] The closer we are to being fully enflamed in love, the blacker the wood becomes, until we are luminous with divine fire. John bids us to take this dark night journey, until the deep caverns of our heart's memory, intellect and will, that were once obscure and blind, are filled with God and rarely and exquisitely, radiate warmth and light to their Beloved. In this transformation of consciousness that takes place as the Spirit penetrates our soul-memory, heart-mind and will, we give to God the same divine light and heat God gives to us. We radiate divine light to divine light. We see, with the eye of our heart, that our Beloved is the divine light of the eye of our heart. We indwell this light-soaked ground.

As this luminous divine knowing through being absorbed in love, becomes present to our heart senses and arises in consciousness, it changes how we see, as every point becomes an enflamed seed, held in this divine oneing energy,

---

[84] 2N: 3.

creating fuller union and communion. The whole cosmos becomes translucently illumed as it is enflamed by the living flame of love. Martin Laird, in his *Ocean of Light,* invites us into "the Mystery, luminous and intimate" into "the Light-soaked ground that is foundational to being human, foundational to light, life and love." Laird says that this light-soaked love, "kisses the lives of each of us, else we would not exist," affirming that this light is, "flowering perpetually in the fertile and unfathomable right now."[85] John illumes this fertile present moment and teaches us to see from luminous oneing love.

Third, this flame of love transforms us in contemplation. As we become more absorbed in love, and enter into the oneness of solitude, shining with the illuminating transcendence of enflaming love, and the caverns of our memory, intellect and will become translucent with divine light, our consciousness transforms into a stable unitive, or oneing consciousness. Our eternal memory, heart-intelligence and loving responsiveness become our initial reference point, rather than the discursive part of the mind. Our mind evolves. Thus, instead of seeing from being separate to what we are observing, or reacting from unconscious motivations, we see from within our mutual indwelling. We respond with the intelligence of the knowing and loving of the Word-Wisdom as we participate in enflaming, enlightening, transforming union. The infused, fathomless, obscure, divine knowledge fills our conscious awareness with transcendent wisdom.

This transformation of consciousness that John articulates, prepares us for an ongoing expanding of what Constance Fitzgerald identifies as a thrilling intersection between the love-knowledge of the contemplative and "participatory epistemology."[86] Participatory epistemology, emphasises that meaning is enacted through the participation of the human mind with the world, so that nature becomes intelligible to itself through the human mind. John shows us how we can only truly become intelligible to ourselves though participatory loving in God, which in turn, awakens us to our innate participation in creation, in God. When the Beloved awakens within us, we see the divine beauty in the whole of creation. Constance affirms how, as contemplatives transformed by Wisdom, we validate the conviction that the relation of the human mind to the cosmos is ultimately not dualistic but participatory. Thus, John shows how our essential

---

[85] Martin Laird, *An Ocean of Light* (Oxford, Oxford University Press, 2019), 25.
[86] See, Constance Fitzgerald, "The Transformation in Wisdom: The Subversive Character and Educative Power of Sophia in Contemplation," *Carmel and Contemplation,* 342. Participatory epistemology has been developed by Richard Tarnas.

knowledge is intrinsically, naturally non-dual. John lays the foundations for the formation of a new pattern of our wholeness in our Beloved, Wisdom-Word, and the blossoming of unitive participatory knowing through love. His insights are fundamental to the awakening of communion consciousness in the noosphere, that we will explore in the next chapter.

Fourth, John shows us how in contemplation our spirit fills with divine light and we know through our union in love. We see from oneness. He enables us to envisage evolving stages of this seeing that is Love's knowing, that is an expression of the mind of the divine heart. What is critical for us to embrace presently is the decisive role of contemplation in this knowing. It is only contemplation that will enable us to return to the ground of divine Wisdom within us, into the ground of divine consciousness itself, opening us to presence in essence, in grace, and in affection, that is evolution rising in us, as us, now. John invites us to stabilise in the fruition of this vision of divine beauty resounding throughout creation. In silent music and murmuring solitude we sing of the Beloved's desire for us, with the exquisite sweetness of the nightingale, who knows the depthless depths of the wound of love. May the night air caress us in the serenity of our oneing in Love's enflaming. We sing with John:

> Soft breathing of the air,
> sweet song of the nightingale above the plain,
> the graceful thicket, where
> a night serene and fair
> brings flame that burns, consuming with no pain.[87]

I invite you into the solitude of contemplation into the luminosity of your deepest centre before we turn into *Communion in Oneing* and join Teilhard de Chardin.

---

[87] C: 39.1.

Praying Contemplatively

*"How gentle and loving…
is your awakening, O Beloved, Wisdom-Word,
in the centre and depth of my soul."*[88]

Embracing Stillness

Your tranquil night stills my wandering spirit,
Inviting me into an abiding repose
as serene silence sings of love
and draws me into the wine cellar of my heart.
I descend gently
tiptoeing softly down the secret ladder
into the point of dawn rising into you.

Ruminating on Scripture

My heart was enflamed, …I was brought to nothing and knew not.

Psalm: 72:21-22.

---

[88]   F: 4.3.

The Music of Silence

Love's silence infuses diaphanous beauty.

Contemplatio

Stirred by Love's urgent longing, I invite you to find a nest of solitude, where you can repose in the quiet embrace of Love's silence, in the tender darkness of the tranquil night. Feel the quiet of night just before dawn.

John invites you take the secret ladder and descend into the wine cellar of your heart. Become attentive to a soft inner glow that radiates from the light of the love of the Beloved, who waits within the wine cellar of your heart's depths.

When you feel centred, at home in your heart-cellar's ground, arouse the delicate spiritual senses and sense the presence of the Beloved gazing, yearning for union with you. Feel the pull of a dissolving love drawing you into a tender embrace.

Imbibe the perfume of the divine lover's presence, the sweet spices of the wine of your love and the Beloved's love mingled. Drink the spiced wine deeply. Feel this infusing. "Spiced wine gives such strength, abundance and sweet inebriation," John comforts.[89]

Become present to the point of the centre of the cellar, to the kiss of spirit in spirit, enflaming with love. Lean, soften, dissolve as love immerses you in the utterly ineffable, intimate union of Spirit making love to spirit. Feel this luminous beauty, radiating beauty through every particle of your being.

---

[89] SC: 25.7.

As Love continues to permeate within you, feel wisdom infuse the sweet, secret, inner wisdom of contemplation, this dark love-knowledge awakening your oneing consciousness. Remain loving in this kiss, absorbed in simple contemplation for as long as you and the Beloved desire.

When it is time to move into the rest of the day, give thanks by living the day with a tranquil heart, infusing serenity into our beautiful world.

Blessing

One in your sweet breathing,
I breathe a serene contentment in to the word this day.
Amen.

III

Communion in Oneing

VII

Centre to Centre

Pierre Teilhard de Chardin

Christ is the image of the unseen God, the first born of all creation.
Colossians 1:15

The very centre of our consciousness, deeper than all its radii;
that is the essence which Omega,
if it is to be truly Omega,
must reclaim.[1]

A sea of marble white headstones rising from a green field immerses me in light. I am looking for Teilhard's grave and realise that the bodily remains of this beautiful soul, now lay at rest, hidden within the communion of his community of Jesuits. I stand still and wait, until silence attracts me to Teilhard's humble burial place. My gaze becomes a beholding, and I feel myself drawn into the energy field of the small cross etched into the metamorphised stone, made up of recrystalised minerals that he loved so much. The tiny cross arising from the IHS, the great symbol of ΙΗΣΟΥΣ, a Christogram of Jesus the Christ, catches my eye. It stills and expands my awareness out into the divine milieu and then draws my gaze to the point where the stone penetrates into earth. As I continue to behold,

---

[1] Pierre Teilhard de Chardin, *The Phenomenon of Man* (London: Collins Fontana Books, 1966). Hereafter, PM. PM: 287.

I am allured by the intense unity of centred being at the centre of the earth and feel love opening and enfolding me into the still point, into Omega. I feel the magnetic pull of the cosmic heart of infinite creativity. I feel the intensity of Spirit enflaming. Teilhard feels so present in this sacred moment in God, his heart aflame, illumed, creatively uniting his passion for God and for the earth, his struggle, his wisdom, his love. I sense how Teilhard is inviting me to become intimate with his insights, formed and reformed by the energy of the evolving creative-union that is at the heart of all his ideas. Many years later Omega draws me to prayer, which I sketch in my journal:

> I yield into the depthless flow of creative union, knitting and knotting flows of luminous light-love energy, to form a point of consciousness. The gathering particles are full, bursting with fecundity as they give themselves to the magnetic pull of Omega. I feel full of light and imbibe a sense of the awakening of birthing eyes that conceive and see union and communion wherever they gaze. The diaphanous radiance of Light illumes blissful perception. Light reflects light, point is within point, awareness and being are one. Yet, I feel drawn into my heart deeper and deeper, until I lovingly know this is Omega pulsating in and through me, in a dynamic all-consuming creative-union.

> Softly, gently, fiercely, vivaciously, I dwell within the Christic centre of the most intense unity of loving energy, gathering, enfolding, knitting, oneing. The centring draws me into an involution, into the pointless point of organic self-giving, deeper and deeper, fuller and fuller. The ground of Love is rising and turning me into Spirit filled light. My body, Christ's body, our bodies turn into glorious Matter as the most potent love amorises. Silence encircles as Presence consumes. Today, images from Teilhard's *Divine Milieu* flow into my awareness, of fullness and of hollow-ness, of activities and passivities, of our diminishments that evolve us into life.

I remember Teilhard's impassioned prayer:

> "at the last moment when I feel I am losing hold of myself and am absolutely passive within the hands of the great unknown forces that have formed me; in all those dark moments, O God, may I understand that it is you who are painfully parting the fibres of my being in order to penetrate to the very marrow of my substance and bear me away within yourself."[2]

Teilhard takes us into the luminous love energy that opens and penetrates the fibres of our being and bears us away, centring us in the most exquisite, creative

---

[2] Pierre Teilhard de Chardin, *The Divine Milieu*, trans. Pierre Leroy (New York: Harper and Row, 1960). Hereafter, DM. DM: 89-90.

point of mystical union in Omega love.³ Now born eternally into this intense creativity, Teilhard is in the fullness of love, one in the one great act of communion. Now, the flaming action of the Spirit that drew him to travel the road of fire is enabling his wisdom born of love, to come into consciousness. Now, this same fire is transforming our awareness into fuller illumination in Omega consciousness. He invites us to feel this passion for the Absolute, to be allured by the Spirit and be transposed by her ever-intensifying blazing love. Through plunging deeply into Matter, into life, into creation, into God, Teilhard shows us how to evolve in centring ever more fully in Omega love,to see how the whole universe is aflame with divine love. Love is creatively evolving within the finite, drawing all things to oneness in the Omega point.

Pierre Teilhard – Aglow with Diaphanous Love

When, towards the end of his life, Pierre Teilhard de Chardin (1881-1955) reflects back on how the enflaming presence of divine love captured his heart: "This happened," he realises, "all during my life, and as a result of my whole life, until it formed a great luminous, lit mass from within, that surrounded me."⁴ Teilhard recognises this great luminous mass, not only within and enfolded around himself, but within and through every being and every event. Specifically, he notes the intensity and the vibrance of colour of this inner light in the interplay of three things: the Cosmic, the human and the Christic, which he develops increasingly throughout his writings. Like a great landscape painter, his dazzling utterances splash before our eyes, crimson gleams of Matter, gliding imperceptibly into the gold of Spirit, ultimately, in his diaphanous words: "to become transformed into the incandescence of a Universe that is Person – and through all this there blows, animating it and spreading over it a fragrant balm, a zephyr of Union – and of the Feminine."⁵ Teilhard awakens us to this Universe that is Person, to the personalisation that is the personalising and amorising of Christ in the Universe. He invites us to inhale the sweetness of this fragrant balm and be transfigured by the waft of the breeze of its essential Union. He draws us

---

[3] Energy for Teilhard is the capacity for interaction, the expression of structure, the most primitive form of universal stuff. Although energy is physical and psychic in the last analysis there is a single energy operating in the world. See, Beatrice Bruteau, *Evolution Towards Divinity* (Weaton: The Theosophical Publishing House, 1974), 129.
[4] Pierre Teilhard de Chardin, *The Heart of Matter* trans. René Hague (London: Collins, 1978). Hereafter, HM. HM: 15.
[5] Ibid.

beyond the limits of masculine-feminine dichotomies and awakens us to the critical integration of a primordial, embodied, ever integrating, unitive consciousness as all things come together in Omega. As a mystic-palaeontologist, Teilhard writes philosophically, scientifically and mystically, identifying "creative-union," which he calls "the ultraphysics of union"[6] and what we have identified as oneing, as the foundational dynamic within the creative process. Subsequently, he crafts a phenomenology of the experience of the rise of consciousness in Matter, which he names complexity-consciousness, that we will see, is the ever unitive, ever oneing, emerging of Christ consciousness that we awaken within, in contemplation. Throughout his mystical and scientific dialectic, he connects the right and left hemispheres of our brain, integrating, linking, drawing us into the convergence of love energy, gathering in the centre of Omega, in an evolving, Christifying oneing.

Teilhard's exquisite prose places us in dazzling light, as it infuses in us a language that can hold the most intimate depths of our nature, and at the same time, enable us to relate what we know mystically to the language of science and our future evolutionary emergence. Never giving up through the struggles of misunderstandings and censorship by his Jesuit superiors, Teilhard composes an extraordinary corpus of books that include scientific treatises, theological reflections, prayers and letters, published in various compilations. His *Divine Milieu, Hymn of the Universe, Heart of Matter, Human Phenomenon, Writings in a Time of War, On Love, On Love and Happiness, The Future of Man, Human Energy,* and *Activation of Energy,* are amongst his most widely known. Teilhard's insights enkindle and enflame our hearts as they enable us to identify the movement of creative union within our own being and within creation, placing us at the face of the emerging forcefield of a consciousness that becomes more unitive. Teilhard's prophetic words shine luminously in the cosmos in ever expanding circles of love. They enflame our hearts and bathe our sensuality in light, making us luminous in our reflection of Omega love. Ultimately, all Teilhard's writings awaken us to the translucent Presence of Omega, who is the divine consciousness within all things, personalising all things and calling us to creatively unite, be illumed and transformed in this animated, dynamic, mystical awareness.

---

[6] Pierre Teilhard de Chardin, *Activation of Energy,* trans. René Hague (New York: Harcourt Brace Jovanovich, 1970). Hereafter, AE. AE: 99.

This Chapter

In this chapter, we will explore how the divine is rising in our consciousness at this point in time, inviting, a oneing consciousness, that is personal, communal and ecological. After immersing ourselves in Teilhard's way of seeing, we will see how Omega Love, expressed through divine Wisdom, is the source of the intrinsically unifying pattern of creative-union, that initiates and realises the rise of consciousness, personally and communionally in the noosphere (the collective spirit-mind).[7] Consequently, we will focus on the organic centration of this creative energy that arises from, attracts and invites us to centre in Christ-Omega. We will see how, as we reflectively turn within into this Omega point and see from within the creative union of Christ consciousness, we choose to participate in the rise of a collective Christosphere. Centred in this Centre of centres, we will then explore how Teilhard's insights illume contemplation today.

Seeing

> Lord, it is you who, through the imperceptible goadings of sense-beauty, penetrate my heart in order to make its life flow out into yourself. You came down into me by means of a tiny scrap of created reality; and then suddenly, you unfurled your immensity before my eyes and displayed yourself to me as a Universal Being. Lord, in that first figure, so near and so concrete, let me savour You at length, in all that penetrates, and in all that envelops – in sweet odour and light – both Love and Space.[8]

In these mystical, impassioned words, Teilhard awakens us to a way of seeing, by sensitising our awareness to the "imperceptible goadings of sense-beauty," to linger, savour and enjoy in "sweet odour and light," how divine love longs for relationship with creation by becoming personalised in us and throughout the universe. Christ penetrates the human heart, within the heart of universal being, filling and enveloping the universe with creative love energy. Teilhard desires that like him, we become lovers of life and of creation so that, like a ray of light in a dark cloud, a crystal drop may spread through the powdery opacity of our

---

[7] In Orthodox theology the *"nous,"* is the eye of the heart, the mind of the heart, or the knowing of the heart. Literally, Teilhard's noosphere is a sphere, a collective of eyes or minds of the heart. The noosphere is a collective consciousness.

[8] "Le Milieu Mystique," from Pierre Teilhard de Chardin, *Writings in a Time of War*, in Henri de Lubac, *The Religion of Teilhard de Chardin*, (New York: Desclee Company, 1967), 250.

limited vision.[9] He yearns for everything to become "not only warm and diaphanous but radiantly transparent,"[10] so that we may bathe in the transparency and truly see with holographic vision the presence of Omega in all things.

Frequently, Teilhard describes himself as a mystic and consistently invites a universal mystical atmosphere,[11] that engenders this mystical way of seeing. This vision Teilhard awakens us to is of living within the beauty of this universe, where God reveals God's self everywhere in a glorious divine milieu. This divine milieu is endless and yet it is a centre where all the elements of the universe touch each other in what is most inward and ultimate in them.[12] This Centre imbibes a centripetal energy that continuously centrates, purifies, presses together, holds in unity all the energies of the universe. Like the other mystics we have pondered, Teilhard reminds us that we will never be able to discern the translucent presence of this centrating energy, unless we plunge into the absolute, become lost in the unfathomable. Teilhard invites us to enter into these unknown depths and awaken what is most intimate and most ultimate within us, urging:

> let us leave the surface, and, without leaving the world, plunge into God. There, and from there, in him and through him, we shall hold all things and have command of all things. ... There we shall find ourselves where the soul is most deep and where Matter is most dense. There we shall discover, where all its beauties flow together, the ultra-vital, the ultra-sensitive, the ultra-active point of the universe. And, at the same time, we shall feel the plenitude of our powers of action and adoration effortlessly ordered within our deepest selves.[13]

This capacity to plunge into the world and into God and so discover this essence, this ultra-active point of pure love energy, where the soul is most deep and Matter is most dense, that is Omega, is our essential first step to seeing. As love circles and unfurls before our eyes, Teilhard calls us to be mystics, who like translucent Matter, only illumined by the light enclosed within it, are bathed in inner light. "This light," he explains:

> is not the superficial coloring that a crude hedonism might discern; nor is it the violent glare that annihilates objects and blinds the eyes; it is the tranquil, mighty radiance born of the synthesis, in Jesus, of all the elements of the world. The more completely the beings thus illumined attain to their natural

---

9	Ibid., 251.
10	Ibid.
11	Ibid., 255.
12	DM: 114.
13	Ibid., 115.

> fulfillment, the closer and more perceptible this radiance will be; and on the other hand the more perceptible it becomes, the more clearly the contours of the objects which it bathes will stand out and the deeper will be their roots.[14]

The more perceptible this light is to us, the more clearly the nuances of the things it bathes stand out. Ecstatically, powerfully, Teilhard awakens this tranquil, yet potent, inner light, rooting us deeply in divine presence and illuminating the next step for us to take along the way of evolving, oneing consciousness. He adds in *Human Energy*, that when we are infused in this light, that which is cold, dead and impersonal becomes: "charged ... not only with life but with a stronger life than theirs; ... they feel themselves seized and assimilated, as they act, to a far greater degree than they themselves are seizing and assimilating."[15] In this light, what looks dead in us is transformed far beyond what we could ever imagine. We are charged to see with the life that is Christ. We expand and see life through the eyes of Omega love. Teilhard places us within the world, within the story of Jesus of Nazareth, within the diaphony of the Christic Heart, within the flow of Wisdom's creativity at the heart of the glowing universe, under the influence of the totalising love of Omega.

Seeing Spirit Shining Through Matter

Teilhard gives a wonderful example of how love penetrated his heart's depths and aroused diaphanous translucent seeing. Adopting the genre of exemplum, in his story, *Spirit of Matter*, he vividly describes a researcher, who could be Teilhard himself, hiking amongst the sand dunes in the silence of the desert, when a small, vibrating "Thing,"[16] swoops down on him. Astounded by its creative power, he senses the "moving heart of an immeasurable pervasive subtlety," and feels "a breath of scorching air" breaking through and penetrating into his soul. Like Elias transported in a fiery chariot into heaven, he becomes radiant as a blazing fire invades him with a force that is both infinitely gentle and brutal, refashioning the fibres of his being and murmuring to the "one secret point of his soul."[17] Notice how this point of his soul is open and can recognise and receive this powerful, swooping, enflaming Thing that he recognises as Spirit.

---

[14] Pierre Teilhard de Chardin, *Hymn of the Universe,* trans. Simon Bartholomew (London: Collins, 1965). Hereafter, HU. HU: "Pensées," 15.88.
[15] Pierre Teilhard de Chardin, *Human Energy*, trans. J. M. Cohen (New York: Harcourt Brace Jovanovich, 1969). Hereafter, HE. HE: 148.
[16] HU: 67.
[17] Ibid., 61.

Echoing the voice of the great "I am" biblical visions, the man interacts with the Spirit and hears:

> I am the fire that consumes and the water that overthrows; I am the love that initiates and the truth that passes away. All that compels acceptance and all that brings renewal; all that breaks apart and all that binds together; power, experiment, progress — Matter: all this am I.[18]

Echoes of his encounter with the eternal feminine resound, where Wisdom-Sophia has this same primordial identity when she declares: "When the world was born, I came into being. Before the centuries were made, I issued from the hand of God — half-formed, yet destined to grow in beauty from age to age, the handmaid of his work."[19] This Spirit is the great "I am," the one who is Presence, the one who Is, the one who is Wisdom embedded into the primordial energy of space-time in the formation of the universe. Mesmerized, Teilhard expands and opens his whole being as the glowing Presence enraptures him, drawing him forward to bathe in its fiery waters, to penetrate into the depths of the universe, into the love of the boundless Essence that permeates the depths of all things. Transformed to the core of his being, his heavy cloak slips to the ground. He chooses to leave all behind and "follow the road of fire."[20] This fire of the love energy becomes the passion that inspires, draws, unites and transforms him.

Teilhard's words carry us into the pathos of this moment of transfiguration where he chooses this enflamed way. He perceives in the heart of the whirling cloud:

> a light ... growing, a light in which there was the tenderness and the mobility of a human glance; and from it there spread a warmth which was not now like the harsh heat radiating from a furnace but like the opulent warmth which emanates from a human body. What had been a blind and feral immensity was now becoming expressive and personal; and its hitherto amorphous expanses were being moulded into features of an ineffable face.[21]

The wild, fiery light reveals a tender, warm, human glance that is the gaze of the Christ, as Wisdom, as Spirt, diaphanously shining from within creation, personalising, transforming our consciousness into the same unitive gaze. This gaze can behold the "blind feral immensity" and see the features of the face of Christ shining through all things holographically. Filled with the sense beauty

---

[18] HU: 61.
[19] "The Essential Feminine," in Pierre Teilhard de Chardin, *Writings in a Time of War*, trans. René Hague (New York: Harper and Row, 1968). Hereafter WTW. WTW: 192.
[20] HU: 67.
[21] Ibid., 67-68.

of this ineffable light, he observes how: "God was shining forth from the summit of that world of Matter whose waves were carrying up to him the world of Spirit."[22] Teilhard is immersed in diaphanous beauty as he sees Spirit shining through Matter, unifying it, divinising it, evolving within it. Like the great prophets of old, he falls to his knees in the fiery chariot which bears him away as he chooses the way of fire. Teilhard's heart is set ablaze.[23]

In this encounter, Teilhard discerns how this energetic, blazing Spirit-fire within Matter is the face, the heart, the body, the blood, the Spirit of the Word incarnate, Wisdom, Sophia, the Christ, rising in the evolutionary process. This becomes his life vocation to give himself fully to the rising of Christ consciousness within the whole of the created being, affirming: "I have no desire, I have no ability, to proclaim anything except the innumerable prolongations of your incarnate Being in the world of Matter; I can preach only the mystery of your flesh, you the Soul shining forth through all that surrounds us."[24] Teilhard invites us into this soul shining from the depths of Matter to become one with this Wisdom Spirit and see every point of energy as a point of Spirit Presence. He draws us into the inner Christic face of evolution, into Wisdom's creative uniting, and awakens the luminosity of the blaze of a holographic Christic vision.

Ultimately, for Teilhard, our whole life lies in the verb *"seeing."*[25] He desires for us to see "essentially" to see the essence of things from being grounded in Love's luminous presence within us and cultivate a vision: "as wide as the skies and the earth and the people of the earth; as deep as the past, the desert and the ocean; as tenuous as the atoms of Matter of the thoughts of the human heart."[26] In nurturing this vast, unitive vision we discover a "deep running, ontological, total Current which embraces the whole Universe."[27] This current is the Christ in evolution being personalised in us by becoming more conscious through us, creatively uniting, evolving, continually growing until the Christ fills every fibre of our being. Teilhard urges us to penetrate into the centre of this ontological current of consciousness and see from within it. Critically, this must include penetrating into the dense, expansive, cosmic quality of the divine milieu, along with centring into the dynamic point of the energies of creative union gathered within

---

[22] Ibid.
[23] Ibid., 36.
[24] HU: 35-36.
[25] PM: 3.
[26] HU: "Pensées," 22.
[27] HM: 25.

our own *nous*, mind, or heart, and the collective *nous*, or heart of all creation, until all is one in our conscious awareness. He urges us to see ourselves in the universe "as the axis and leading shoot of evolution,"[28] affirming that "we are evolution."[29] Evolution is rising in our consciousness from the dynamism of our creative union with the divine in all things. This is the point we are at now, and it is so critical in this moment of climate crisis, that we become this leading shoot of evolution and enable humankind to evolve in a collective, unitive consciousness. We are the point where Christ Omega is coming to consciousness, where the Christ is continuing to incarnate in creation. Ever seeking for us to be this creative point, Teilhard develops a comprehensive theory of the foundational nature of the creative-union that releases this evolutionary energy of rising Christ consciousness.

Teilhard develops an insightful theory of the rise of the awareness that is Christ-Omega, or Christ consciousness.[30] And importantly, he does not limit this rise of Christ consciousness to human beings, who must separate themselves from the world in order to be contemplative. For Teilhard, contemplation is at the heart of the evolutionary story of the universe. This rise of Christ consciousness occurs within the wholeness of the divine milieu, within the world. Teilhard infuses us with a sense of wonder at the immensity, the depthless-ness, magnitude, rhythm, novelty, movement, and structural unity of the collectives within creation that he so highly cherished. At the same time, he grounds us in our own inner universe that holds all this energy of the outer universe, within the convergence of our centre in the Christ-Omega.

Teilhard shows us how Omega holds within its radius, the essential unity of reflectivity, or what we have been identifying as the most intimate inter-penetration of divine Love in Love, or as oneing. Although, this language of "reflectivity," that Beatrice Bruteau later calls "reflexivity," has developed with a variety of technical meanings today, for Teilhard reflectivity has its source in Omega. Omega is the supreme unitive point of convergence, who attracts us to be present in presence in this pointless point of infinite union that is the Omega point. And this reflective capacity, to turn within and reflect back within our-

---

[28] PM: 40.
[29] Ibid., 256.
[30] Broadly speaking, for Teilhard consciousness is the substance of the heart of life in the process of evolution. See Bruteau, *Evolution Towards Divinity*, 129. Substance in this context is the essence, or the evolutionary amorising love of Omega who is the source of all consciousness. Consciousness has an organic converging movement active within it.

self, within the awareness of Omega itself, is evolving. Thus, we could say that reflectivity holds an organic oneing energy that is evolutionary. Teilhard emphasises the supreme role of Omega in this reflective oneing, who is both beyond, and within, this essential unity. In the cyclical movement of the turning within to the ground of our heart into Christ, into Omega, we find ourselves being transformed into an ever more intensified oneing, that is the capacity to see from oneness within Christ-Omega. Teilhard affirms how loving and lovable Omega is, at this very moment, this point in time.[31] Omega is so supremely attractive, so supremely present that when we are present within this loving point, we are present to Love's evolutionary movement. Teilhard's insights confirm how essential contemplative prayer is for the natural evolutionary process to flow. We will now see how this occurs through endless creative union.

Endless Creative Union

"Deus create uniendo," God creates by uniting,"[32] Teilhard says simply. And he adds in his *Activation of Energy*, "To unite, to form one with something, is to be immersed in it; … to become a particle within it."[33] Teilhard is affirming how God immerses God's self in the world, becoming a particle within it through Christ becoming human, placing the intimacy of the divine persons being in one another within the Trinity within creation. Christ, in the person of Jesus of Nazareth, plunges into the natural process of creation, placing creative union in the heart of the material universe. Thus, the gracious, vivacious intimacy of this shared love within the Trinity is poured into the soul of creation, making creation an expression of divine loving with the capacity to share in and express the same divine outpouring and receiving of love. Teilhard explains this Christification:

> Because Christ, who is the principle of *universal vitality*, has sprung up as man among us, he has put himself in the position of, and forever has been, actively curving beneath him, purifying, directing, and superanimating the general rise of consciousness into which he has inserted himself. By a perennial act of communion and sublimation, he is aggregating the entire psyche of the Earth to himself. And when he has thus gathered everything together and transformed everything, then, in the final act of rejoining the divine focal point he has never

---

[31] PM: 295-296.
[32] HM: 226.
[33] AE: 263.

left, he will close in on himself. ... And then as St Paul tells us, "There will be only God, who is all in all."[34]

The reverberation of the intimate fertile shared loving of "all in all" resounds, as Teilhard affirms how Christ is the principle, the fundamental unity, the Centre, who places the foundational pattern of creative or mystical union within creation. Christ is the origin of universal vitality, the infinitely fertile archetype of creative union, within the human heart. Christ is the ground of divine consciousness within us, who instils in us the initial unitive spark, that we have seen with all the mystics, who becomes Person in us by rising in our consciousness, enabling us to become truly human. Christ is the one whose loving energy has the power to embrace the plurality of all things, who gathers together the whole mind, or *nous,* of the earth, into the highest density of creative union in Omega.

Teilhard further stresses the power of love expressed in this Christic unifying principle, by identifying its essentially unitive nature with the eternal feminine, or Wisdom-Sophia. Paul's identification of Christ, as the power and wisdom of God (1 Cor 1.24) resounds,[35] and Julian's expression of Christ as deep Wisdom and Mother harmonises. Wisdom sings of her unifying qualities:

> Everything in the universe is made by union and generation —
> by the coming together of elements
> that seek out one another,
> melt together two by two,
> and are born again in a third.
> God instilled me into the initial multiple
> as a force of condensation and concentration.
> In me is seen that side of beings
> by which they are joined as one,
> in me the fragrance that makes them
> hasten together and leads them,
> freely and passionately,
> along their road to unity.
> Through me, all things have their movement
> and are made to work as one."[36]

---

[34] Pierre Teilhard de Chardin, *The Human Phenomenon. Pierre Teilhard de Chardin*, trans. Sarah Appleton-Weber (Brighton: Sussex Academic Press, 2015), 211.
[35] See Kathleen Duffy, "Sophia: Catalyst for Creative Union and Divine Love," in Ilia Delio, *From Teilhard to Omega*, (New York: Orbis Books, 2013), 31, who acclaims Sophia's identity with Wisdom 7:25-26 and affirms how Sophia reveals herself as the divine *ousia*, the very nature of God residing in the core of the cosmic landscape.
[36] WTW: 192.

We can inhale the opulent fragrance of Wisdom's fecund desire for union within us that imparts a natural yearning to unite and be generative. We can taste Wisdom's luminous unifying presence that incites a centre to centre intimacy. We can touch her simplifying force of condensation and concentration that knits, ones and engenders ever fuller union. And so we can see why Teilhard highlights the "creative" nature of Wisdom's passion to foster union, stressing how the coming together of elements in a centre to centre union always brings creativity, transformation, novelty, diversity and an emergent quality of something more. Moreover, the love-making of the ecstatic energies uniting, creates something new, that is more than the sum of the parts. Teilhard comes to see how these new entities formed by centres, uniting centre to centre, are Wisdom expressing herself in the soul of collective humankind. Accordingly, Wisdom's luminous presence continually instils in us a desire for fuller union, making us "super-personalized," or superlatively personal in radiating love from our Christic-self. Wisdom incites in us a desire to be "super-centred,"[37] ever more condensed and concentrated in the dynamic of creative union in the Omega point. In following Wisdom's drawing and recollecting within our centre, we become creatively differentiated, more uniquely ourselves as transcendent-human persons, whose loving participates in the ever more reflective, unitive, communal consciousness field of Omega love.

Thus, there is a sense in Teilhard's understanding of this grounding principle of creative-union, of an evolutionary God, who initiates a desire for union and communion within creation. Reciprocally, God is then affected by creation's growth towards fuller unity. Although, through all things being held eternally in the Christ we are already one in Christ-Omega, divine Wisdom infuses an ever-centring desire to give all that we are to the drawing of the Centre of Centres to become more fully one in Christ. We are now at the point in the evolutionary cycle, where we must consciously, and actively join together, in response to Wisdom's magnetic desire. Teilhard is suggesting that the future is a naturally unitive love that comes to meet us in the present moment, inciting creative union. And critically, our choice to meet in the creative union of this present moment is necessary for the fulfilment of the work of Incarnation. Teilhard's vision releases our potential for uniting together in creative mystical union and seeing all of

---

[37] AE: 117.

creation within our oneness in Christ. It is natural for us to be in communion, or oneing consciousness in the divine.

Creative Union Evolving

Engaging our imaginations and sense of wonder, Teilhard the scientist, elaborates on the dynamic of creative union evolving. He outlines the process of successive progressions in evolution from the first appearance of consciousness in non-being, to the gradual development of consciousness in biodiversity, to the formation of the animating spirit of the soul within humankind, to our personalisation and communion of all in the mystical body of Christ. All manifest within the inner dynamic of creative union. This creative union of centre to centre uniting, occurs from the tiniest molecular level connecting and forming cells. This union of cells leads to the formation of organisms, with organisms uniting to form species, over and over again. Teilhard stresses the origination point of the bursting forth of light and fire from the original cosmic singularity.[38] He accentuates how, without losing this original point, gases and particles burst forth, groping,[39] and randomly come together, to form new knot-like elements that enable the emergence of something new. Sometimes these knots join other knots and form even more complex knots. This ongoing creativity of points, uniting centre to centre and bursting forth with generativity, creating something more, springs up in the cosmos like:

> knots spaced out along a cord, or like the folds into which a single curtain falls, or the eddies forming on one and the same surface, everything that moves and lives in the universe represents, in one particular aspect, the modifications of one and the same thing; and every monad, if it looks into itself, can find that thing as the initial point at which all things make contact in their inmost essence.[40]

Echoes of Julian's knitting and oneing resound, as Teilhard describes the enfolding, knitting and oneing of knots in an endless process of elements bonding, creatively uniting centre to centre and forming a woven tapestry of

---

[38] See, Kathleen Duffy, *Teilhard's Mysticism. Seeing the Inner face of Evolution* (New York: Orbis Books, 2014), 58-59.
[39] 'Groping' is a searching blindly or straining towards finding a way forward. It is, he says, "*directed chance.* It means pervading everything so as to try everything, and trying everything so as to find everything." This energy of groping creates the profusion in nature. PM: 121-122.
[40] WTW: 21.

more complex inter-related entities. Everything is inter-related and interconnected within a wholeness that is: "endless and unutterable, so closely woven in one piece that there is not one single knot in it that does not depend on the whole fabric."[41]

In short, the interweaving of unitive knots in this fabric continues to evolve until the pressure of love creates a small shift in the tangential energies and initiates a radial concentration of energies in the centre.[42] As the cosmic spindle forms a reflective consciousness, we begin to know that we know.[43] This reflective consciousness, assists us to become aware of our Christic nature and to recognise Wisdom's unitive presence in Matter. Critically, this stronger reflexivity marks a major turning point because before this, consciousness creatively united intrinsically. Now, in the rise of reflective consciousness, evolution must be accomplished though consciousness. We must choose to be immersed in the power of Wisdom's self-giving love.[44] We must cooperate with her ongoing task of Christifying the universe, by activating Christic consciousness within us, because God creates by uniting with us, creating from within us. It is only this chosen, increasing, interiorization that will produce a greater unicity of energy and the increasing complexity of Love's amorising the universe.[45]

Reflective Human Nature

Our capacity to be self-reflective, to know that we know, and to know that we know from within the Christ-self within us, brings us to a critical point in evolution. As we actively participate in the involution within the depths of our heart, and ruminate within the point of creative union, unitive conscious awakens. The contemplative wisdom of a oneing heart-awareness arises, enabling us to recognise the radiance of Wisdom's unifying presence and enter

---

[41] Pierre Teilhard de Chardin, *Science and Christ*, trans. René Hague (New York: Harper and Row, 1966), 79.

[42] For Teilhard, all energy is psychic. Tangential energy links all elements at the same order, complexity and centricity, while radial energy, draws towards ever greater complexity and centricity in a forward movement. PM: 63-64.

[43] This reflective power of consciousness, "can only subsist by means of a double movement which is in reality one and the same. It centres itself further on itself by penetration into a new space, and at the same time it centres the rest of the world around itself by the establishment of an ever more coherent and better organised perspective in the realities which surround it." PM: 191.

[44] See, Pierre Teilhard de Chardin, *Man's Place in Nature*, trans. René Hague (London: Collins Fontana Books, 1966), 121.

[45] HE: 97.

into her ever unitive vision. We become a person, a flow of love energy, an expression of the personalisation of our own differentiated unique personhood within the body of Christ Omega. In Teilhard's words: "As soon, ... as, through reflection, a type of unity appeared ... the sublime physics of centres came into play. Having become centres, and therefore persons, the elements could finally react directly as elements to the personalising action of the Centre of centres."[46] This reflection that enables unity, is:

> the power acquired by a consciousness to turn in upon itself, to take possession of itself, as of an object endowed with its particular consistence and value: no longer merely to know oneself; no longer merely to know, but to know that one knows. By this individualization of himself in the depths of himself, the living element, which heretofore has been spread out and divided over a diffuse circle of perceptions and activities, was constituted for the first time as a *centre* in the form of a point at which all the impressions and experiences knit themselves together and fuse into a unity that is conscious of its own organization.[47]

When consciousness passes from divergence to convergence in this centre where we know that we know, we plunge into a growing and irreversible unification, as we are knit together, in union with all other centres, in Christ. In the last resort, Teilhard affirms, "the reflective centres of the world are effectively 'one with God'."[48] We are one in the oneing, in the communion of this reflective centre of Love.

This sublime physics of centres complexifying, as centres centre upon centres, with increasing depth, consciousness and intensity, increases the amount of concentrated spiritual energy and awakens us to the dynamism of inter-centric energies. Teilhard confirms the importance of this centring, inter-centring dynamic, when he says:

> it must be centre to centrer and in no other way that they establish contact with one another ... it is the "intercentric" energies that we have above all to identify, to harness and to develop if we would make an effective contribution to the progress of evolution within ourselves.[49]

We must surrender to Love's magnetic centring force and be drawn into her synthesising inter-centric loving flow. In his "Reflection on Love and

---

[46] PM: 298.
[47] Ibid., 183.
[48] Ibid., 338.
[49] HU: "Pensées," 122-123.

Happiness,"[50] Teilhard summarises the process of the releasing of these inter-centric energies, identifying a threefold movement in this "centrogenesis," from centration, to decentration, to super-centration.

The first movement of centration, or centring within ourselves, involves locating, centring in, and awakening the centre of our own heart and living authentically from this centre, in the creative, unitive, centring energy of onening of love. This personal centration then prepares us for the awakening of Christ consciousness which, in turn, initiates a second movement, of "decentration." In decentring, we centre in our essence, and then de-centre by extending our centred awareness, and freely choosing to unite, heart centre to heart centre, with others in the Centre of centres. This collective of centres in the Centre, in the Omega point, then creates a "supercentration," that has a yet to be conceived intensely communal unity. Wisely, Teilhard counsels:

> we cannot reach our own ultimate without emerging from ourselves by uniting ourselves with others, in such a way as to develop through this union an added measure of consciousness a process which conforms to the great law of complexity. Hence the insistence, the deep surge, of love, which, in all its forms, drives us to associate our individual centre with other chosen and specially favored centres: love, whose essential function and charm are that it completes us.[51]

This deep surge of love that encourages us to seek others and decentre for the sake of centring, animates communion. It then instils in us a super-centration, or consciousness of all in all, of *oneing* in Omega. In centring in Christ and sharing in Wisdom's vitality in inciting and harnessing the inter-centric energies of love in creative union, a collective world heart-mind, a noosphere (a sphere of *nous*, or sprit-mind) forms which we can actively choose to evolve.

So reflectively turning to our centres, until we yield beyond the turning, into the natural energy of Sophia within us, is our essential task now. We are being invited to follow the attraction of the ever lovable Omega and plunge into the unfathomable depths of our oneing in Christ in the *kenotic* loving exchange of creative union, creating a fuller union, a more dynamic oneing. We must surrender into the dynamism of creative union in the Omega point within us and learn how to grope, to risk, to yield into the darkness of unknowing, into the

---

[50] Pierre Teilhard de Chardin, *On Love and Happiness* (San Francisco: Harper & Row, 1984). Hereafter L&H. L&H: 64-69.
[51] Ibid., 67-68.

spaciousness that creates the potentiality for fuller union, for a more intense oneing, beyond our current notions of union. This personal centration in the Centre of Centres, that evolves into a decentration, that leads to a super-centration, is critical for the evolution of Christ consciousness in the noosphere. In Teilhard's ever unitive vision of creative union, contemplation is essential for our evolutionary growth.

The Noosphere

Teilhard first became conscious of the inter-centric energies of the noosphere in the trenches at the front in World War I, when he confronted the opaque darkness of the fear, despair, horror and seemingly unending suffering of war. Vividly, he writes in his notebook of the moon shining on blackened and bloodied trenches covered with barbed wire, that illumed his sense of our common humanity.[52] The stark contrast between the luminosity of moonlight and the sharp metal of barbwire infused a dialectic between hope and despair, as Teilhard wonders, what is it that is rising up from the dimly outlined trenches and asks, "Is it the Moon, or is it rather the Earth, a unified Earth, a new Earth?"[53] Woven together in a tapestry of suffering, Teilhard sees a unified earth. Similarly, in *Human Phenomenon,* he emphasises Wisdom's unitive presence in this earth consciousness, as he envisages glowing light rippling from the first spark of conscious reflection. "The point of ignition grows larger," he says. "The fire spreads in ever widening circles till finally the whole planet is covered with incandescence."[54] The fire within glows as it becomes the fire without.

This image of the noosphere forming like ripples of fire expanding as they glow outward from the first spark of consciousness, helps us envisage how the noosphere is intrinsically connected to the centre of consciousness, to the spark, to the light of the divine transcendence, to Omega within us.[55] The fiery energy of this spark, this light within matter within human beings, naturally forms into

---

[52] 'La Grande Monade' HM: 183. Written in the trenches, about 1917, Teilhard also referred to the noosphere as the "Anthroposphere" emphasising the human sphere.
[53] HM: 184.
[54] PM: 182.
[55] We are reminded that the *nous,* in the Orthodox tradition, is the eye of our soul, or heart that is noetic, transcendent, unborn. When purified it can become fully conscious of the light of grace, knowing God and the inner essence of things. Literally the noo-sphere is a sphere, a surface equidistant from a centre, created by the oneing of the *nous* within humankind. We will see how Beatrice suggest we can noetically coincide in the noosphere and be conscious communionally.

a communion of minds, a *nous*, a heart-mind, thinking-spirit, or common soul of humankind, which Teilhard pictures as enfolding the planet in the incandescence of transcendence. As we communionally draw our consciousness within, into the point of the spark, its luminous energy expands without, like an envelope, folding and enfolding. "The earth makes a new skin," Teilhard observes. "Better still it finds its soul."[56] The earth finds its soul, its *anima mundi* in the reflective consciousness of the noösphere. Teilhard sees that this divine spark igniting ever more dense energy fields of conscious reflection is not only our own soul: it is the soul of the earth. The noosphere gives expression to our essential oneness. We dwell within a noosphere, a communal soul that is conscious, can reflect on itself and know that it knows communionally.

Later, reflecting back over the progression of his insights, in *Heart of Matter*, Teilhard confirms this lustrous living membrane that is: "not only conscious but thinking, and from the time when I first became aware of it, it was always there that I found concentrated, in an ever more dazzling and consistent form, the essence or rather the very Soul of the Earth.[57] Again, Teilhard emphasises the oneness, the unicity of this conscious thinking human-earth soul, or *nous*, as he delimitates the development from the primordial disposition for self-arrangement and self-involution, to "a critical point 'of reflection', which releases a whole chain of the specific properties of the human."[58] At this point of reflection, a new capacity to reflect within develops. The germinating principle, or spark of divine consciousness within the marrow of the Noosphere, awakens.[59] Within this lustrous living membrane of the soul-mind of collective humankind, there is a natural attraction to centring within. In centring and creatively uniting, we reach a critical point of reflection, releasing a new capacity and consciousness of union and communion, in the germinating principle that is the consciousness of the Christ. We become communionally Christ-conscious.

Christ-Consciousness

This is where we are invited to be at this phase of the evolutionary journey, to awaken within this germinating principle and actively participate in the rising of collective Christ-consciousness within the noosphere. Teilhard foresees that it

---

[56] Ibid., 183.
[57] HM: 32.
[58] Ibid.
[59] Ibid.

will be a critical moment when human beings wake up to this ocean of human creative energy of collective consciousness and embrace the complete configuration of this one world. When we see that we have the same luminous centre, are encircled in the same light, and feel this amorising love energy vibrate in the fabric of our being, a lasting transformation will occur. He affirms:

> One and the same influence animates and holds together everything that thinks. … One single circle embraces all Spirit, and imprisons nothing... We can hardly perceive this higher and uncircumscribed unity of the Universe ... the most we can say is that at certain times a wind greater than we, coming we know not whence, passes through our soul.[60]

Though we can hardly perceive this "higher and uncircumscribed unity of the Universe," Teilhard wants us to perceive it, to have a sense of the energy of the exquisite oneing of this unified forcefield which is an expression of the union that is rippling out from Omega. Gradually, as we share in these higher inter-centric energies, and knots of creative-union form, greater complexity emerges creating a "super-centration," or intense mystical union of collective humankind in the Christ, forming a Christosphere, the sphere where the consciousness of the noosphere transforms into the mystical consciousness of the body of Christ.

In this Christosphere we are so grounded in the Christic centre that we are, "ultra-reflective," so reflective within our heart, so centred in the Christ self within us, that Christ consciousness emerges personally and communionally. We see from within our oneness. n this super-centring of essence within essence, the oneing of Love evolves into circles with an increasing radius of one single great humanity aglow from within. The beauty of this unitive collective heart-mind leaves Teilhard in awe. He acclaims: "O wonder-laden Centre! O immense sphere! O God!"[61] Teilhard assists us to sensitise to this wonder laden centre who is Christ Omega longing to be personalised and come to fuller consciousness. In doing so, he enables us to create a Christosphere in this centred sphere of the human-earth-heart-mind. He calls for us to surrender into this converging energy of love and give ourselves to Omega's creative influence. Together, one in Omega, we meet each other "wanting, hoping for and loving the same thing at the same time."[62]

---

[60] HM: 191.
[61] Ibid.
[62] L&H: 69.

Illuminating Contemplation

Contemplatives who become absorbed and centred in Christ, in Omega, in contemplation, in Teilhard's view, becomes a centrating force in the universe. Our contemplation enables the rise of unitive Christ consciousness to occur personally and communionally in the noosphere. Teilhard plunges us into the depths of creation and enables us to realise our identity in the burning centre of Christ, drawing us into Omega love, right in the centre of the heart of the world. He affirms:

> when I contemplated your Godhead, I had the rapture of finding a personal and loving Infinite; ... And now I know more: the very multitude of my race comes to life in your humanity; the breath that gives solidity and harmony to its scattered elements is not a Spirit whose higher nature is disconcerting to us, it is a human soul that feels and vibrates as I do; it is your very soul, Jesus. I know, too, that, in a supreme condescension to my yearning for activity and change, you offer me this higher, definitive, world which you concentrate and shelter in Yourself, but you offer it unfinished, so that my life may draw sustenance from the intense satisfaction of, in some small way, giving You to Yourself.[63]

Our role in this unfinished work of longing to evolve, is to give Christ to Christ's self within the finite. With this beautiful sense of reflectively illuminating the Christ, we will focus now on four ways Teilhard illuminates contemplation today.

First, Teilhard gives us the gift of seeing from within the translucence of essence. He floods our consciousness in divine radiance, bathing us in the lucid, unifying spiritualising energy of Wisdom. He instils in us Wisdom's desire and her potential for an evolving creative union, heart centre to heart centre in the heart of Christ, in Omega. He sensitises us to the aroma of Wisdom's presence, to the fire of her passion, to the translucence of her wisdom, ever revealing how we one we are in Christ. In all that Teilhard writes, he longs to unify his interior vision with the material creative process, and show through his exploration of creative union, that the entire evolutionary process within creation is a vast movement of unification, converging in the heart of Christ. As we immerse ourselves in this finely integrative, dynamically animating oneing, we become a flow of creative union ourselves, centred and aware in centre to centre connection in Omega. The more we celebrate our fleshy material nature and recognise the presence of Spirit

---

[63] WTW: 52.

connecting and interlacing particle after particle of our being, the eyes of our Christic energy field expand and pour out love-wisdom creativity. The more we become this love energy, the more our hearts beat with this amorising love, the more Christ rises as the heart centre of Matter. This activates a stronger Christ consciousness, or capacity to see from the eyes of our transcendent nature in Christ. This theory of creative union, Teilhard feels, lays a foundation for further development in the future, which it is now our turn to develop. It has philosophical advantages in that it dissolves boundaries between the many and the one. It reconciles any separation between Matter and Spirit showing how Spirit locks together and interlocks the elements that constitute the world.[64] And, this theory of creative union, he says, satisfies us mystically: "because it reduces all the world's movement to a communion. Communion becomes the unique and essential act of the World."[65] Teilhard's cosmogenesis places all of creation within the mystical body of Christ. Here, we see as creation animated by ever-intensifying Omega love.

Second, contemplation is the engine room of actively and creatively forming a stronger noosphere. We spiritedly shape what is sometimes called a "we" space, or conscious communion of hearts. In discovering the shared ground of our contemplation together, by entering into the depths of the ground of shared heart-spaciousness and finding language for this creative union of amorising energy, we participate in the evolution of Christ consciousness. This communion of hearts takes us beyond all egoic distinctions, especially gender distinctions, into a natural contemplative, collective *nous*, a spirit filled global thinking heart-mind that is one with the ground of divine unity. This collective heart-mind responsively nurtured by the energy of oneing, can engage tenderly with and embrace all those too vulnerable to take this inner journey at present. As well, it can enter into the shadows of the collective unconscious, and shower light into the limited, fearful, violent, barren, places in the human psyche. Moreover, because this heart-mind, is intrinsically part of the soul of the earth, we necessarily listen and respond to the wisdom of earth. In learning to consciously enter into the ground of silence, into the energy field of heart in heart communion, into Wisdom's endless unitive creativity, our lives as contemplatives strengthen the bonds of creative union and place unitive love wherever love feels absent. We can create a Christosphere.

---

[64] HM: 205-206.
[65] Ibid., 206.

Third, as Omega Love's passionate longing to attract, connect and draw all things into convergence continues to unfold, it is critical that we unite *only* centre to centre, in the cosmic point of Omega. Anything else but personalising centre to centre heart loving, such as ego to ego fusion, has the potential to create boundary violations, rather than true unity. The unity of the noosphere must be centred in our originating spark of Omega, that we have seen with the other mystics. The energy of the inter-centric energies, and their informational flow must be Omega love energy. For as Ilia Delio reminds us, "the noosphere is a superconvergence of psychic (spiritual/mental) energy, a higher form of complexity in which the human person does not become obsolete but rather requires more being through interconnectivity with others."[66] And more being means fuller union, richer communion. Ilia affirms, the noosphere is the rise of a cosmic spiritual centre, the rise of God.[67] As awareness of the field of the spirit endowed thinking mind of the noosphere strengthens, we grow in our capacity to live oned, inside the mind of Christ, as Christ's mind lives in our mind. We are one in the point of centred Christ consciousness, and the field of inter-centric Christic consciousness.

Fourth, Teilhard's assurance that the gradual increasing and expanding of the rise of Christic collective consciousness, is so full of hope. In this collective we are held within the fertility of Wisdom's creative, unifying, enfolding, love. And exquisitely, in every moment of this growth, Wisdom sings: "I still held them within me, and taught them to bear the burden of a greater consciousness. I was able to stand before them, matching, circle for circle, the concentric zones of their desires, as the proper form of their beatitude."[68] Wisdom holds us within this dynamic creative-union that attracts, connects and draws us to be the heart of Christ, to be radiant Omega love, to be a field of inter-centric energies of flowing love.[69] When Teilhard writes to his friend Lucile, his heartfelt words come from this expansive, unifying, common field of shared love. He pens:

> I feel that in spite of the miles your presence is with me, – or still more truly, – in me. I enjoy this idea (perfectly "scientific", I believe) that distance does not exist but for what we call "Matter." Gradually, – and according to the proportion of a mutual love, – the Spiritualized elements of the world are

---

[66] Delio, *Making All Things New*, 111.
[67] Ibid.
[68] WTW: 193.
[69] "Love," Teilhard says, "is by definition the word we use for attractions of a personal nature." HE: 145.

converging into a common and deeper centre, in which nothing whatever can separate them. There I will find you."[70]

May we find each other as the spiritualised elements of the world become diaphanously transparent in Matter converging into a common and deeper centre, where nothing can separate us. May we give Christ to Christ's self.

I now invite you to join Teilhard in contemplation before we turn to Beatrice.

---

[70] Letter from Hankow, 1934, Pierre Teilhard de Chardin and Lucile Swan, *The Letters of Teilhard and Lucile Swan,* eds. Thomas M. King and Mary Wood Gilbert (Scranton: University of Scranton Press, 1950), 15.

Praying Contemplatively

Christ consumes with a glance my entire being.
And with that same glance, that same presence,
he enters into those who are around me and whom I love.
Thanks to him therefore I am united with them, as in a divine milieu,
through their inmost selves, and I can act upon them
with all the resources of my being.
Christ binds us and reveals us to one another.[71]

Embracing Stillness

O Loving centre of all that is,
creative, evolving, Presence, Omega
the urgent longing of my heart
is to plunge into the wild abandon of love
and converge in the energy of your loving.
Still, silence and centre my gaze in your Omega Point.
Dissolve my isolation.
Envelop me in the energy of your attraction to me.
Gently, draw me home.

---

[71] HU: 119.

Ruminating on Scripture

I am the Alpha and the Omega.

Rev 21:6

The Music of Silence

Gentle silence encircles and centres in pools of love.

Contemplatio

"Let us leave the surface and, without leaving the world plunge into God,"[72] Teilhard invites. Teilhard longs for us to centre in the Omega Love that is the Centre of centres, the centre of our heart and the centre of all being. So, I invite you to find a quiet place, where you can come to silence and stillness.

Become attentive to your innate yearning for Omega, as you centre into your heart. Harness your breath, your mind, your senses, the marrow flowing through your bones, every fiber of your being, the energies of your loving and plunge into the spacious darkness of luminous Presence. Yield into the potency of the magnetic pull of this Centre of Love drawing you.

In communion with all life, become aware of your body as part of the earth. Gradually release any tension, as you relax into the endless horizons of yourself, held in the divine milieu. Breathe in the divine fragrance that suffuses the universe. As you breathe, notice how your breath is inspired by the flow of Spirit everywhere present, love flowing, enfolding, filling, melting, oneing.

---

[72] HU: "Pensées," 139.

Gently, encircle the wanderings of your mind into your heart, plunge your awareness into Love's darkness and melt away into Omega's drawing. Continue to encircle and lean into the innate presence of Omega, permeating and centring softly, darkly, intuitively.

When you feel centred in a centration, drawing on your heart energies, yet without conceptualising, extend your love into the multi-centres of the noosphere, in a decentration. Feel infused in the luminosity of the noosphere.

Sense the super-centration of the ever-expanding circling and encircling drawing all things into Omega. Dissolve in the circling, encircling, stillness, into oneing of Love.

Softly, gently continue to release into Sophia, the Spirit of Omega, encircling, encompassing, enfolding, embracing, enclosing, knitting, oneing. Sink into this exquisite radial energy, that unites and draws all things into a more intense unitive consciousness, or oneing awareness.

Savour your oneness with the earth, all creatures, all human beings. Delight in the communion of oneing love.

Stay in this circling encircling stillness for as long as you feel drawn.

When you feel drawn to finish the prayer time, rest in gentle silence, in an ambiance of gratitude, yielding into the unitive Presence creating the future reality of All in all.

Blessing

Omega Love,
Centred in you Omega
in your ever-centring presence
I encounter the world as your body and blood.
May every breath I take, every response I make
harness the energies of love into your encircling oneness.
I hold all who suffer in the tender embrace
of your creative union
in the healing love of the future's fullness.
Amen.

VIII

Enstatic-Ecstatic Communion

Beatrice Bruteau

Be transformed in the renewing of your mind.
Romans 12:2

*The self-realized person is present in the world
as a valley of peace and a fountain of joy.
There is a kind of gentle bubbling of happiness
and kindly humor just under the surface all the time,
because the person knows that at the root of being,
in the secret place which is the place of the great secret,
there is that Infinite Act of Love that makes every being to be,
and that no matter how bad things may appear to be here
on the surface, somehow, at the depth,
all is well and all manner of thing is well.*[1]

"All is well," reverberates throughout the cosmos, as Beatrice magnifies Julian's words of hope that are so needed in this time of ecological crisis. As I compose this chapter, the land is parched and dry. Earth's cry has become a wail, as closed hearts continue to ignore her soul wisdom. The dryness explodes into ravaging

---

[1] Beatrice Bruteau, "In the Cave of the Heart: Silence and Realization," *New Blackfriars* Vol. 65, No. 768-770, 1984, 319.

fire, destroying wildlife, plants, people, homes. Fire rages and smoke billows for months, infusing the once fresh air with unbreathable fumes. In the face of all this tragedy, and sadly so much indifference to global warming, Beatrice opens up the ground of hope for us, as she sheds even further light on how we can develop the participatory love knowledge of contemplation, that we explored with John of the Cross. Beatrice enables us to feel the libation of suffering creation and enter into our communal indwelling in the ground of all being, into the point of creative union in love. Beatrice takes us into the placeless, "secret place which is the place of the great secret," so that the obscure, divine love-knowledge imbibed in contemplation, may shed its light. It is here in the ground of our heart, in the ground of love, that we discover the original creativity that can assist our evolution beyond this impasse.

In praying with the prophetic insights of Beatrice, this infinite act of love draws me into its silent ground, into what Beatrice calls the *kolpon*, which we will explore in this chapter. This exquisite *kolpon*, hollow, emptiness, is where Jesus is in the bosom, or heart-womb of the Father, making the unseen God known (Jn 1:18). This *kolpon* evokes the silent-womb-heart of infinite creative union or oneing, where all is in all (Col 3:11), in an endless divine begetting. It signifies the womb-like placeless-place of divine contemplation, the fertile divine consciousness, the archetypal point of revelation, holding all things, within all things and yet beyond all things, that is infinitely creative, evolutionary. While still staying in the energy of the prayer, I record in my journal:

> Love infuses, absorbs my whole being in contemplation, dissolving old patterns of seeing and knowing, as I awaken in the silent-womb, *kolpon* heart, in your *contemplatio*, that is always original, because it is you beloved Trinity. You, O Trinity of absolute self-giving, pour out *agape*, dissolving, annihilating, old constricting images, of who I am, and who we are as earth-beings. The silence, the stillness is so fecund, fertile, verdant, you endlessly express what is within through your Word, Jesus, enfleshing love into creation. I dissolve into the point where your silence resounds, and your Word becomes flesh. I sense the pointless point, the kiss of enstasy that is infinitely fertile, ecstatically evolving ever new ways, to creatively express your transcendent beauty within the cosmos. You infuse me in your divine creativity, where my soul, the soul of every human being and the soul of creation, one, infusing, as light illumes light, in the heart knowing of *cardio gnosis* oneing.

This is my prayer, and it is also a communal prayer, because entering into the ground of the silent womb *kolpon,* where we are held in the intimacy between the Father and the Son, between Silence and Word, is intrinsically relational. In this exquisite between of being in one another, in the oneing, we are naturally communal. The prayer reminds me of times when my contemplation has been more overtly communal, when I have entered into this sacred *kolpon* spaciousness, into the relational energy field of oneing, intentionally, to pray for the world, with a trustworthy friend, and with retreat communities. In these communion-consciousness prayers, we meet in the ground of the *kolpon,* in the point of divine contemplation, where infinite Silence speaks the Word, and the luminous intensity of the intimacy of love naturally pours out in expansive Spirit directed creative union. These communion-consciousness prayers leave us with a sense of one love, one consciousness flowing through our hearts, flowing through the soul of the earth, trees, all creatures, knitting all into the flowing of the love of the Trinity. Together, in communion, in the awakened consciousness of the noosphere, we embody how the one heart-mind of divine love, tenderly holds the suffering of the earth. We enter into the divine embodiment as the world and pass through into the creativity of divine love-making, into the hidden ground of hope. We participate in a communal reflexivity, where in the oneing, experience enfolds into the divine, unfolding as our lives. Beatrice explores the dynamic of this evolution of communion consciousness extensively.

Beatrice – A *Theotokos* or God-bearer

Graciously, harmoniously, Beatrice Brutuea (1930-2014) affirms the beauty and holiness of creation, envisaging creation as the ecstasy of God: "God's ecstasy creates the world, and the world's ecstasy realises God. And you are right in the midst of it," she proclaims.[2] Creation is the *Theotokos* is, mother of God, or God-bearer. Creation is like a fertile womb that gives birth to transcendent divine love in and through the finite. In this sense, Beatrice herself is a *Theotokos* is, as her words are spoken from communion with the Word - the Logos principle of John's gospel, who becomes flesh. Conceived in the intimacy of the womb of silence, incarnated in her heart, explored in her mind and shared with the world, her words from the Word, open us to the same self-realisation. She is a true *schola contemplationis*, one who leisurely seeks stillness and silence in contemplation and gives expression to the insights that arise.

Throughout all her writings, her logic, her capacity to synthesise and her prophetic vision resonate in our hearts drawing us beyond the limits of the mind,

---

[2] Beatrice Bruteau, *God's Ecstasy: The Creation of a Self-Creating World* (New York: Crossroad, 1997), 179.

into the ever-flowing waves of luminous heart seeing. Beatrice takes us into the Omega point, into the apex of maximum complexity coinciding with maximum centricity. Intently, systematically, she awakens the enstatic point of pure stillness within us and draws us out in a fecund ecstasy enabling us to create a future wholeness and fullness in Omega. Graciously, she grounds us in the wonder of the divine consciousness rising in us, as us. Beatrice crafts a comprehensive vision of how we may evolve in our current evolutionary awakening. Integrating wisdom from the Christian mystical tradition, Vedanta, Sri Aurobindo's insights, philosophy, mathematics, and science, her language is dense and eclectic. Artistically, she draws us into the depths of contemplative prayer, and expands the horizons of our thinking as her mystical metaphysics takes us into the heart of our oneness in one love.

Radically optimistic, Beatrice encourages us to be also. She reminds us of our deepest truth that we are in union with the Absolute, the Infinite Being, God.[3] This wisdom is timely, in the face of so many critical events at this time in our evolutionary development such as climate change, the development of uncontrollable viruses, the proliferation of nuclear weapons, the displacement of peoples from their land, and the necessary and unnecessary chaos that the collapse of hierarchical structures brings. Beatrice urges us to take the grand option, by becoming more conscious through activating the energy of love, or *agape* within us, and responding with Love's creativity. What is needed, she suggests is the activation and sharing of human energy, which she defines psychically as, thinking, knowing, loving and willing. "It is the most intimate energy we are asked to commit to a new union," she says, "we are being asked to give ourselves as persons in order to create a higher level of new being."[4] Beatrice encourages us to be revolutionary by creating a gestalt shift in our whole way of seeing and being in relation with one another. "Any revolution worthy of the name," she affirms, "must be primarily a revolution in consciousness."[5] Beatrice fosters this revolution of consciousness, by returning us to the ground of Trinitarian consciousness, and awakening communion, or *perichoretic* consciousness. Beatrice awakens a capacity to arouse our contemplative vision and see clearly, on the basis of experience, how we are always participating

---

[3] Beatrice Bruteau, *Radical Optimism: Practical Spirituality in an Uncertain World* (New York: Crossroad Publishing, 2002), 10.
[4] Beatrice Bruteau, *The Grand Option: Personal Transformation and New Creation* (Notre Dame: University of Notre Dame, 2001), 3.
[5] Beatrice Bruteau "Neo-feminism and the Next Revolution in Consciousness," *Crosscurrents* Vol. 27, No. 2, 1977, 170.

within the ground of creative union. We indwell within the oneing love of the enstatic-ecstatic Trinity.

This Chapter

In this chapter, having affirmed Beatrice as a *Theotokos*, we will now ponder how she inspires the rise of a unitive, or oneing consciousness within us, that awakens into communion consciousness. We will begin by immersing ourselves in the enstatic-ecstatic oneing of the Trinity. Subsequently, we will focus on the I-I enstatic-consciousness that awakens from this Trinitarian ground against the background of the evolutionary rise of self-reflexive consciousness. This will lead into the awareness that awakens when we are in Christ, within the flow of original creative freedom that initiates the rise of communion consciousness. Finally, we will draw out how this evolution of Christ-consciousness itself, illuminates Christ consciousness today.

Enstatic-Ecstatic Oneing

Divine Love's enstatic-ecstatic sharing of God's self as *agape* in creation is foundational for Beatrice. She stresses that the Trinity is a community of persons who are both one and many, infinite and finite, enstatic and ecstatic.[6] Transcending all categories and descriptions, a person, she emphasises, is one who is a self-giving, universally loving energy centre, a flow of *agape*, who continuously shares self, seeking the good of all.[7] Thus, this field of flowing *agape* of the three persons of the Trinity is potent, alive, fertile, initiating the deepening and expanding of its consciousness within creation. Beatrice stresses that each person is transcendent, a pure "I AM" who is "unmodified, indescribable, unclassifiable, incomparable."[8] As well, each person is immanent Being that is "self-diffusive, active, and being-communication."[9] She highlights how the first person, or poise of the Trinity,[10] is the purely transcendent, the

---

[6] Bruteau, *God's Ecstasy*, 27.
[7] This comes from Danial Walsh who describes a person as transcendent, formless, unborn, immortal. Person describes who one is. Nature in contrast is specified and defined, describing what one does. See, Beatrice Bruteau, "The One and the Many: Communitarian Nondualism," in *The Other Half of My Soul*, ed. Beatrice Bruteau (Wheaton: Quest Books, 1996), 273. Bruteau, *Grand Option*, 9.
[8] Bruteau, *God's Ecstasy*, 28.
[9] Ibid.
[10] "Poise" emphasises equilibrium. It is a balanced, calm, motionless stance.

infinite, the absolute, the creator.[11] The second person is the Incarnate, the transcendent divine community becoming incarnate in creation, while the third person is the gift of the emergence of Sprit from the Incarnation being realised.[12] In this self-giving as transcendent, incarnate and realised, God empties God's self and takes form in matter. Over billions of years, the material cosmos evolves, until it becomes self-conscious enough to realise that it is being created by God. Consequently, the self-conscious, God conscious universe, then realises that it participates in this divine creativity and is necessary for the ongoing work of incarnating the divine in matter. Reciprocally, creation becomes a *Theotokos*, a God bearer and gives birth to God, enabling Matter to return to God.[13] We notice the resonance with Eckhart here, as we participate in giving birth to the divine in creation and the birth of what is incarnated into God.

Beatrice draws on John's prologue to clarify the central role of the Incarnation in the Trinity's self-sharing. She highlights: "No one has ever seen God; the only begotten God who is in the interior (κόλπον *kolpon*) of the Father, that one *exegetes* (ἐξηγήσατο *exehesato*) (Jn 1:18)."[14] What is important to illuminate here, is the intimacy of relationship between the Father and the Word in the *kolpon*. Literally, a *kolpon* is a wrap with a hollow that is used to carry a lamb, or a child.[15] As we have seen, this *kolpon*, often translated as bosom, evokes the hollow where Jesus is in the bosom, or heart-womb of the Father, making the flesh of Jesus the dwelling place of the unseen God. Jesus, in turn, becomes the *kolpon*, as he holds, reveals who God is in the world. *Kolpon* evokes the silent-womb-heart of infinite creative union or oneing, where all is in all (Col 3:11), in an endless divine begetting. It signifies the womb-like placeless-place of divine

---

[11] Beatrice acknowledges the three "poises" of Brahman developed by Aurobindo. Brahman is "the one without a second" and yet is also "all this," making Brahman transcendent and immanent. For Aurobindo, when we enter into the silent void, beyond form and activity, we realise the transcendent poise of Brahman, as well as energies pouring out into activities in the universe. In brief, the first pose is being. The second poise is Cosmic Consciousness, (the intelligence and power immanent in all of nature). This conscious energy is transcendent (*Siva*), divine consciousness (*Chit*), that is also divine creative energy (*Sakti*, the feminine principle), that is powerful, dynamic and concrete. Aurobindo's third pose is becoming manifest as the multitude. Conscious persons can enter into all three poises, and see themselves as limited and separate, as well as transcendent and universal, because they have these three triune consciousnesses within. See, Beatrice Bruteau, *Worthy is the World: The Hindu Philosophy of Aurobindo* (Rutherford: Associated University Press, 1971), 48-49; 255-258.

[12] Bruteau, *God's Ecstasy*, 21-22.

[13] Ibid., 22.

[14] Ibid., 38; also, Bruteau, *Grand Option*, 124.

[15] "Science, Fear, God and the Mystical," Episode 3, *National Catholic Reporter*, Podcast, August, 2009.

contemplation, the fertile divine consciousness, the archetypal point of revelation, holding all things, within all things and yet beyond all things, that is infinitely creative, evolutionary.

The Incarnate Word is enstatically within the silent womb-heart of the unseen God, in pure Self-awareness in contemplation and, at the same time, speaking, or revealing, the unseen nature of God within creation, enabling humanity to see God. Beatrice affirms how, we, as persons in the cosmos, one in the Word, participate in this exquisite intimacy in the contemplation within the heart-womb, where infinite and finite, being and consciousness one. As persons, we mutually indwell each other in an intimate oneing in the Word, in the pure awareness of the hollow-womb of transcendent love. We could further say that the *kolpon* is the source, the ground, the womb of divine consciousness, that the Word gives expression to by exegeting, interpreting, translating, making God known. Still, Beatrice emphasises its root meaning "to devise."[16] The Word breathes, speaks, devises new ways to creatively express the beauty of the transcendent God within the cosmos. The Word proclaims throughout all creation: "May you be."[17] What is spoken, Beatrice affirms is, "truly, wholly and thoroughly 'God' and truly wholly and thoroughly 'cosmos'."[18]

In developing this Trinitarian perspective, Beatrice emphasises our union within this divine creative loving, or oneing. "If God is love," she acclaims, "then God must be a 'quest for union,' for oneness. The love-relations must be intrinsic to the oneness, must be total self-giving mutual indwellings, drawing all into a vital, living oneness."[19] Within this dynamic relationality, of differentiating and drawing into oneness, the divine persons remain within themselves, in enstasy, yet simultaneously express their differentiated-identity, giving themselves ecstatically, creating *perichoresis*, an encircling dance of one in another. Encircling and inter-penetrating creates endless oneing, infinite Presence in Presence, exquisite *circumincession*,[20] a circle dance, as the Trinity-Lovers pour out their hearts into each other, in the I-I self-giving of pure self-awareness, forming a communion of wholeness-oneness. In the encircling *perichoresis*, each enstatic Lover gives self to the other person in ecstasy, unites in the loved one's enstasy, and together as one, in I-I being-in-one-another, they love the third

---

[16] Bruteau, *God's Ecstasy*, 38.
[17] Ibid.
[18] Ibid., 139.
[19] Ibid., 36.
[20] "*Circumincession*" is the Latin term for circling. See, Bruteau, *Grand Option*, 56.

Beloved.[21] The three persons become one "I," one consciousness, one mind. The encircling enstatic-ecstatic burgeoning of one in another flows endlessly as each lover loves and contemplates the other. Each acts as both Lover and Beloved. Each is both one and many. The whole Trinity is an exchange of creative union, one in another in communion. Each expresses *fiat* to the other and says: "May you be."[22] This pattern of I-I, enstatic-ecstatic loving, then continues in the incarnation as the Trinity lovers become flesh through the Word. This same delightful vivacious loving expands into the finite, making us an expression of *agape's* enstatic-ecstatic self-giving.

Enstasy

Enstasy, for Beatrice, points to our pure, transcendent luminous within-ness. In mystical literature, enstasy, denotes the experience of the exquisite inner tranquillity of being grounded and remaining, resting, standing within one-self in God.[23] In Julian, enstasy is our enclosure in the Trinity, as the Trinity is enclosed in us. It is the deepest centre of mutual indwelling, the still point, where our consciousness infuses into divine consciousness, into the divine self-realization. Enstasy is a self-knowing that comes from a profound standing in one's self.[24] It describes the *stasis*, the energy-less energy, the shimmering stillness, the pure silence that is creative-union, where we pass into the within-ness of divine persons. Enstasy identifies the pointless point of our essential consciousness, the centre of our selfhood, the heart of our heart, where we are a person, a lover, where we are "I."[25] In this realised union, the beloved knows the Beloved as the Beloved experiences self-knowing. We enter into the depths of our heart into our enstatic reality, we indwell the intimacy of the Trinitarian I-I-I stillness of being in one another. We come home to what Beatrice identifies as our true face, or transcendent personhood.[26] Here our conscious awareness is the divine conscious awareness, our will is the divine will. Here we naturally express

---

[21] Martin Buber originally made a distinction between an "I-It" subject-object relationship that sees the other as separate, and an "I-Thou," face to face relationship, where love is encountered and received from the other. See, Bruteau, *God's Ecstasy*, 30.
[22] Ibid., 29.
[23] Ibid., 27.
[24] Ibid., 76.
[25] Bruteau, *God's Ecstasy*, 84. *Enstatis* describes *Saccidananda*, the point where awareness is identical with being. See, Abishiktananda, *Prayer: A Spiritual Classic for Forty Years* (Norwich: Canterbury Press, 2006), 79.
[26] Ibid., 9-10.

the creative freedom of the Trinity creating by loving. Ultimately, we arise from the Trinity's contemplation of itself in enstasy and mystical union in ecstasy.

Ecstasy

Literally ecstasy denotes standing outside oneself.[27] Although we have seen that ecstasy can denote rapture, passion, intoxication, extreme joy, or sexual pleasure, for Beatrice, ecstasy is the movement of *kenotic,* outpouring *agape*, as in the Philippian hymn (Phil 2:6) that celebrates the fertility of self-emptying. It is the emanating dynamic action of exuberant Trinitarian love creating. This:

> ecstatic movement outside the God community happens (is going on) for the same reason that it is going on inside the God community: It is the nature of the God community to behave so. Theistic theology calls this agape, self-giving love, and metaphysics can call it the natural pressure of Being to expand, to be more and to give Being, to be in every possible way.[28]

Thus, although God is enstatic as formless *agape*, God does not remain in enstasis, transcendently within God's self; God empties out, manifests, taking the form of a servant (the cosmos), pouring forth love, enabling the formless to take form in the finite.[29] And crucially, it is this same ecstatic, self-giving *agape* that is inherent within our transcendent personhood.

Beatrice affirms:

> Our "I," our personhood, is not a product of God's action, something left over after God's acting has ceased. Rather it is God's action in the very actuality of acting. We are not a thing but an activity. This is why God's activity of ecstatically moving out to us is an act of coinciding with our activity, just as our union with God will be our ecstatically moving out to God in an act of coinciding with God's activity. This is also why it is only a naked "I am" transcending all the descriptive attributes of one's nature and history, that can perform the ecstatic act.[30]

In the depths of who we truly are as I, we are an expression of God's ecstasy, God's action acting, a flow of ecstatic *agape*, a *perichoresis* of expanding love energy. And the invitation is for us to realise this ecstatic creativity, as God's

---

[27] Ibid., 9.
[28] Ibid., 84.
[29] Ibid., 9-10.
[30] Bruteau, *Grand Option*, 75.

ecstasy creates the world and our ecstasy realises God and be consciously present in the midst of this.[31]

Moreover, always remembering that the enstasy-ecstasy of *agape* flows as one reality, like quantum fluctuations oscillating between physical nothingness and something-ness, appearance and annihilation, Beatrice affirms the dynamic life enhancing nature of enstatic-ecstatic *agape* that acts through us.[32] She also likens this enstasy-ecstasy dynamism to dancing, because, "the dance is precisely the dancer in the act of dancing."[33] Like Shiva Nataraja's cosmic, encircling dance, the infinite dance of enstatic-ecstatic energy joyfully expands outwards, as the inside dancers turn into the outside-ness of the dance. The dance is enstatic-ecstatic *agape* that is Omega drawing us forward into a future of love communing. Beatrice calls us to nurture our enstatic awareness, by centring into the depths of our heart, within the field of enstatic-ecstatic *agape* and responsively participate in the dance. She awakens us to how we live in a field of potent, alive, fertile love energy in a deepening, expanding conscious participation. This suggests that the ground of consciousness is enstatic-ecstatic, relational, ever revelatory. When we turn into this enstatic movement within the ground of our heart, our reflexive capacity enhances, infusing a greater awareness from within the consciousness of divine enstatic-ecstatic *agape*. Language draws us into unitive unknowing, as we seek to illuminate the self-awareness of the Trinity, or Trinitarian consciousness, that we return to in contemplation. So what does Beatrice mean by consciousness?

I-I Enstatic-Consciousness

In a general sense, Beatrice affirms consciousness is universal. It is the great natural force of cosmic energy that includes everything,[34] that enables us to know and to respond to the environment.[35] Consciousness, as Teilhard describes it, is the "within-ness" of things, "the substance and heart of life in the process of evolution."[36] And, theologically we might say, consciousness is the origin-less awareness that arises from the three divine persons' enstatic-ecstatic

---

[31] Bruteau, *God's Ecstasy*, 179.
[32] Ibid., 84.
[33] Ibid., 39.
[34] See, Bruteau, *Evolution Towards Divinity*, 130.
[35] Beatrice Bruteau, "Teilhard and Creative Freedom," *Prabuddha Bharata* Vol. 86, 1981, 455.
[36] Pierre Teilhard de Chardin, *The Phenomenon of Man* (London: Collins Fontana Books, 1966), 198.

contemplation, expressing themselves in creation. In keeping with this sense of consciousness as arising from the enstatic being within, in pure oneness, Wayne Teasdale, a friend of Beatrice, emphasises how unity is the basis of consciousness. "Unity," he affirms, "is the "golden string" the very thread of identity, allowing each successive moment of the stream of moments called life to be related to the centre of knowing, to a subject who can claim each experience as one's own."[37] Teasdale stresses that consciousness is the deep ontological unity that runs through and sustains all that is and can be. Beatrice sensitises us to this spaceless, placeless, objectless, transcendent, substantial heart of life, this awareness that is essentially unitive within us. She awakens us to how this evolutionary consciousness is ever revealing itself more fully to us. And she affirms how the Word is still devising new ways to express the ecstasy of divine life through the natural process of creation. Thus, this consciousness, this aware-ing that is only released in contemplation, is Christ-Omega, drawing us into a future wholeness-oneness that is uniquely diversified and differentiated. Through stirring our innate desire for creative-union and activating our evolutionary impulse to become more fully who we essentially are, Omega-consciousness draws us forward beyond the limits of our present egoic consciousness. Christ-Omega awakens a more expansive capacity to see and respond from this Omega ground of consciousness that is essentially, our origin, our being and our fulfilment.

When Beatrice asks more technically, "what is consciousness?" in *God's Ecstasy*, she says we find it impossible to say specifically what consciousness is, because we only know what consciousness is by being conscious. This means that in being consciousness, in perceiving, in knowing that we know, we are always within consciousness as subject. We cannot objectify consciousness, as if it were separate from us, and try to say what it is, in terms of something else. Consciousness is a primary first cause, a ground reality, a fundamental force that cannot be examined as an object. We experience consciousness as the original source, the fullness of being, the ultimate witness. Thus, consciousness is the source, or ground of our personhood that can only be accessed subjectively, by being conscious. Beatrice summarizes her position:

> this consciousness view is the direct access to the intrinsic nature of Being. What is "known" in the "mystical experience" is the ontological structure of the

---

[37] Wayne Teasdale, "Christianity and Eastern Religions," in Beatrice Bruteau, *Other Half of Our Soul* (Wheaton: Theosophical Publishing House, 1996), 132.

Whole. Because we ourselves exist on every level of the Whole. We are the incarnational union. We are not only "one side" of it, the finite, objective material side. We are the union of intrinsic/extrinsic, subjective/objective, absolute/relative, infinite/finite. It is the nature of being to be this way. Therefore we are this way. We know ourselves as being this way; thus we know Being is this way. The knowing and the being are one. That's mystical.[38]

"We are the incarnational union," rings throughout the cosmos, creating more unity, deeper communion, intricate oneing. This point of union, this field of oneing, where the knowing and the being are one, where awareness is identical with being in the infinite luminosity of divine love, is the contemplative consciousness that Beatrice awakens in us. She seeks for us to attain the pure self-awareness which we truly are. She takes us well beyond thinking, or understanding God as other, as object, into our enstatic, subjective experience of being "I," in the one "I." Her vision resonates with Julian's prayer of oneing, when she invites us to be present to the Christ who says: "I am the ground of your prayer," or "I am the ground of your heart-awareness, I am the ground of your consciousness." In this awakening, awareness and being intersect. We realise that the oneing between the Silent-womb and the Word is the same oneing in the ground of our heart-womb. We awaken within the enstatic I-I intimacy of the divine oneing, that in its enstatic nature is simultaneously ecstatic.

Consciousness Rising

Beatrice converges on Teilhard's exploration of self-reflective consciousness, highlighting the growth in the more intense reflexivity, of turning, or enfolding the awareness of our discursive-mind, into the awareness of our essential "I," or heart-self.[39] In the early phases of this reflexivity, while we have a sense of our transcendent nature and desire to reflect and cultivate an inner life, there is a

---

[38] Bruteau, *Grand Option*, 162.
[39] Beatrice's development of "reflexive consciousness" resonates with Eugene Halliday's "Reflexive Self-Consciousness." Halliday suggests that consciousness can become "reflexive," completely self-transparent and continuously aware of its own presence and nature and we can promote this reflexive state when observing something by turning our own consciousness back into the self. This is consciousness itself, the "I am," the self that is always subject. Reflexivity frees us from object-identification, enabling us to observe from within the ground of consciousness itself. See, Eugene Halliday, *Reflexive Self-Consciousness*, published by the Melchizedek Press, 1989. https://en.wikipedia.org/wiki/Reflexive self-consciousness.

demarcation between every day consciousness and heart awareness.[40] Our discursive-mind that is easily distracted and reactive is the dominant power, while our heart-mind frequently lies dormant.[41] Importantly, the discursive mind is not separate from the heart-mind, we are one mind. However, it is limited, diminished, partly blinded, operating on a different level to the heart. When we are dominated by the discursive mind, we see and make choices through the dualism of subject-object perception. Therefore, although we can observe a situation, examine possible desirable outcomes and objectively choose amongst alternatives, the stimulation comes from without, activating what Beatrice calls "choice freedom." Choice freedom is always limited and though it can manifest under the guise of discernment, it is not discernment, for it arises abstractly, from outside our centre.[42] Not yet stably grounded in our heart, at this depth of limited reflexivity, it is easy to become blindly caught in a mindset that objectifies, distinguishes by properties, descriptions and attributes and demonizes difference. Without being consciously aware, we can find ourselves locked in this negativity and impotent within the reaction net of the karma trap, reproducing unhealthy patterns of behaviour.[43] This constricted and conditioned mindset distinguishes and excludes anyone who is different to the dominating group who holds power.

To illustrate this, Beatrice draws on the metaphor of sharp objects, first describing how in this negative dynamic, an ego-centred, aggressive, obsessive consciousness, establishes a domineering model. In this domination model value comes from being sharp. As a result, all sharp items are considered to belong to the one highly sort after class, thus rejecting and excluding all unsharp objects. The objects that are the sharpest, become prized and those associated with the sharp objects are acclaimed. All others are scorned. The emotions of honour, or scorn, attach to each class, resulting in a domination paradigm.[44] This pattern of

---

[40] In Bruteau, "Teilhard and Creative Freedom," 456, Beatrice notes the development of the instinctual impulse of the DNA molecule to duplicate itself by producing another DNA molecule exactly like itself. She notes the evolutionary growth of cells recognizing and distinguishing themselves as separate from other things, distinguishing between like and unlike and taking action against unlike cells. Gradually, a critical threshold is reached, the unifying interiority complexifies and becomes reflexive, conscious of being conscious and reflectively free.

[41] Aurobindo stresses this when he says that Supermind, or the divine mind within our heart, pervades all the forms of the world as an indwelling Presence. See Bruteau, *Worthy is the World*, 107-108.

[42] Bruteau, "Teilhard and Creative Freedom," 457.

[43] See, Bruteau, *Grand Option*, 79.

[44] Ibid., 24-26.

perceiving persons as different, as other, is violent, destructive, and all too familiar. Only a revolution in consciousness, through the awakening of what Beatrice describes as a "neo-feminine consciousness", can displace this negation.[45]

Neo-feminine Consciousness

Neo-feminine consciousness is a participatory consciousness that transcends the dichotomies of masculine feminine stereotypes and dismantles the power of the domination paradigm evident as it manifests four critical qualities.[46] First, it is an intellectual, intuitive consciousness, that nurtures the uniqueness of individuals as a whole, esteeming embodied-transcendent personhood, valuing each one equally as a person, not an abstraction, or a role. Second, this intuitive consciousness establishes identity not by mutual negation, but by mutual affirmation. It does this by integrating rationality and precision, while always fostering the development of relational, participatory, communal consciousness. Thirdly, this neo-feminine consciousness perceives existentially, rather than essentially, valuing lived experience in creation. It transcends the limits of purely essence-based categories and connects with the lives as others as persons, entering into and celebrating the sheer life energy of "I." Fourth, neo-feminine consciousness arises from the ground of spirit as an act of spirit. It sees holographically, appreciating each real concrete being as unique.

In order to develop this revolution in consciousness, we must journey within and do the necessary healing work and contemplative practice that will enable us to become more deeply reflexive. We continue to turn within the ground of our heart, until our transcendent heart-self awakens as "I," in Christ who dwells at the centre of our being. This includes connecting all our conscious faculties, our intellect, will, imagination, bodily awareness and action, in single hearted, single pointed awareness to this original Christic consciousness. In this, Beatrice affirms, a holographic, relational world of direct perception awakens. Our Christic vision emerges, initiating a new level of love bonding. This deeper reflexivity of single pointed self-realisation in Christ, initiates the creation of creative selfhood, which Beatrice identifies as *self-establishment by self-creation*.[47] Here the freedom that emerges from the transcendence that

---

[45] Ibid., 29.
[46] See, Bruteau, "Neo-feminism and the Next Revolution in Consciousness," 170-182.
[47] Bruteau, "Teilhard and Creative Freedom," 458.

reflexivity makes possible, enables us to truly discern from our oneness in Christ, in the Trinity, in creative freedom.[48]

Reflexively In Christ

"Once your eye becomes single, everything is flooded in light,"[49] Beatrice reminds us. Once we turn into the radiance of the enstatic ground of our heart, where awareness is identical with being in Christ in the Trinitarian self-sharing, we become open to Love's evolutionary movement. In yielding into the centrifugal force of Love's magnetism, gathering, recollecting, knitting, all our ways of knowing into a single focus, a single mind, we release into the point of pure consciousness. We become translucently awake to the Christ-self, aware beyond any perception, or thought. In this awareness, the intimate luminous wisdom of divine consciousness radiates from within us and we see from oneness. Our eye is naturally oned. Organically, the luminosity of the intimacy of the divine love-making that is the ground of who we are, shines in us incandescently. We see through the divine light flowing in us how everything is flooded in light. When our eye is single and realises that it is the seer, then we are enlightened. In drawing us into this illuminating vision, Beatrice highlights some important nuances about the nature of this deeper reflexive response that creates a single eye and grounds us in our centre, in the luminous Omega point.

Although some spiritualities consider any reflexivity, or awareness, to be a hindrance to union with God, it is important to note that the intensely reflexive loop of consciousness that Beatrice encourages is in keeping with the mystics we have been exploring. Even, Meister Eckhart who encourages a bare mind, describes the point, the spark of enlightenment, that we receive in our passive intellect in the bare awareness of contemplation. Beatrice desires for us to appreciate that our mystical union is God's mystical union with us.[50] And she emphasises that contemplation is an "activity" arising freely out of God's ecstatic activity. Thus, what Beatrice is encouraging is a turn within, into the depths of our origins in divine mystical union, until even the most delicate turning, or centring, gives way into our transcendent self, our "I," who is Christ, and we participate in Christ's ecstatic Trinitarian self-sharing. Like so many of the mystics who prepared this mystical ground for her, Beatrice seeks to return us to

---

[48] Ibid., 457-458.
[49] Bruteau, *Radical Optimism*, 65.
[50] Ibid., 75.

our concrete experience of releasing our awareness beyond the conceptualisations of objectifying consciousness. She seeks for us to live at the point between being and consciousness within the consciousness of the Wisdom-Word, in the *perichoresis* of the Trinity flowing in and through us. Here we are a person, truly ourselves as a Word spoken in creation, as an expression of Trinitarian the love energy of *agape*. Beatrice encourages us to cultivate a "concrete intelligence," that produces concrete existential knowledge of ourselves as a transcendent person.[51] Concrete, stresses experiential. We must experience our sense of self as transcendent of all categories, until only our Christic nature is illumed. But she warns us not to be too literal about what we mean by experience and confuse metaphors for the heart-felt awareness of our transcendent self in Christ, with metaphors of the field energies of ethic, or astral bodies.[52] Rather, we simply draw our sensual awareness, along with our mind into a single focus, to coincide with, and experience our self as person in Christ.

Wholistically, as enfleshed, inspirited heart-minds, we fold into the enfolding, encircling, gravitational force of our centre, into our transcendent personhood in Christ. We centre and "noetically coincide" in Christ. "Noetic" draws on the Greek νοῦς *nous*, intellect of the heart, and νόησις *noēsis*, meaning inner wisdom, direct knowing, or coming to a subjective understanding through the *nous*, intellect, or eye of the heart. Whilst "to coincide," from the Latin *coincidere*, literally to fall upon together,[53] suggests a turning of our awareness, into the ground, into the *nous*, eye, mind or consciousness of our heart, so that our outer awareness and inner awareness awaken simultaneously as they one. Beatrice affirms how in this contemplative vision of noetically coinciding, we cease looking at our self as an object and coincide with our self, so that there is no outer and inner self only one self in God. Coinciding initiates a liminal metamorphosis, as the over-lapping of our consciousness becomes more translucent, and we see from within the focal point of our heart-self-being, at the centre of our soul. Beatrice likens this to two spotlights overlapping and shining into a single point and becoming one light, the point of overlap of petals at the centre of a rose,[54] or a solar eclipse as all our ordinary ways of seeing are blotted out, until just as everything disappears the crown of light of the corona bursts

---

[51] Ibid., 163.
[52] Ibid., 55. These energy fields are more unrefined, subject to boundary violations, and as we will see, well before the transcendent centre described in Beatrice's mystical rose metaphor.
[53] https://www.etymonline.com/word/coincide
[54] Bruteau, *Radical Optimism,* 116-119.

forth with breath taking beauty.⁵⁵ All sense of separateness, or subject-object poles, dissolves in Love's transcendence. Effortlessly, the single eye of the vivid, expansive eye of the ground of our heart perception, rises up and pours out, expanding in space-time, boundlessly like luminous molten lava. Our single eye, our enstatic "I," opens into the energetic vibrancy of the endless oneing wisdom of love. Our heart mind, our "I" perceives with the illuminated clarity of holographic vision. It knows, simply, purely, lucidly, that it is the oneness.

Beatrice gives a powerful example of noetic coincidence in the table scene (John 13:23), where the beloved disciple reclines into the breast, or bosom, heart-womb (κόλπῳ *kolpō*) of Jesus. Just as we saw Jesus in the hollow, the silent womb-heart of the Transcendent One, here we have the beloved disciple, who could be either John of the gospel, or Mary of Magdala, representing all Beloveds, leaning into Jesus, into the depths of his luminous *kolpon* heart-womb. Graciously, Beatrice invites us to centre in our heart and place ourselves within the burning radiance of the presence of Jesus, into each person's alluring centrality. She invites us to imagine Jesus embracing us from behind and lean back into him as subject, in an intimate ecstatic self-emptying and yielding of our heart into his heart. We continue to lean, until we lose any sense of separateness and both our luminosities merge enstatically in a still, translucent, being-in one-another.

As we lean into the magnetic current of heart infusing into heart and yield into his centre, Beatrice affirms:

> We are coming to know the Sacred Heart from the inside, inside his consciousness, and inside our consciousness. And our 'inside' comes to be more and more coincident with his 'inside.' His Heart is becoming the Heart of our heart.⁵⁶

Abiding in silent still being in one another, all imagery falls away as we noetically coincide. We indwell heart in heart, nestled in the *kolpon*-heart-womb. We are centre in centre, translucently luminous, shining with divine self-knowledge. In the dazzling intimacy of being in one another, we are not only conscious of original consciousness. We are the ground of consciousness, the ground of awareness itself. We are the awaring. We are the loving. This way of

---

⁵⁵ Beatrice Bruteau, "Prayer and Identity," in Thomas Keating et al, *Spirituality, Contemplation and Transformation: Writings on Centering Prayer* (New York: Lantern Books, 2008), 108.
⁵⁶ Bruteau, *Radical Optimism*, 98.

noetic coinciding does not produce duality; it creates a deeply intuitive, lucid oneing awareness of ourselves as active participants in the original divine loving that imparts wisdom and exudes creative freedom.

This is where nondualism, or we might say oneing comes in, Beatrice affirms. To say that we cannot know Jesus as an object, is to say we cannot know him as another, we cannot look at him, remain outside of him. To know in the most intimate mystical sense, we must enter inside Jesus, enter into his own awareness, know by returning to the ground of his consciousness in us, becoming Jesus, by being Jesus at the cellular depth of how Jesus lived in the divine heart-womb. One with Jesus in the transcendent hollowness of mystical union, the unitive illumination of a oneing consciousness arises and floods us with enstatic in-sight. In this oneing, the heart of Jesus, opens us into the mind of Christ, into the ecstasy of Trinitarian loving, into the fullness of Omega. We realise "the mind of Christ Jesus" (Phil 2:5) is the ground of our heart-mind. We recall Julian beheld from within this heart consciousness when she was drawn into the wound of her vulnerable lover and saw a delectable place large enough for all humankind to rest within. Clare gazed and participated in the mirror of eternity. Teilhard gazed at the picture of the sacred heart, was magnetically allured into its radiance, entered into its centring consciousness and participated in the whole of creation becoming a sea of glowing matter.[57] Here "All is in All" (Col 3:11). Thus, the heart-womb ground is ontologically intimately personal, relational, communal.

From this ground of consciousness, original creative freedom rises up with all the creativity needed to create a future in Christ. In Christ we are an act of creative freedom, of initiative, of self-originating self-giving.[58] Beatrice affirms: "So when we come into being as our experience of God's union with us, or when we attain our destiny as an experience of union with God, what is happening in both cases are the two self-giving activities are confluent."[59] We flow together. This suggests that as we become more silent and still and illuminated by the awareness that rises from the natural light of the ground of our heart-mind and stabilise in being and seeing from within this union in the intimacy of oneing, we perceive the grounding unity, the oneing of all creation, because oneness is all there is in the luminous depths of God. We perceive from within the endlessly

---

[57] Pierre Teilhard de Chardin, *Hymn of the Universe,* trans. Simon Bartholomew (London: Collins, 1965), 41-45.
[58] Bruteau, *Grand Option*, 75-76.
[59] Ibid.

unitive flowing light of divine creativity uniting by differentiating, in an exquisite union that makes every person and every created thing so uniquely beautiful. The invitation for us is to be creative union, to be this field of oneing, to be the flow of love energy, the creative freedom that self-creates. Our task, Beatrice suggests, is to exist "as a unitary overflowing act."[60] Images of Mechthild's flowing light of the Godhead, resound. Can we be the union that imparts flowing light? Can we be a hollow heart-womb of "creative freedom" that creates as we act? Can we be the oneing that creates communion and awakens communion consciousness?

Communion Consciousness

In freely choosing to be a flow of love energy, a unitive point that creates, ever fuller, richer, more inclusive life, this capacity to see from within our shared inter-personal unity heightens along with our desire to enable our sense of our essential unity to flourish. Lucidly, Beatrice describes the radiance of the enstatic energy that naturally emanates when we stabilise in our centre. Her compelling words dance in our consciousness as they resound with our lived experience:

> We no sooner touch this 'still point" at the core of our being, this immutable at the heart of mutability, than we discover it as an explosion of energy. Our "I am" is simultaneously a "May you be," also. We find that the energy of existence that we are is necessarily a radiant energy. It streams out from us in every way. It seems to be the nature of that which is "I am" to say "Let it be." This is what we might expect, since our free luminous energy originates in the common point of our mutual interiority with the creative God, with the one whose proper name is I AM and whose characteristic energy as creator is Fiat, "Let it be."[61]

In centring into this still point, ecstatic divine energy pours forth. We, like each person in the Trinity giving self to the other, are simultaneously drawn out ecstatically in a *perichoresis*, an encircling dance of giving self to another, awakening a *perichoretic* consciousness. We pour out the radiant energy of *agape* and all we desire to say to each other and the whole of creation is "May you be." Notably, Beatrice identifies the energy that arises from this intimate point as "spondic" energy. Spondic, from the Greek *sponde* (σπονδεῖος) emphasises an outpouring, a libation. Spondic energy rises up like a spring in the

---

[60] Ibid., 116.
[61] Ibid., 166.

heart, springing up unto unlimited life, pouring out love abundantly. Interestingly, the plural for spondic is *spondai*, denoting a peace treaty, because the libations poured out in a ritual express a commitment to peace and alliance.[62] Thus, spondic energy is a libation, an offering of mercy and compassion, a pouring out of Love's abundance to another, to creation, offering a commitment to being-in-relationship. Spondic energy is personal, boundless, endlessly *kenotic*, ever unitive, hallowing all it touches as it flows in the enstasy-ecstasy cycle. Therefore, as we direct our transcendent spondic heart-self toward another's spondic centre, this originally free act of loving generates the possibility for communion consciousness.

When we create a sacred, silent communal heart space with another, meet each other as persons, as transcendent flows of love energy, turn into our heart, pour out *agape*-love and go deeper into the ground of consciousness, we become transparent to each other. We meet in a subject-presence in the ground of heart awareness. We meet in the One who says, "I am the ground of your prayer," that we encountered with Julian. We meet in the ground where there can be no object. Here, there is one Christic body, one heart, one mind of Christ, one Word, one Love, one energy field of oneing, one Omega consciousness that is intimately accessible in this communion. The Christ rises in the mutually indwelling shared loving of our spondic centres oned, speaking though our "I," manifesting in our "We." This essentially unitive "We" becomes a luminous, spondic centre of consciousness, one-self, one in the *perichoresis* of the Trinity. Together, we are inside the ground of the heart, as subject, in an immediately felt whole that is self-luminous. In this wholeness, pure Spirit flows freely. Such differentiated unity is clear, boundless, yet free of any attachment, or boundary violations. This is pure communion, oneing in the One. As we allow each other to express what arises as "I," from this sacred ground, Christic consciousness clarifies. Reciprocally, as each gives voice to our "We," even stronger resonances emanate from the ground and dance and infuse colourful energetic vibrations of the Christ-presence. The pearl of the communal evolutionary impulse is activated in our world.

This communal heart mind naturally imparts a greater awareness of our wholeness, including in ourselves all of creation and the whole of cosmic expression. The energy of oneing heightens imparting deeper union, stronger connectivity and fuller being. In this consciousness, creative freedom abounds.

---

62   Bruteau, "Neo-feminism and Communion Consciousness," 16.

Moreover, we can choose to activate our communal will, and unite with other spondic centres and form a noosphere infused with the mercy, compassion, peace and the desire for greater connectivity that spondic energy manifests. We form what Patricia Albere has called a *"spondasphere,"*[63] a sphere of spondic relationships. As we align our centre with the *enstatic* centre of others, and this new level of bonded heart-energy forms in *Omega*, a communal "mind" of Christ manifests as *Amicus*-communion, forming what Beatrice calls "a communitarian non-dualism."[64] Beatrice reminds us:

> The more the Cosmos-Community evolves towards self-realisation, the more the Person-Community succeeds in incarnating itself as Cosmos-Community with the fullness of the divine values, so that the fullness of the Godhead can dwell in the Cosmos corporally.[65]

The fully realised person, present in the world as a valley of peace and a fountain of joy, becomes a fully realised Cosmos-Community. There can be no separation because all we are is a Holy Wholeness.[66] We are one. This is the evolutionary moment to activate this luminous spondic energy and celebrate our wholeness within the "Infinite Act of Love that makes every being to be."[67] Contemplation enables the self-realisation of this holy wholeness.

Illuminating Contemplation

Contemplation, for Beatrice, is being so united within the energy field of intimate creative union in God, that we live the divine life. We are an expression of oneing. Beatrice affirms that whilst initially, contemplation was thought of as a movement of consciousness from the world to God, now we recognise that contemplation is a manifestation of God in the world. Contemplation is,

> a movement of consciousness from God, with God, in God, *as* God, out into the world, a movement in which the divine consciousness and my consciousness, flowing together, stream out in love and in creative, healing, beautifying energy to create the world and make it even better."[68]

---

[63] See, https://evolutionarycollective.com/global-virtual-practice-community/
[64] Bruteau, "The One and the Many," 304.
[65] Ibid.
[66] Ibid., 305.
[67] Bruteau, "In the Cave of the Heart," 319.
[68] Bruteau, *Radical Optimism*, 132.

This major paradigm shift in emphasis from leaving the world to find God, to living the divine life in the world, invites us to live the fullness of enstatic-ecstatic *agape* in the world, expanding our notions of contemplation as simply focused on our personal experience of God, into a communion consciousness sensitivity. Beatrice affirms how: "the apophatic experience itself disabuses us of the notion that we have any such thing as 'our contemplation,' or even any separate substantiality. In the Night of the Absolute, everything is empty."[69] As all distinctions and all possessiveness vanishes in contemplation in the emptiness of the Absolute, the silence of the *kolpon* heart-womb, we lose all distinctions between the Absolute and the world. Indeed, the world we thought we left to find God, "by not speaking, by not thinking of any form, by not identifying ourselves with our particular egoic point of view," frees us to discover:

> that the very distinction of the Absolute from the world, carried to the limit, destroys the distinction of the Absolute from the world. The contemplative, having attained union with the Absolute, discovers that the Absolute is engaged in creating the world; and so, the contemplative too, as united with the Creator, must engage in self-emptying into the world. Once coincided with, the Transcendent--initially set over against the relative, the embodied--reveals itself as self-expressive as the relative, the embodied, the world.[70]

In leaving all discursive knowing and centring in the dark radiance of the spondic centre, we awaken in our "resurrection body." Beatrice affirms, "having lost 'the body,' the finite and the relative, for the sake of the Infinite and the Absolute, we find ourselves again in the finite and the relative, as glorified by conscious recognition of their being the Body of the Divine."[71] Calling us to live now in contemplation, in our resurrection body, as the body of the divine, in the world, we will draw out four key insights that help sustain contemplatives today.

First, for Beatrice contemplation is a dance of *agape*. The sacred dancer, searching for God through dance, intuitively practices a double form of meditation, Carla DeSola affirms. The dancer is centred on the "still point" within her, where spondic energy arises like an unlimited spring in her heart, pouring out love abundantly. At the same time, the dancer is aware of what she is experiencing. She moves with a strong sense of her heart centred in God, and while holding this awareness, she also perceives her centre as flowing throughout

---

[69] Bruteau, Beatrice. "Eucharistic Ecology and Ecological Spirituality," *Crosscurrents* Vol. 40, No. 4, 1990, 491.
[70] Ibid., 491.
[71] Ibid.

her whole body.[72] This is what Beatrice calls us to be, a dancer dancing the divine dance, centred in the still point of the Infinite and poured out, flowing into the world, into the future, as Love incarnates and expresses itself as the finite. When we live within the awareness of this enstatic-ecstatic flow, the dancer, Carla avows:

> allows it to shape her body into myriad forms, creating rhythmic and dynamic fluctuations. Her movements, in turn, affect the space around her. She is one with all that is happening. Drawn by the beauty of this stream of movement, she is as a river flowing onward, giving "voice" to a song from within. Or she can become a tree, motionless except for leaves that shimmer and flutter, whispering as the Spirit moves. Drawing from the varied gifts of the world, or incarnate life around us, she even becomes like the *Theotokos*, the God-bearer whose ecstasy will give birth to divine life.[73]

This vision of ourselves as a *Theotokos*, a God bearer, living awake in the full wakefulness of the consciousness of enstasic-ecstatic *agape*, empowers us to respond to the heart-ache and division in our world from within our oneness. Radiating the spondic luminosity of mercy and compassion we give voice to the song within and creatively bare God in the world.

Second, the evolution of communion consciousness is critical for the future of the planet. It is only from this mutual indwelling, where we know by communion, that we will find, in creative freedom together, what is needed for our evolutionary future. Beatrice reinforces Aurobindo's vision that, "for the complete and perfect fulfilment of the evolutionary movement, illumination and transformation must take place on every level of the individual, not only individuals but in the collective life of individuals."[74] A whole new sphere, a collective of enlightened persons is essential. Our task, Aurobindo's affirms, is to realize the divine symbol within ourselves, and then "reproduce, multiply and ultimately universalise it in others."[75] From this perspective the universalising of unitive consciousness becomes fundamental, because within the collective, Trinitarian intimacy expresses itself in the collective, in all of us, together. As the Trinity's unity expresses more unity through multiplicity, it then contemplates this unity in the multiplicity. Therefore, as we learn to coincide,

---

[72] Carla DeSola, "The Ecstasy of the Dancer and Perichoresis," in *Personal Transformation and New Creation: The Spiritual Revolution of Beatrice Bruteau*, ed. Ilia Delio (New York: Oribis Press, 2019), 189.
[73] Ibid., 189.
[74] Bruteau, *Worthy is the World*, 250.
[75] Ibid., 251.

heart in heart, in the *perichoresis* of the enstasy-ecstasy of the Trinity, the luminosity of the radiant spondic-energy that pours out, iridates a whole new level of persons in communion. Moreover, a more potent, truly discerning communal wisdom and vision emerges, that is truly inclusive and life enhancing. It is only through awakening in the noetic coincidence of being in one another in communion, in the ground of consciousness itself, that we can activate original, creative freedom, and solve the current crises. These crises were formed through the limits of choice freedom, reinforced by our incapacity to go within and awaken the consciousness of the ground of our heart. The awakening of communion consciousness is critical. And critical to this awakening is contemplation.

Third, in contemplation we choose to create communion, through meeting with others in silent, still awareness and activating the Christic ground of "we." This exchange of heart energy not only facilitates deeper communion amongst human beings; we necessarily overlap with the soul the earth, the heart of matter. The centre of our being and the centre of earth's being coincide. We realise we are the earth, and we are evolving in our capacity for an earth-human heart presence from our more intense reflexivity of turning into the heart. In this creative-union awareness, we realise that we are earth's awareness. We feel the pain, the heartache of the land, our betrayal of creatures, along with the rich potential for newness, as we face so many world catastrophes, especially the climate crisis. Consequently, in Beatrice's understanding, as we are becoming personally and communionally self-aware, our earth-human-communion consciousness is evolving. In this awareness then, we are not separate from the changing climate. Climate change is not happening "to us." We are climate change. In this evolving earth-human communion consciousness the divine voice becomes stronger, Love's intrinsically bonding energy, deepens and expands. We are reminded, "where two or three are gathered in my name, there I am with them" (Mt 18:20). To be gathered (συνηγμένοι *synēgmenoi*) is to be recollected, turned in towards each other's centre, to be stably grounded in the Christ centre, and to awake as a unitive self-creative consciousness. When the totally free creativity of this awareness flows, we have the capacity to draw on the mystical gifts and the science we already have and trust the innate generosity of creativity. Meeting in the transcendent ground of Christ consciousness and activating spondic radiance releases the evolutionary impulse of the collective intelligence of the noosphere that Teilhard foresaw, enhancing a greater convergence in Omega and the formation of a Theosphere. We celebrate the Holy Wholeness.

Fourth, our vulnerable sacred hearts must reawaken and burn with the blissful serene presence of the Beloved, Andrew Harvey inspires.[76] Beatrice returns us to this burning heart that is our natural state of being. She does this by showing us how to awaken the heart of our heart-mind and take the next step in attaining a new level of reflexivity, by entering into Christ, the creative Logos, the one in the heart-womb of pure transcendence. She calls us to delve into the unfathomable depths of the creative intimacy of our shared centre and discover the seeds of heart awareness that are beginning to shoot and blossom forth now. Grounded in this centring Absolute, she then calls us out, to live on the edge of tomorrow. She awakens us to the emerging allurement of living in Christ inspired by a natural Christic awareness illuminating the mind of our hearts. She calls us to enter into the transcendent freedom of Christ, into the heart of creativity itself, into the heart of every person, into the heart of the earth, into the one Heart-Self. She calls us to be Christ-like, eucharistic, food for all. She calls us to be revolutionary in enabling the wisdom of our radiant heart to glow incandescently and radiate abundant life. Hence, as we face the climate crisis together, in human-earth communion, in the ground of contemplation, we know that hidden in Christ: "somehow, at the depth, all is well and all manner of thing is well."[77]

One in this incandescent flow, I invite you to join Beatrice in contemplation before we turn to Ilia Delio.

---

[76] Andrew Harvey, *Activating your Divine Transfiguration,* Study Course, Shift Network, November, 2019.

[77] Bruteau, "In the Cave of the Heart," 319.

Praying Contemplatively

...what Jesus is communes directly with what one is, passing the meditation of either's behaviours or description. As the descriptors melt and evaporate before the burning radiance of each person's central reality, so the words that would capture those descriptions fail, and silence supervenes. The two luminosities gradually grow together.[78]

Embracing Stillness

Heart of all hearts, Love of all Love
Bathe our mind, our sensuality, our spirit in your silence
as we recline into your heart,
into the enfolding, encircling magnetism
of your heart-centre, rising in our heart-centre
in a translucent heart in heart, centre in centre awareness.
Soak us in the incandescence of your communion
as our enstatic being in one another
overflows in ecstasy pouring out love.
Amen.

---

[78] Bruteau, *Radical Optimism*, 132.

Ruminating on Scripture

The disciple, Jesus loved, reclined into his *kolpon* heart-womb.
John 13:23

The Music of Silence

Silence communes infusing unceasing circles of radiant kindness.

Contemplatio

Following in the tradition of the beautiful sacred heart prayer that Beatrice develops, this is an intrinsically communal contemplation that may be prayed alone, or with another person, or persons.

After finding a quiet place of solitude and coming to stillness, I invite you to enter into the depths of your heart and recline with Jesus at the last supper. Awaken the senses of your heart and feel yourself, reclining, more and more as you lean back into the *kolpon*, heart-womb of the one you love. Sense the intensely intimate fertile silence of this *kolpon*-heart-womb receiving you. Repose in the silence.

As you feel the tranquillity of repose, sense into the magnetic yearning of the heart of Jesus drawing you deeper into his heart. Feel yourself yielding, seeping, beyond your bounded self, back and down and in, towards your centre, where your heart infuses into the heart of Jesus, until you become absorbed in Jesus.

Softly, abide in the oneing, becoming more and more inside each other, as your consciousness and the consciousness of Jesus one. Feel the love energy of this sacred heart ground as your inside coincides with his inside and his heart becomes the heart of your heart. As you gently abide, one in each other, feel all descriptions of yourself melt and evaporate. You are one in the burning radiance of the one heart.

Gently, continue to release into this oneing love energy. Sense your heart and the heart of Jesus oneing in this one heart awareness. Feel yourself coinciding in the intimacy of the divine *kolpon*, in the Silence speaking the Word, as the Word infusing your consciousness ones. Dissolve into the silent love of Love's Trinity, into the communion of all hearts one in the Trinity. Flow with the inflow-outflow of *agape*.

Remain loving in this intimacy of Silence and Word oneing within this *agape* loving for as long as you feel drawn.

When the Spirit stirs you to behold from within this sacred heart consciousness, become present to the *agape* energy of communal consciousness as all humankind indwell, heart centre in heart centre.

After this contemplation, prayerfully record in your journal the wisdom that arises.

Blessing

May I/we dance
in the radiance
of the communion consciousness
of one in another
in the Trinity.
Amen.

IX

A Holy Wholeness

Ilia Delio

*My desire is that they may be encouraged in heart
and united in love, so that they may have the full riches of
complete understanding, in order that they may know the
mystery of God, namely, Christ,
in whom are hidden all the treasures
of wisdom and knowledge.*
Colossians 2:2

*I know that transformation is possible
and that we live many lives in the course of our existence.
Every time I died, I was born anew:
reincarnation and incarnation,
not as returning life but as rebirthing life,
as Word becoming flesh:
a spiraling incarnation, by which I have begun to glimpse
a bit of heaven and the grandeur of God stretching before me.*[1]

---

[1] Ilia Delio, *Birth of a Dancing Star: My Journey from Cradle Catholic to Cyborg Christian* (New York: Orbis Books, 2019), 205.

The diaphany of God shining through the transparent world, luminously oneing, drawing all things into a fuller consummation in Omega wholeness is where Ilia Delio is inviting us to be, at this phase in our evolutionary journey into living our oneness in God. As I write this chapter it is winter. Last night there was a luminous full moon that rose early, shining softly, as it was cradled in a mauve sky. Her humble stillness awoke my essential stillness, centring and yet drawing me into the void of the infinite vibrating field of Love's oneing, where we are one. As I settle into prayer, the moon and the mauve sky are still within me in the oneing. I feel tender, enfolding, unfolding flowing light, wrapping me in the winter stillness, enveloping and inviting me to draw all my senses within, to flow with the wrapping, until my awareness centres in my heart. My breath deepens and opens into spacious oneness, as the blood flowing through my veins yields. My body aching with the pain of a fall, with the pain of the world, softens and feels drawn into tender embrace. The enfolding, flowing, infusing, gentles and absorbs the pain. My senses fuse into a tranquil abiding and the marrow of my bones melt into love. My mind rests, gives way, descends into my heart and dissolves into the void of cosmic mind. The enfolding, flowing, tender infusing of being becomes lighter and lighter, creating translucent points of luminous stillness. All is the oneing. The timeless luminosity of embracing love ripples out with a serene glow of light infusing light. I am a flow of love. I am the sheer, shining emptiness of the embrace of silent love.

This prayer holds within it, the unquenchable desire of my heart to live a life of oneing love, to be aware of and to participate in the flowing light of Christo-Sophia. I desire to respond to Love stirring and drawing us into this next evolutionary movement of living the fullness of oneing that is the wholeness of being. And Ilia's compelling insights at the beginning of her memoir, *The Birth of a Dancing Star*, mirror my desire to live in this oneing. I desire to be this shining emptiness that is so extravagantly fecund. Ilia affirms our oneness in being: "one God empowers one flow of love through the one cosmos of life."[2] Subsequently, she speaks of the injustice we have inflicted on the cosmos by separating science and religion as two distinct spheres of unrelated knowledge, or even worse, she laments, removing ourselves from "the equation of love."[3] Ilia suggests that all the questions on how science and religion inter-relate are really the question of being itself. And essentially, all this is related to how we

---

[2] Ibid., xiii.
[3] Ibid.

recognise the fluidity of the inner-outer flow of life. The poetry of Rilke, that Ilia introduces her memoir with, so vividly holds this central dilemma of how we see our relationality. Rilke expresses our essential desire grounded in divine desire:

> Ah, not to be cut off,
> not through the slightest partition
> shut out from the law of the stars.
> The inner – what is it?
> if not intensified sky,
> hurled through with birds and deep
> with the winds of homecoming.[4]

May we truly know that one God empowers one flow of love through the one cosmos of life. May we know that we are this intensified sky hurled through with birds. May we know we are the fullness of the moon, the shining of the stars, the empty void, the flow of love and the winds of homecoming.

Open and optimistic, as Julian of Norwich was, in an age of turmoil and crisis, Ilia grounds us in hope. She creates an expansive canvas, as she envisages both scientist and mystic as harmonious voices together, enabling the creation of a fresh and vibrant new melody of love evolving. Her wisdom and insights feel so consistent with what I have come to know about soteriology, that salvation is the oneing of Love. Ilia affirms, that salvation is to be made whole.[5] And this wholeness creates such a profound centricity, and fullness of love in Christ, we find it unbearable. The love is overwhelming. Ilia calls us to live from within this fullness in Christ and awaken a quantum consciousness. She shows us how quantum consciousness is essential for the evolution of our mystical awareness today. Ilia's Christophany of Omega love that inter-weaves science, theology and spiritual ways of knowing, immerses us in a future fullness of oneness in divine Love.

Ilia Delio – A Dancing Star

Ilia Delio, (b.1955) a vibrant Franciscan theologian, is one of the contemporary prophetic voices who is inspiring me on this evolutionary path of oneing. Immersed in Franciscan mysticism, Ilia invites us to embrace the *kenosis* of the

---

[4] Cited in Delio, *Birth of a Dancing Star*, xiii.
[5] Ilia Delio, *The Unbearable Wholeness of Being: God, Evolution and the Power of Love* (New York: Orbis Books, 2013), 69.

poverty of being that draws us into fuller oneness in Christ, that we entered into with Clare. Well studied in theology, and the evolving insights of contemporary science, Ilia is delving deeply into the synthesising point where theology and science meet. Ilia is a prolific writer who is widely published and read. Her website, *Centre for Christogenesis* makes the most recent scholarship on our evolutionary convergence in Omega available to all. Her early research in science, followed by her extensive study of Bonaventure and then Teilhard's mysticism, laid the foundations for her ground-breaking trilogy, *The Emergent Christ, The Unbearable Wholeness of Being* and *Christ in Evolution* to emerge some years ago. In her later writings, she draws out the nature of our essential wholeness within Omega love in her *Making All Things New* and *Hunger for Wholeness,* and *The Hours of the Universe: Reflections on God, Science, and the Human Journey*. Always at the cutting edge, she also explores the future potential of technology and transhumanism, in *Re-enchanting the Earth: Why AI Needs Religion*. Ilia calls us forward into a future one in Love's Trinity, where the transcendent personhood of our identity in Christ may emerge in Omega consciousness.

Ilia assists us to be deeply present within the stirrings of love so that Christ consciousness may emerge and stabilise. Her Christophany of Omega love, that inter-weaves science and spiritual ways of knowing, situates us within the future fullness of oneness in divine love. Ilia's Christic path is well summarised in her memoir, *The Birth of a Dancing Star*:

> The path into the world of meaning and truth is the path into the human heart. If you want to know how science and religion are related, first come to know the deepest truth of yourself. This is what I realized when I looked into the night-time sky: I saw myself in the stars and the stars within me. The God who created the heavens is the same God who is alive and active in my heart. God who is the absolute power of love, the power of my life, is the power of the future.[6]

Ilia invites us to discover anew the power of love, the vision of the heart, and harness its energies in our lives, to create a future wholeness in love in Omega. She calls us to come home to our own Christic nature, as she is doing, and Christify life through loving.

---

[6] Ibid., 205.

In an age where the rationality of science and the fast progression of technology has separated us from our Christic nature and our mystical unitive way of knowing, Ilia offers a way forward. Sadly, in this contemporary climate, while we know intellectually and technically, we do not know intelligently, because our predominant model of research disregards the wisdom of the heart as the researcher objectively observes, divides and separates. Individual parts are examined in isolation, rather than exploring from within the naturally synthesising vision of unitive consciousness. As Beatrice reminds us: "Intelligibility, insight into the nature of the reality – is to be had in each instance on the level of synthesis, at the point where unity is finally achieved."[7] Intelligibility comes at the point of union, in the oneing point. Ilia affirms this synthesising role of the observer when she says, "The whole is actualized by the observer, who transforms the perceived data into wholes; each perceiver is a 'particular actualizing of the whole.'"[8] We must see from within the wholeness, and in the seeing, actualise the whole. We must look more deeply into this synthesising wholeness beyond what we can observe empirically. As quantum physicist David Bohm confirms, reality "is no thing and … it is also not the totality of all things (i.e., we are not to identify 'reality' with 'everything')."[9] In this contemplative way of knowing through love, with the quantum consciousness, that Ilia develops, we are ever sensitive to this "no thing," to the more, to the whole that is greater than the sum of the parts, to the endless creativity of creative-union, in this exquisite evolutionary journey of Love's oneing.

This Chapter

Having met Ilia, we will focus on the power of love, noting the underlying influences on her, of the mysticism of Bonaventure's crucified Christ and Teilhard's Christ-Omega. We will then explore how Ilia invites us to awaken a Christic quantum resurrection consciousness. Since Ilia draws on the research of physicist David Bohm, as she expands on this wholeness of being that we are, we will spend some time exploring Bohm's development of "holomovement," and ponder how this holomovement relates to our metaphysics of oneing. This

---

[7] Beatrice Bruteau, Beatrice Bruteau, *Evolution Towards Divinity* (Weaton: The Theosophical Publishing House, 1974), 31.
[8] Ibid.
[9] David Bohm, *Wholeness and the Implicate Order* (London: Routledge, 2002), 76.

will lead to seeing how Ilia invites us to nurture a quantum heart-body-mind, that is the mind of the risen Christ. Finally, we will explore how, through grounding us in Omega love and strengthening our quantum, Omega consciousness, Ilia offers fruitful insights into how contemplation is necessary for this next evolutionary impulse to flourish in this quantum, cosmic, divine milieu.

The Power of Love

Relentlessly, Ilia speaks of love as the ultimate mystery of being and of truth. Love is the ground of all being, the metaphysical foundation of all that exists, the essential cosmological energy. "Love is a passionate force at the heart of the Big Bang universe," she affirms. Love is, "the fire that breathes life into matter and unifies elements centre to centre; love is deeply embedded in the cosmos, a cosmological force."[10] Love-energy is the grounding energy, the amorising energy of the universe, creating. Love is the within of things, the immanent power amorising, unifying all of creation, personalizing, by becoming conscious in us, drawing us into the fullness of our identity in Christ. Grounded in Christ, Ilia continues: "Love is the integrated energy field, the center of all centers, the whole of every whole, that makes each whole desire more wholeness."[11] Ilia stresses Love's personalizing nature as the centre of centres, the whole in every whole, that makes us more united, whole, one. And as we have seen, this oneing love is not a naïve union of undifferentiated oneness. We are one and yet differentiated in Love's unifying holy wholeness. Every person, creature, thing is distinguished within Love's oneness, is valued and has a part to play in this wholeness. We are one and many, as Beatrice affirms. Thus, we simultaneously, perceive both our oneness and our uniqueness. At this moment, Omega is inciting a desire for this consciousness of our wholeness, so Ilia invites us to be present to this divine desire within, to attend to the discomfort this unbearable wholeness of being can incite and respond to love's promptings. This creative, spontaneous, novel, integrating, wholeness is always opening us into deeper consciousness, more unity, more centricity, more love.

Thus, empowered by love, "the wise person," Ilia says, "thinks with the heart."[12] This is where we find ourselves now, learning to think with our heart, and enable the synthesis of what our mind knows about the evolution of the created world

---

[10] Ibid., 43.
[11] Ibid., 44.
[12] Ibid.

and what our heart knows about love. We must, Ilia affirms, "liberate the spark within, the inmost center (*scintilla animae*), a freedom beyond freedom, a self beyond all ego, a being beyond the created realm, a consciousness that transcends all divisions, all separations."[13] And importantly, do this in the world. As Ilia affirms, we must allow the flash of the Absolute to recognise itself in us,[14] in our own hearts in creation. We must be a luminous mirror of eternity. And as we discover our own incarnating role in creating a new creation, our Christic consciousness emerges, and we know our oneness in the body of Christ. Ilia defines this consciousness as "the mindfulness of awareness that underscores in some way, evolution's direction."[15] Ilia calls us to nurture this evolutionary awareness and follow the Spirit's promptings in the creative, cosmic transformation of evolution becoming conscious of itself, through us. Ilia calls us to be so at home within the interior depths of our inner universe, and so at home in the outer universe, that there is no dualism between inner and outer. All is one in Christ Omega. Ilia summons us into the depthless depths of the divine mystery of Christ, human, divine and cosmic, expressing the fullness of Trinitarian love. She calls us to live in this love and be evolution becoming conscious of itself through our lives.

In her memoir, Ilia gives voice to a sacred moment, when she looked into the night sky and was immersed in love. She comes to see:

> Deep within the cave of my heart, a depth that belongs to me alone, I recognize a fire that burns brilliantly and glows with warmth. Through that glowing fire I see the outline of a face, the face of Christ, but I also see my face, and then I begin to see Christ's face as my face. Sometimes I cannot tell Christ's face from my own face, and all at once I recognize a single face whose eyes are looking inward and outward. The word "God" doesn't seem to capture the infinite depth of my soul that stretches toward an endless horizon. By its sheer unlimited being I know I must be divine life, because it is life other than my own and yet entangled with my own life.[16]

This fire that burns and glows as it creates, that feels like a burning star, this centre of centres in the depth of the cave of her heart, is the face of Christ. In gazing into the cave of her heart, Ilia knows irrevocably, through love, that she sees the mirror of love endlessly reflecting the oneing in being that we saw with

---

[13] Ibid., 141.
[14] Ibid.
[15] Ibid., xxi.
[16] Ilia Delio, *Birth of a Dancing Star*, 202.

Clare. Christ's face is her face, and her face is Christ's face. There is only one face looking inward and outward. Ilia's Christic face sees with heart vision, as her eyes look inward and outward simultaneously, dissolving the perceived separation between the inner and outer universe, Matter and Spirit, in a union that enables her to see how Matter is diaphanously infused by Spirit and Spirit manifests as Matter. Ilia sees, she knows that she knows with her heart knowing, that she is in the stars and the stars are within herself. She beholds and sees the absolute power of love. Ilia offers us a deep theology of our evolution towards a greater awareness of our holy wholeness in love, the holomovement of all things in Christ, the centre of centres.

In clarifying what she means by Christ, Ilia says: "Christ is probably the most inclusive term we could use to talk about God's presence, Christ is the one who draws together, who unifies the new creation."[17] Ilia places us in the centre of Christ, into the midst of Christ's personalizing all things, drawing all things into convergence in the Omega point. She invites us to love from our heart's depths, in Christ, in a holy wholeness. In Ilia's words: "Christ belongs to the whole. Christ symbolizes the personal centre of love that bursts forth in Jesus and empowers our own lives to converge in love. Christ represents the capacity of every person to live in love and hence in God."[18] She invites us to live the fullness of this wholeness in Christ in love. "Love is the core energy," she says, "of cosmic personalism, the depth of being and dynamically unitive."[19] Ilia affirms all we have been reflecting upon. In love we are one, in Christ, in the dynamism of evolutionary oneing.

Creatively, Ilia points out that the Hebrew word for one is *ehad*, and the word for love is *ahavah*.[20] In mystical numerology, each Hebrew letter has an equivalent so that when the numbers are added together, oneness and love are equivalent. Furthermore, when each word's numerical value is added together, it is the same value assigned to the holiest name YHVH. Ilia highlights how, in Hebrew spirituality, God is oneness and love.[21] Ilia continues, "out of our oneness in love is our being in love and our desire for oneness. Love is the whole and every person belongs to the whole."[22] Ilia teaches us how to evolve in our

---

[17] See, https://uscatholic.org/articles/201103/universal-savior-ilia-delio-reimagines-christ/
[18] Delio, *Unbearable Wholeness*, 105.
[19] Ibid., 106.
[20] Ibid., 108.
[21] Ibid, quoting the research of Danial Matt.
[22] Ibid.

capacity to enter more fully into the fountain fullness of Love's presence within our own heart, within the heart of creation and live the fullness of our wholeness in this love. Profoundly touched by the unbearable wholeness of being, and a desire to plumb the depths of evolution as a movement of convergence and complexity, Ilia invites us to see how the evolution of life is essentially towards integral wholeness.[23] She calls us to embrace a catholicity, from *katholikos,* of the whole, so that we may orientate the whole of our lives towards making wholeness.[24] This includes attuning to the physical order, living in harmony with the stars, having a sense of the cosmos, including both physical and spiritual things. Ilia invites us to turn together as one, to enter into the oneing and awaken a Christic mind that is essentially communal, universal, all embracing of the whole.[25] So the awakening of a Christic mind is the awakening of wholistic vision. It is the awakening of Omega within us. Ilia helps us enter into the enflaming love-knot of this oneing point, into the spark, the scintilla, the Omega point within us. She draws us into the synthesising point in Christ, where her research into Bonaventure's ecstatic union and Teilhard's convergence of all things in the Omega point coincide, as we will now see.

Influences: Bonaventure's Christ and Teilhard's Omega

Ilia's early research into Bonaventure expressed in *Crucified Love* and *The Humility of God*, lay a foundation for the theology that emerges in her writings. In all that she writes, Ilia affirms that because God is love, the spiritual journey from God, in God, to God cannot be simply one of intellectual contemplation, that takes us away from the world. Contemplation involves the union in love with the primordial mystery of love, expressed in the world and as the world.[26] Steeped in Bonaventure's love mysticism, Ilia draws on his seminal vision which we explored with Clare, of creation as a mirror translucently aglow with the beauty of divine love. "So it appears that the entire world is like a single mirror," Bonaventure affirms: "full of lights that stand in the presence of the divine Wisdom, shedding light like burning coals."[27] Bonaventure elaborates on this

---

[23] Ibid., xxi.
[24] Ilia Delio, *Making All Things New: Catholicity, Cosmology, Consciousness* (New York: Orbis Books, 2016), xi.
[25] Ibid.
[26] Ilia Delio, *Crucified Love: Bonaventure's Mysticism of the Crucified Christ* (Quincy: Franciscan Press, 1998), 59.
[27] Zachary Hayes, *Bonaventure Mystical Writings* (Phoenix: Tau Publishing. Kindle Edition, 1999), Loc. 984.

luminously burning presence of divine Wisdom radiant within creation, when he says:

> The created world is a kind of book reflecting, representing and describing its maker the Trinity. At three levels of expression: as vestige, as image and as likeness. The aspect of vestige is found in every creature; the aspect of image only in the intelligent creature ... the aspect of likeness in those creatures that are God conformed through these successive levels, compatible to steps, the human intellect is designed to ascend gradually to the supreme Principle, which is God.[28]

Ilia immerses us in this book of creation and awakens us to this trace (vestige) of the divine in all creation, drawing us into the intimacy of how the fountain fullness of divine love pours out into the entire web of life. Every created thing, from a grain of sand to the largest creature, holds the vestige, the trace, imprint, the footprint of divine loving. All of creation has a centre of divine presence, a within-ness, or what the Franciscan, Duns Scotus identifies as *haecceitus* a "thisness" that is unique and knowable only by God.[29] Bonaventure affirms: "God is contemplated not only through them, as by His traces, but also in them, in so far as He is in them by essence, potency, and presence."[30] This essence, potency, and presence within creation gives creation an inner point of creative union, a within-ness, an inner life, a soul, an energy field, or what contemporary science is calling a "god-particle."[31] While this sense of God within creation, naturally affirms creation's essential value, dignity and rights, there are further implications for the evolution of Christ consciousness. It must include ecological consciousness. For as we become more one in Christ, in the Christic image and likeness, grace floods us with the gift of seeing from oneness in the trace (vestige), in the luminous footprint of the divine within all creation, holding creatures in being.

---

[28] *Breviloquium* 2.12, cited in Ilia Delio, *Christ in Evolution* (New York: Orbis Books, 2008), 60.
[29] Delio, *Christ in Evolution*, 61.
[30] Bonaventure, *The Journey of the Mind into God*, Chapter 2, Paragraph 1. https://www.discerninghearts.com/PDF/Bonaventure%20Journey%20of%20the%20Mind%20Into%20God.pdf
[31] This Higgs boson, or God particle, was identified by the Scottish quantum physicist Peter Higgs in 1964. It is an invisible, universe-wide field that gave mass to all matter after the Big Bang, forcing particles to coalesce into stars, planets etc. https://en.wikipedia.org/wiki/Higgs_boson

While reflecting on what contemplation means in this unfinished process of psychic-spiritual-material life,[32] Ilia qualifies how, in her recent understanding, contemplation is "mindful relationality" or "minded matter." Coining the term "*econoesis*" or "*matrnoeisis*", from *nous* – mind, *eco* – household relationships, or *matra* – mother, her term, "*econoiesis*" connotes conscious interbeing life and mindful creative union that includes the whole of nature. This emphasis on "eco" and "mother" also brings us back to Julian's homeliness of the divine household that includes all, and the importance of integrating Christ deep wisdom and mother consciousness into this ecological vision. In nurturing this shared consciousness within the divine trace within creation, we strengthen an ecological communion consciousness and enhance the ecological dimension of the noosphere. In encouraging us to see from within this ecological wholeness, Ilia invites us to truly contemplate the book of creation, not as subject reflecting on creation as object, but by being one, in the dynamism of God in creation, and creation in God, awakening conscious inter-being and mindful creative union and contributing to the evolution of the whole.

In *Crucified Love*, Ilia highlights some striking aspects of Bonaventure's understanding of ecstatic union, stressing that union is not an exclusive privilege. Mystical union is for all. Like the mystics we have been exploring, Bonaventure seeks for us to turn into the highest point of the mind (*apex mentis*), to the sublime, or most transcendent, numinous point of affectivity (*apex affectus*), where we are so single pointed, we pass into the divine. This involves stilling and calming our body and conceptualizing mind. Bonaventure stresses the Trinitarian presence within this *apex mentis,* that reflects an eternal memory grounded in the divine Eternity, an intellect grounded in divine Word and a will grounded in divine Goodness.[33] And he upholds this inner capacity to enter into the memory, intellect and will when we turn within our soul, until our sensual ways of knowing naturally release into our heart-senses and we abide in love.[34] In his *Soul's Journey to God,* Bonaventure says: "Consider…these three powers, and you will be able to see God in yourselves as in an image, which is to see

---

[32] Ilia Delio, "Econoeisis: a New Contemplative Paradigm, Ω *Spirit: Centre for Christogenesis* (July, 2021), https://christogenesis.org/econoeisis-a-new-contemplative-paradigm/.

[33] Here, Bonaventure draws on Augustine, (see, Ch. 1) and so is resonant with Julian, the *Cloud* author, Eckhart and John of the Cross.

[34] For Bonaventure, the physical senses are always rooted in the spiritual senses, and so endure in all phases of our union in love until they give way in ecstasy. See, Delio, *Crucified Love*, 63.

through a glass darkly (I Cor 13: 12)."[35] He suggests that when we turn into our heart-self, as if entering into a mirror, all our sensual ways of knowing rest and release into what feels like an exquisite divine darkness, in union in love. Bonaventure's language enflames: "In its burning desire, the soul becomes not only an agile flame swift to rise: it even transcends itself, entering mystical darkness and ecstasy through a certain wise unknowing."[36] This luminous, flame of dark, ecstatic, being in one another, infuses "a wise unknowing," or a "learned ignorance."[37]

Like the *Cloud of Unknowing* author who is so in harmony with this "wise unknowing" that we only discover through love, Bonaventure gives some delicate nuances into the way in which we know in this wise unknowing that Ilia highlights. Again, paradox is needed here, as Bonaventure helpfully describes how our mind, "sleeps," and at the same time "keeps vigil." He stresses that it is our affectivity within our mind, that keeps vigil.[38] Meanwhile, our will is so delicately attentive, keeping watch that our active mind remains still, at rest. In this delicate attentiveness, in the intimacy of Love's ecstasy, we hear secret words that are unrepeatable, because they are only in the heart. "Hence," Bonaventure says, "because nothing can be expressed unless it is conceived, or conceived unless it is understood, …the intelligence does not speak."[39] In this ecstatic loving, a conception takes place that we intuit through love that is beyond the knowing of our intellect, for the intellect cannot speak. In silent, still, being in love our heart knows.

Ilia makes a critical point about the role of our heart senses in this conception, as for Bonaventure, the heart senses of hearing and sight belong to the uncreated Word, smell to the inspired Word, taste and touch to the incarnate Word.[40] Thus, in this union in love in Christ, grace so floods our soul that the senses of our heart hear and see the divine presence in the world through the eternal Word in us. We see with transcendent eyes. We inhale the fragrance of the divine in the world through the inspired Word within us. We taste and touch through the Word enfleshed in us. Our heart senses express how one we are in Christ, as we see

---

[35] Bonaventure, *Journey of the Mind*, 2.1.
[36] *Hexaemeron*, quoted in Delio, *Crucified Love*, 62.
[37] Ibid., 63.
[38] See, Ilia Delio, *A Hunger for Wholeness* (New York: Paulist Press, 2018), 41. Ilia mentions the influence of Thomas Gallus (1219-1247) on Bonaventure who emphasised that we reach ecstatic oneness and awaken the *scintilla synderesis* in the *affectus* through loving.
[39] *Hexaemeron*, quoted in Delio, *Crucified Love*, 63.
[40] Ibid.

through a mirror darkly, until the dark wisdom of wise unknowing pours back into our conscious awareness. As our heart indwells the uncreated Word and is infused in the aroma of the inspired Word, tasting and touching the fleshy incarnate Word, we become truly intelligent, because we learn to see from our oneness in the Word, through our union in Love.

What I see Ilia inviting us into, in her later writings, is the evolutionary movement of awakening this heart intelligence so we can "think with our heart," because we see from within this union in love in the eternal Word, who is the Wisdom of God, enfleshed in us. This awakening of the mind of the Word, or the mind of Christ within us, and fostering our understanding from our participation in this mind, then enables us to reclaim the intellect that we released into love. Reflexively, love can then inform reason and reason can then be informed by love. Nurturing this gift of a mystical, heart, sense-perception from within the Word, who is the uncreated, incarnated, and inspired Logos within our heart, awakens a capacity to synthesise the wisdom of our mystical consciousness, with the reason we see expressed in science. We then "think with our heart," creating a dialectic between love and knowledge. And if we add Julian's being wise in mind with the wisdom of Christ our mother, this way of seeing with a Christic mind that senses through the eternal, inspired and enfleshed Word, who infuses oneing wisdom, has enormous implications for the development of a quantum consciousness, where, in Ilia's words, our "whole brain is enabling the whole person to connect with the whole environment."[41] *Econoesis* evolves.

Teilhard de Chardin, is the other influential voice in Ilia's theology, especially in her development of Bonaventure's appreciation of our oneness with the Word in the *apex mentis*, in our most transcendent point of affectivity, in the point of pure love. In a fascinating chapter in *Hunger for Wholeness*, Ilia shows how the various interpretations of the point within the soul (*the synderesis*) that we have seen especially in Julian, the *Cloud of Unknowing* seer and Eckhart, laid the foundations for Teilhard's development of Omega.[42] Ilia describes this principle of Omega that Teilhard magnified:

> Omega is the presence of something in nature that is wholly other than nature distinct yet intrinsic, autonomous and independent, yet deeply influential on nature's propensity towards complexity and consciousness. This Omega is

---

41 Delio, *Making All Things New*, 150.
42 Delio, *Hunger for Wholeness*, 35-43.

irreducible to isolated elements, yet accounts for the "*more* in the cell than in the molecule, *more* in society than in the individual, and *more* in mathematical construction than in calculations or theorems." Omega is the most intensely personal centre that makes beings personal and centered, because it is the attractive centre of love that empowers every love.[43]

Inviting us to be ever attentive to this more, Ilia continues to amplify Teilhard's insights that:

> As the principle of centration that is within, it [Omega] is also independent of nature and thus escapes entropy, so that it is ahead of nature as the prime mover. Omega therefore emerges from the organic totality of evolution and is the goal towards which evolution tends. It is operative from the beginning of evolution, acting on pre-living, cosmic elements, even though they are without individualized centres, by setting them in motion from the beginning, as a single impulse of energy. Omega is the absolute centre of every whole that makes wholeness in nature not only possible but intensely personal.[44]

Omega is the principle of centration, the Centre of centres who is both within creation, the more within creation and ahead, drawing us into greater convergence and oneness. Omega is within creation as the highest state of centricity and complexity and yet beyond creation, calling us beyond into a fuller unity in Omega. Centred in Omega, all of life has a centre that participates in this Centre of centres and we as human beings have the capacity to become conscious of this centring love energy that resides within our own heart, awaken from the centre and see from the centre with Omega eyes.

Moreover, this quality of "more" that Omega incites, and Ilia highlights, immerses us in awe and wonder and carries us into silence, as exquisitely, beyond our wildest imaginings, Omega continually lavishes creation with more. The source-less source of all love, the groundless ground of all being, the silence that speaks the Word/Wisdom, the life force, the power, the potential, the abundance, the fullness of the endlessness of love begetting love, faithfully, steadfastly, streams forth within creation. Omega is the organic totality of evolution, the One who makes all things one, the All who makes all things all. Omega is the attractive centre that enflames every love.

Centred in Omega love and held in creative unity, creation bears within its innermost being, this pattern of divine inter-flowing love gradually drawing all

---

43 Ibid., 35.
44 Ibid., 35.

things into the creative-union of oneing. And as we have seen, we experience this Omega presence as the enstatic, ecstatic, dynamism of the oneing, enfolding, enclosing love of the Trinity. This fountain fullness of Trinitarian love energy overflows into creation. And, creation, in turn, expresses the same fountain fullness. Ilia invites us into a deeper mystical union with Christ in creation, in the dynamism of being drawn into oneness in Omega. She stresses how: "Creation is the Beloved of God and the becoming of God in Love. God is in matter and matter is in God."[45] Ilia invites us to awaken a quantum consciousness and responsively participate in this becoming of God in creation.

Awakening Quantum Consciousness

Guided by Ilia, we will now see, how when we journey into our soul, we discover the outer universe mirrored within our own inner universe. This in turn, draws us out into the outer universe to see the inner divine presence within all things, in an endless mirroring of microcosm and macrocosm that the quantum world sensitizes us to. Following in the tradition of Bonaventure, Teilhard and many others, Ilia carries their foundational wisdom forward as she takes us into a new dynamic phase in this process of becoming one in Omega. She invites us to become so turned within the ground of our heart, aware that we are aware, sensitive to our oneness in the ground of consciousness, that we are the field of oneing love into which we gaze. A stronger field awareness awakens, and we develop a quantum consciousness. Invitationally, she says:

> The mirroring of microcosm and macrocosm, human person and universe, finds renewed meaning today in light of evolution and quantum physics. In a particular way, quantum physics has opened up a new relationship between mind and matter in such a way that we can say the soul is returned to matter.[46]

Ilia then defines the soul within a quantum context, as the field of the mind, the ground of consciousness, the centre of inner freedom, the power of self-determination, the seat of co-creativity, the depth and breadth of all existent life.[47] And she stresses the interrelatedness between consciousness, space, unity and love, within the mind. In this sense, the mind includes the "*nous*," the intelligence of the mind of our heart. The mind is the unified field of pure consciousness that is spacious, oneing love.

---

[45] Delio, *Unbearable Wholeness*, 69.
[46] Delio, *Hunger for Wholeness*, 41.
[47] Ibid.

Specifically, for Ilia, on a human level, the mind includes, "the brain as well as the body, the senses and emotions, as well as the environment of interaction."[48] Far more than limited to chemical reactions in our brain, "the mind," Ilia says, "is not so much an organ as an informational flow."[49] This informational flow, of oneing vibrating energy is constantly giving birth to itself, generating new cells and neural pathways in our brain. Mind is in a constant flux of connectivity, forming new connections, expanding new horizons, achieving new levels of consciousness.[50] "Mind is where a sense of the whole – catholicity – becomes a reality,"[51] she says. We might say "mind" in this expansive context, is the ground of Love's oneing in the cosmos, that is Christ-Omega gathering all of creation in an eternally centrating love.

Drawing on quantum physics,[52] which Ilia explains is the behaviour of matter and energy at molecular, atomic, sub-atomic, nuclear and microscopic levels, Ilia awakens a microscopic sensitivity within us. She alerts us to the tiniest particles, to the intricacy of the inner flow that makes up one whole expanding field of consciousness. She immerses us in the fundamental light energy, in light's electron-magnetic radiation shared in the flux of light-waves, relating how researchers in quantum mechanics now realise that light behaves both as waves and particles. In this quantum world, there is no dualism between matter and energy. All objects manifest both wave like and particle like behaviour. In other words, what we think of as matter is actually a manifestation of energy, of quanta, or little bundles of vibrating energy manifesting themselves out of an infinite field, communicating with each other.

As well, quantum theory enables us to realise that light, once understood to manifest primarily as cosmic rays of light-waves, actually exhibits photons, or little quanta of energy. Sometimes light behaves as a wave, and at other times as

---

[48] Delio, *Making All Things New*, 149.
[49] Ibid.,150.
[50] Ibid.,151.
[51] Ibid.
[52] Quantum mechanics highlights how we are made of star dust billions of years old. Our matter and energy contribute to the life of the universe and when we die will continue to live on in matter and energy as it evolves. All matter and energy is inter-connected. Last century, the German physicist Max Plank saw how radiation in the form of light or heat is not omitted in a continuous stream, but in bundles of energy or "quanta." He postulated that energy is made up of both waves and particles. Energy can be in more than one place at the same time, although it does not exist in ordinary space time, until we observe it as a particle. Quantum waves hold potential energy. They can collapse, cease to exist and appear in existence somewhere else. Our observation of a quantum object simultaneously affects its twin object no matter how far apart they are. See, Diarmuid O'Murchu, *Quantum Theology* (New York: Crossroad, 2004), 29.

a photon. Researchers concluded that when light looks like a particle, it is a particle, when it looks like a wave it is a wave. In a quantum world, nothing is real unless it is observed. Our participation in observing is critical to the outcome. Ilia affirms:

> It is a participatory universe with no distinction between the process of observation and what is observed; that is, there is no line between subject and object. Reality is what we observe. At the most fundamental level of existence there is no discrete piece of inert matter. Rather, there are clusters of interrelated probalistic events that change their nature when observed. In this sense there is no objective reality; only what we can observe can be known. We are actors therefore, rather than spectators.[53]

In this quantum perspective, matter is not composed of separate elements, but is interconnected by waves spread out infinitely linking everything. Everything exists within a complex web of relations in which the observer creates the final link in a chain. In this view, separation is an illusion, because everything is in relationship to the whole. In this web of relations, the observer and what is observed are one.

Moreover, we, as observer, create a crucial connection in the chain of connectivity and affect the outcome of what will happen, not only where we are observing, but non-locally. This quantum interconnectivity crosses the boundaries of space and time, operating in the spaceless-ness of infinity. Morphogenic fields form when our observation of quanta creates a history. These morphogenic fields are made up of living energy that hold information, memories and habits. A morphogenic field forms in space-time and continues to live on beyond space-time. In this quantum vision, everything is interconnected in wave flows, affects and is affected by the whole, because the relational flow of energy is the relationship itself. As Ilia says, we live within an undivided wholeness and the consciousness we bring to this wholeness helps shape the whole. Ilia summarizes, "to be is to be related."[54] Ilia draws on the research of physicist David Bohm as she expands on this wholeness of being that we are, that is a holomovement.

---

[53] Delio, *Making All Things New*, 149.
[54] Delio, *The Emergent Christ: Exploring the Meaning of Catholic in an Evolutionary Universe* (New York: Orbis Books, 2011), 28.

Holomovement

David Bohm's sense of undivided wholeness, or what he calls, the implicate order that he sees in a constant holomovement, is first explored by Ilia her *Christ in Evolution*, and developed in her later books.[55] Ilia specifically relates Bohm's understanding that we are wholes within wholes, to the contemplation of Christ, who is the energy of creative union, of the oneing of this wholeness. Bohm is of particular interest to us, because he had a developed mystical consciousness himself, being not only a professor of theoretical physics, but also spending considerable time with Krishnamurti exploring the notion of consciousness. Albert Einstein called him his spiritual friend, while the Dalai Lama called him his scientist.[56] Like Ilia, who gazed into the night sky and saw the expansiveness of the stars within her own self, shining through her being, taking her into a depthless oneness in being, David Bohm also has a numinous experience when looking at the night sky.

Quantum physicist, David Schrum tells of a time when he was walking with Bohm gazing at stars shining in the dark sky. He recalls how Bohm observed that although, ordinarily, we think of stars as objects shining from far out with spaces in between them, there is another way we can look at the sky. When our gaze shifts to the wholeness of the space of the sky, we can see a vacuum, an empty space that is a plenum, a fullness that is alive with interconnectedness. Bohm further sees that the material objects in this vast expansiveness are like little bundles, little vacuums in a vast sea. He recognises that the night sky is one whole living organism, and the little bits we call matter, are tiny wholes within the whole. Bohm notes that in a cubic metre of this plenum, within the seething creativity of this invisible vacuum, there is more energy than in the entire visible universe.[57] Bohm sensitises us to the oneness expressed in this quantum vacuum that while on the surface seems non-visible and seemingly empty, is in fact an information-filled plenum, the ontological relational ground that underlies the multiverse.

---

[55] Delio, *Christ in Evolution*, 144.
[56] Paul Howard, *Infinite Potential: The Life and Ideas of David Bohm*, see, https://www.youtube.com/watch?v=Xudo0Vz61wk
[57] Ibid.

Bohm emphasises the fecundity, the possibility and the potentiality of this void-like emptiness that characterizes this field awareness. In opening us to this way of seeing with quantum, oneing eyes, Barbara Fiand reminds us that this:

> pure vacuum is omnipresent. The Buddhist concept of *shunyata*, seeing space as "empty and yet full of potential," is perhaps the closest any spiritual insight has come to addressing it. Brian Swimme calls it an "empty fullness, a fecund nothingness." It is the ground of the universe–not, as was previously thought, inert matter, but seething, rather, "with creativity, so much so that physicists refer to [its] ground state as 'space-time foam.'"[58]

Seeing space as empty and yet full is critical here, for the emptiness has its own exquisite mystical consciousness. And Bohm draws us into this empty fullness that is at the ground of the universe, into its undivided wholeness, that he calls the implicate order. Implicate, stresses the within-ness of this fundamental level of reality that continuously, implicitly, enfolds in on itself, as it simultaneously unfolds outward in the explicit order. This enfolded order within, or we could say the soul of the universe, is often ignored by scientists, who tend to focus on the external, abstract explicit order.

At present our thought patterns are shifting from concentrating on isolating and observing distinct parts of the explicit unfolded order, to strengthening our capacity to explore the one flow of being that has both an implicit enfolded, explicit unfolded movement. And Bohm warns us that we need to be aware of the "ever-changing flux of process in which thought passes into nonthought while non-thought passes into thought, so that it cannot be regarded as fixed."[59] This "non-fixed distinction," he says, "evidently requires the free movement of intelligent perception, which can, on each occasion, discern what content originates in thought and what content originates in a reality that is independent of thought."[60] He notes that "ultimately, the actual movement of thought embodying any particular notion of totality has to be seen as a process, with ever-changing form and content."[61] Bohm provides the example of the incompleteness

---

[58] Barbara Fiand, *Awe-Filled Wonder: The Interface of Science and Spirituality* Madeleva Lecture in Spirituality (New York: Paulist Press, Kindle Edition, 2008), Loc. 114.
[59] Bohm, *Wholeness and the Implicate Order*, 76.
[60] Ibid.
[61] Bohm adds, "Even this statement about the nature of our thinking is, however, itself only a form in the total process of becoming, a form which indicates a certain order of movement of the mind, and a certain disposition needed for the mind to engage harmoniously in such movement. So there is nothing final about it. Nor can we tell where it will lead." Bohm,

of examining still photographs of a speeding car, without taking into account the actual experience of the movement of the car that has a sense of an unbroken, undivided process of flow.[62]

Through his extensive research, Bohm shows how everything exists within this flow, or what he identifies as a holomovement. In Bohm's words:

> the holomovement is the basic reality, and that all entities, objects, forms, etc., as ordinarily seen are relatively stable, independent and autonomous features of the holomovement. ... The basic order of this movement is therefore enfoldment and unfoldment. So we are looking at the universe in terms of a new order, which we shall call the enfolded order or the implicate order.[63]

Bohm further highlights the flowing nature of this movement when he writes: "The implicate order has its ground in the holomovement which is, ... vast, rich and in a state of unending flux of enfoldment and unfoldment."[64] In Bohm's view, "the movement of enfolding and unfolding is ultimately the primary reality."[65] This suggests that the inner order of the whole of the universe is enfolded into each part, and this enfoldment in each part, in turn, helps determine what each part is and will become. Thus, this enfoldment and unfoldment is the basic energy flow that is.

Again, in Bohm's words:

> *what is* is the holomovement, and ... everything is to be explained in terms of forms derived from this holomovement. Though the full set of laws governing its totality is unknown (and, indeed, probably unknowable) nevertheless these laws are assumed to be such that from them may be abstracted relatively autonomous or independent sub-totalities of movement (e.g., fields, particles, etc.) having a certain recurrence and stability of their basic patterns of order and measure.[66]

For Bohm, holomovement is the basic reality. He is suggesting that reality is made up of wholes within wholes, within a wholistic movement of enfoldment and unfoldment, and so he sees the whole multiverse in terms an enfolded order.

Wholeness and the Implicate Order, 80. In his discussion with Krishnamurti they explore how when thought moves into no-thought, time ends, so that perhaps we could say that thought is time. J. Krishnamurti & David Bohm - Brockwood Park 1980, "The Ending of Time," Conversation 14. https://www.youtube.com/watch?v=Ivs6o7M45Es.

62 Bohm, Wholeness and the Implicate Order, x.
63 Ibid., 25-26.
64 Ibid., 185.
65 Ibid., 25.
66 Ibid., 226.

From this holomovement perspective, Ilia continues: "what may appear like permanent structures are only relatively autonomous sub-entities that emerge out of the whole of flowing movement and then dissolve back into it in an unceasing process of becoming."[67] Within this holomovement, space and time emerge as forms flowing from the holomovement. Space-time becomes a reality in the explicit, or unfolded order, when we observe from this space-time consciousness. Otherwise all that is, exists in potential, in the enfolded holomovement. Towards the end of his book, Bohm reaffirms:

> the holomovement which is 'life implicit' is the ground both of 'life explicit' and of 'inanimate matter,' and this ground is what is primary, self-existent and universal. Thus we do not fragment life and inanimate matter, nor do we try to reduce the former completely to nothing but an outcome of the latter.[68]

Bohm is suggesting that we can only have insight into this primary ground of the holomovement at the level of synthesis, because the holomovement is both life implicit and explicit. In this holomovement spirit cannot be fragmented from matter. When we awaken our deep absolute mind and return to the enfolded unity of the ground of consciousness, we intrinsically participate in the empty fullness, a fecund nothingness of the holomovement. We awaken within the oneing of the holomovement. Importantly, in this wholistic perspective, wholeness is not a static oneness, but a relational, dynamic wholeness-in-motion, and endless oneing in which everything moves together in an inter-connected process. Ilia affirms that Bohm highlights three important ideas for our evolutionary growth in consciousness of our wholeness in this holomovement in Christ. First, she affirms Bohm's stress on the relationality of being that exists as unbroken wholeness in a system. Each part is connected to the other part at the quantum level. Second, Ilia upholds how systems are in movement, or in holomovement and she emphasises the dynamism of this process creativity. And third, because reality is relational and in constant flow, Ilia affirms, it has endless depth. Bohm, Ilia says, "directs us to think in wholes, relationality and depth."[69]

Bohm's imagery of enfolding, unfolding that identifies enfoldment and unfoldment as the whole enfolded in each of its parts, resonates with Julian's portrayal of Christ wrapping, enfolding and unfolding in us, or as Ilia says of our

---

[67] Ilia Delio, *Personal Transformation and New Creation: The Spiritual Revolution of Beatrice Bruteau* (New York: Orbis Books, 2017), 122.
[68] Bohm, *Wholeness and the Implicate Order*, 247.
[69] Ilia Delio, *Emergent Christ*, 29.

wholeness in Christ. The enfoldment-unfoldment imparts a holographic sense of ourselves enfolded, enclosed and *beclosed* in the Trinity, as the Trinity is enclosed in us. And this appreciation of this holographic holomovement is consistent with our heart awareness of oneing. Furthermore, Heidi Russell suggests that:

> Analogously, we can image the Source of Love as the implicate order of wholeness with the Logos as the enfolded holomovement and the Spirit as the unfolding of the holomovement. The Triune God of Love enfolded into our very being is at the core of who we are as persons. The explicate order is the mechanistic or external relationships among the parts (or subwholes).[70]

Thus, we could say that this holomovement is the *"wholomovement"* of the flow of the love of the Trinity, the ground of consciousness itself. Ilia affirms how through the mystical awareness that awakens in contemplation, we know this ground and can have a sense of the holomovement of love evolving and drawing us into a fuller convergence in Omega. She calls us to embrace this new paradigm that begins within our essential unity, our oneness, our holy wholeness, and experience through contemplation, how the inner universe is part of the outer universe.

In fact, Ilia affirms that the inner and outer universe are not simply part of each other, they *are* each other. The within and without, the enfolded and unfolded are a seamless unity. The whole is in the part and the part in the whole. In this endless, depthless, oneing love, we see that the experience of separateness is an illusion of a disconnected mind. Our challenge is to free ourselves from this illusion of self-separateness and enable the wholeness of the holomovement to manifest in space-time by bringing our awareness into its primordial ground. Ilia affirms: "For where the distinction between outer and inner universe is transcended in a flow of unbroken wholeness, there lies our transformation into new existence, that is a new way of seeing the world and relating to the world as a whole."[71] Ilia invites us to cultivate a silent, still, mind that can centre within our heart's depths, enter into "the empty fullness," "the fecund nothingness" that is the holomovement, contemplate our wholeness in Christ, beyond all observer/observed limitations and activate a quantum consciousness. In this

---

[70] Heidi Russell, *The Source of All Love: Catholicity and the Trinity* (Catholicity in and Evolving Universe) (New York: Orbis Books. Kindle Edition), Loc. 548.
[71] Delio, *Hunger for Wholeness*, 82.

contemplation we enter into quantum resurrection as we awaken our resurrection body.

A Quantum Heart-Body-Mind

In her *Making All Things New*, Ilia affirms that a quantum view envisages a person as a constellation of relationships, inner and outer. Communion is our essence and things and events that were once perceived to be separate are integrally linked within the holomovement of the whole. Matter is made up of particles relating to each other in waves of constant energy exchange so that all that is takes place in the enfoldment and unfoldment of the whole. This unending process in an entangled field of energy exchange, makes the pattern that we are part of all that is to come. We are in essence whole makers, in an undivided wholeness, creating a future wholeness.[72] While our awareness of space and time occurs at the level of the explicit, and is recognised by our discursive mind, the depthless-ness of our heart-mind, oned in the ground of consciousness itself, realises the infinity of the present moment. From this quantum perspective, Ilia invites us to awaken a quantum consciousness that strengthens the sense of holomovement between our discursive mind and our depthless silent heart-mind and give us a constant flow of holographic wisdom knowing. This holographic vision becomes ours when through contemplation, we awaken in our resurrection body, living in Christ within an activated luminous mind body oneness. We have the same mind as Christ Jesus, crucified, risen and in us now.

Ilia explains that our bodies are entangled through a quantum field of "electrical bio-photon resonances" that are in constant flux. Thus, our minds have a capacity to awaken to the depthless depths of the holomovement of all things, in the whole that is beyond space and time. In the fecundity of the empty-fullness of the implicit order, we become aware of "a quantum field consciousness," which Ilia calls "quantum consciousness." We realise our mind participates in this quantum field of consciousness that transcends the divide between an individual and the world, between human beings and nature.[73] I would also suggest that this quantum consciousness transcends the divide between our discursive thinking mind and our heart mind. Here, we see how when we enter into our mind, in a subject in subject presencing, into field awareness, we gain insight into the nature

---

[72] Delio, *Making All Things New*, 62.
[73] Ibid., 149.

of the universe. We see there is in fact, no inner and outer, but one dynamic wholeness centred in God-Omega. This wholeness, oneness, is what the research of quantum physics affirms. Ilia points out: "there is no outer universe without an inner universe; there is no matter without consciousness."[74]

This means that the gift the mystics give us in showing us how to awaken within the ground of our mind and see from oneness is critical to this next evolutionary step. What we realise about the inner universe of our consciousness in God is that it has as much to contribute as quantum science has, in telling us how the universe works. Ilia reminds us:

> The inner universe is not secondary to the outer universe; rather it is the outer universe on the level of consciousness. It is here that the soul encompasses the field of the mind where intellect and emotions are integrated into a transcendent oneness with God.[75]

As Ilia quotes Teilhard: "If we are to progress or evolve, however, we must release ourselves from religious individualism and confront the general religious experience, which is cosmic and evolutionary and involve ourselves in it."[76] We must involve ourselves in this shift in consciousness, beyond the dualisms of inner and outer universe, and strengthen the flow between the wisdom of the heart and the intellect, personally, communionally, cosmically and awaken within the consciousness of oneing. Ilia calls us to this wholeness reminding us that "when the whole brain is enabling the whole person to connect to the whole environment, catholicity is alive."[77]

A Christic Mind

In developing how we might awaken a quantum consciousness, Ilia draws on Paul's seminal comment in his Letter to the Philippians, where Paul insists: "In your relationships with one another, have the same mind (ίδια μυαλό του Ιησού Χριστού *ídia myaló tou Iisoú Christoú*) as Christ Jesus" (Phil 2:3-5). Literally, the translation reads: "let this mind be in you that is also in Christ Jesus." Paul is telling us that we can let the very same mind that is in Christ, crucified and risen, arise in us. In a quantum view, we know we already share in this mind at the enfolded implicit level. Our response is to turn within, into our I, our, subject

---

[74] Delio, *Hunger for Wholeness*, 43.
[75] Ibid.
[76] From Teilhard de Chardin, *Human Energy*, quoted in Delio, *Hunger for Wholeness*, 33.
[77] Delio, *Making All Things New*, 150.

in subject identity, and enable the realization of Christ within us, to unfold explicitly. In this realization in space-time, we participate in the ongoing incarnation of the mind of Christ in humanity.

Importantly though, although this mind of Christ, this same consciousness that we share, is intimately ours, from a quantum perspective this mind is not something else, it is the holomovement, a totally loving awareness field that we all participate within. Thus, the mind of Christ is intrinsically communal, a "communion consciousness," we could say. Paul would have none of this language, but he understands this crucial communal dimension when he advises, that it is in our relationships with one another, that we have this same mind. The mind of Christ is the communal mind of the body of Christ. The mind of Christ is a field of enstatic-ecstatic loving, a holomovement, a dynamic oneing consciousness. When we activate this Christic mind intentionally, we create pockets of energy that form a stronger morphogenic field of the mind of Christ in the every-day consciousness, of our explicit, unfolded state of activity. Ilia invites us to awaken this quantum Christic mind, and create, "a 'mind-fullness' of *the Now that is*, ... a mind that is not merely in creation, but a mind that is creating evolving the world into something new."[78] The mind of Christ is an evolutionary mind.

Omega Love In Our Midst

Ilia takes us into the everlasting newness of the now that is, into the oneing flow of the holomovement of Christ consciousness becoming more stable in our every-day awareness. Her words expand us into the primal flow of Christ consciousness that is Omega holding us within an expanding fullness of the holomovement of Love's becoming. She delights:

> Omega love is in our midst, and this love is our power, our hope and our future. Remain in this love, because this love is the fire of life itself and will endure forever. Be the co-creator you are made to be: emblazon this world with the grandeur of God.[79]

At present, the ever-fertile presence of God-Omega, who is the ground of all being, the underlying consciousness of flowing love energy, is evolving and drawing us into a new consciousness of our wholeness in God. God-Omega is

---

[78] Ibid., 155.
[79] Ibid., 190.

rousing our hearts, inciting a thirst to see and to respond to the flow of love within evolution's movement at this sacred moment in time, so that we may centre in and contribute to the divine desire that continually loves and creates anew.

This stirring is intimate, taking us into the depthless waters of our hearts. It is also expansive, communal, environmental, universal, opening us into the fullness of an ever-expanding universal wholeness in love. In this naked moment, Omega's luminous presence is rising within the whole of creation, gathering together all the disparate voices, all the disharmony, all the scattered pieces of our past separating consciousness, knitting, oneing and centring us in love and enabling us to participate more fully in a further phase of centring in the communal mind-body of Christ deep Wisdom, Word and Mother who is Omega. This movement flows from the desiring, yearning, longing of God-Omega, thrusting us into a new phase of awareness of how we are one in the oneing of the holomovement of the wave particle, enfolding and unfolding of divine life embodied in creation.

We have affirmed how Omega is the grounding principle within evolution, the Centre of centres, the flow of Love energy, the pointless point from whom all life emanates. Within this perspective, everything in the universe occurs within the unifying spiralling flow, emanating from the infinite divine fullness of love into the finite, continuously drawing all creation into an evolving, eternal, divine unity. Ilia upholds this wholeness in relationality stressing how:

> every aspect of life, from the smallest to the complex, is centred in Omega. This divine presence is divine Love, so we can say, divine Love empowers evolution through created energies. As love-energy combines disparate elements into new unities, consciousness rises; as love and consciousness rises in evolution, so too does unity and wholeness.[80]

This endless flow of divine love empowering evolution immerses us in awe and wonder and carries us into silence, as exquisitely, beyond our wildest imaginings, Omega continually lavishes us with more love. The source-less source of all love, the groundless ground of all being, the silence that speaks the Word, the life force, the power, the potential, the abundance, the fullness of the endlessness of Love begetting love faithfully, steadfastly streams forth within creation. Omega is the organic totality of evolution, the One who makes all things one, the all who makes all things All. Omega is the attractive centre that

---

[80] Delio, *Making All Things New*, 176.

enflames every love. Centred in Omega Love and held in an ongoing creative unity, creation bears within its innermost being this pattern of divine interflowing love, enfolding, and gradually drawing all things into fuller and fuller creative-union of oneing. We experience this Omega presence as the holomovement, that is the enstatic, ecstatic, dynamism of the oneing, enfolding, enclosing love of the Trinity. This fountain fullness of Trinitarian love energy overflows into creation. Creation, in turn, expresses the same fountain fullness of conscious interbeing, which we make consciousness through contemplation. It is our invitation now to become a conscious expression of this luminous fountain fullness.

Illuminating Contemplation

The heart of contemplation is love, for Ilia. She sees finding time for silence and solitude as fundamental to the awakening of our resurrection body with an enlightened Christic mind. Contemplation is centring in intensely personal Omega love, yielding into Omega's magnetic concentration, into an inner single pointed being in one another that then enables us to emerge and live with resurrected quantum field awareness in a holy wholeness. Ilia writes:

> To know God as the wholeness of love is to enter into oneness at the heart of all life. That is why prayer and contemplation are essential for the next stage of evolution. Without the eye of the heart or the inner space to welcome the new ways love shows itself in others, we cannot love toward greater unity.[81]

In contemplation we come to know God as the wholeness of love drawing the wisdom found within our inner universe and the holiness of matter in the outer universe into one multiverse of cosmic illumination that is *Christogenesis,* the birth of Christ, in creation and the evolutionary shaping of the earth into the body of Christ. As the flow from within the inner ground of our heart overflows into the created world with divine creativity, we become more one, more whole in the intense loving of Omega. In contemplation we intentionally, creatively give birth to the Wisdom-Word through the entangled energies of matter, becoming an entangled amorising centre of love. Ilia's wholeness of being and the harmony of the catholicity that emerge from this holy wholeness in these Love energies, transforms our consciousness. Awakening this oneing consciousness within our inner universe is core to this task. Ilia brings this great tradition of contemplation

---

[81] Delio, *Unbearable Wholeness,* 112.

and places it within the heart of the scientific world. We will explore four fundamental ways she illuminates contemplation today.

First, Ilia invites us how to see from within the oneing of the holomovement, to see that what is, is the holomovement, enfolding and unfolding infinitely. Contemplation, for Ilia, draws us into the next level of reflexivity, of the whole of creation being oned, subject in subject, in Christ Omega that Bonaventure and Teilhard foresaw. Contemplative prayer prepares the ground of our heart for the grace of this awakening, opening us into the luminous risen life of the mind of Christ. This is the mind of Christo-Sophia, expressed in Christ-Omega. As Omega gathers all things into the field of Love's begetting, we see how whole, how one we are, in the body of Christ. This ontological ground in the holomovement of Christ-Omega, affirms and extends our hermeneutic of oneing, that we have seen in all these mystics, offering us a new sensitivity to the soul of the earth and the quantum field, wave-particle fluidity. It reminds us how important our observation is to the way evolution emerges. When we enter into this Christogenesis in the ground of our being and awaken from within the love energies in the oneing of the holomovement, we assist in the infinite expressing itself in the finite. However, if we bring a negative, separating, selfish glare to the process, we create more fracturing in the universe. If we are indifferent, dispirited, unaware, we contribute to this collective shadow, sabotaging life. It is critical, at this phase in the evolution of Christ coming to consciousness in us, that we release all that we are into this ever-loving wholeness and help activate a fuller wholeness.

Second, at this quantum level of reflexivity Ilia urges us to embrace, we have the same mind as Christ-Jesus. This mind has the *kenotic* pattern of dying and rising, awakening a quantum resurrection consciousness in us. This is for Ilia, a Christic luminous, risen-body-mind. Hence, this is what Ilia means by wholeness, "nothing can separate us from the love of Christ" (Rom 8:3-9). This luminous Christic mind that is the ground of consciousness, beyond the dualism of thought and no-thought, knowing and unknowing, experiences the flow of no-thought and thought harmoniously in a naked now. Our thoughts infused by no thought, overflow with Logos-Sophia perception. In this contemplative awareness, our mind is not separated into cognitive discursive consciousness and heart-consciousness. With one mind, oned in Christ, we see and know that the inner universe is the outer universe. And there is no outer universe without an inner universe. This luminous body-mind sees wave particle fluidity, in the fecundity of the vacuum plenum, the potential empty fullness, the ever-conceiving nothingness. Importantly, this Christic mind cannot be objectified because, it is the holomovement. We cannot talk about Christ consciousness as if we are looking at Christ consciousness. Christ consciousness is the ground of consciousness we already are, the totally loving awareness field that we all participate within. In this oneing holomovement of holy wholeness, we are the risen body of Christ. All is in All.

Third, Ilia wants us to know that our contemplation activates a communal, quantum, luminous mind whose lightness radiates in our bodies. In actively converging in Christ through meditation, we can create a stronger morphogenic field of quantum consciousness that is inclusive of all creation. In a time when the collective shadow is haunting our world, living the *kenotic* path of dying and rising and learning to stabilize in resurrection, in the vision of our oneness, in the light of oneing love is critical. Oned in Christo-Sophia and grounded in the holomovement in the enfolding, unfolding wave-particle fluidity enables us to, as Ilia says, "think with our heart." In this eternal flow, the thought-non-thought dichotomy dissolves. This luminous empty mind infuses a clarity, a vividness, in a oned, oneing, oneness, that opens us into a vast field of wisdom knowing, that organically informs our thinking, while always keeping thought open to new possibilities. This enables us, as Ilia says, "to continuously search for truth, for sheer transparent being that radiates life."[82] We remain open in the wonder of the present moment oneing is us. We become a transparent portal, in the *apex mentis*, in the Omega point, where time and eternity meet in an evolving oneing. Whole making becomes ever present in our consciousness as the divine incarnates, and we in turn, in the holomovement, incarnate the divine. This is what Ilia calls a "spiralling incarnation."[83] This spiralling, birthing, rebirthing is sourced by an ever generous, compassionate renewable energy, an abundance of amorising love. In this love there is fullness for all.

Fourth, Ilia is a dancing star, joyfully dancing within our central star Christ-Omega. She is radiant in bringing science and spirituality together within the Christian story of love. With David Bohm, she opens new vistas for an essential dialogue between quantum physics and spirituality. Together, they invite us into the newness of a spacious, fecund, vacuum of this present moment of the dynamic, enfolding, unfolding, holomovement of Love's oneing, to become a

---

[82] Delio, *Birth of a Dancing Star*, 207.
[83] Ibid., 211.

oneing field. "Quantum physics should bring us to our knees in the wake of mystery," Ilia writes:

> and meditation may be our most effective technology for curing our illness. For the inner universe shapes the outer universe; consciousness is governed by the attraction of love; how consciousness and love flow, so goes space. What we love or fail to love influences our spatial differences and the distance between us affects what we become both personally and collectively.[84]

This oneing consciousness that is evolving, as we awaken in our quantum, resurrection body, is the source of creative possibility for a future of greater unity, beyond the current social, economic, political, ecological crisis we now face.

Ilia affirms:

> The more I travel inward, the more God there is than self, and, truthfully, the further I go the less I can speak of either God or self; there is simply an entangled fire of love. In the search for who I am I find God, and in finding God I find my 'self' as no separate self but being itself, flowing into and out of an unquenchable power of divine love.[85]

Ilia brings us into the spiraling luminous future in Omega, into our indwelling within the entangled fire of Love's oneing. She grounds us in the holomovement of the fiery point of incarnation-re-incarnation where Silence conceives and ecstatically births the Word, the Word conceives, births and returns us into the Silence of Love's oneing.

In Conclusion

As the pages of this book have turned, we have explored the luxuriant multi-hued canvas of contemplation as oneing and developed a metaphysics of oneing. We have seen how contemplation awakens a unitive, or oneing-heart-awareness. We have conferred with nine wisdom figures from within Christian love mysticism, seeing how the tradition of contemplative unitive seeing is evolving within Western Christianity, and has an enormous contribution to make to the awakening of the translucent seeing of a oneing consciousness in this time. We have considered how an awakened luminous oneing-heart-awareness returns us to our Christic identity in the Trinity, integrating the past and placing us in the

---

[84] Delio, *Hunger for Wholeness*, 106.
[85] Delio, *Birth of a Dancing Star*, 203.

fertility of the future, meeting us in the oneing-point of this naked moment. We have participated in how the grace of contemplation immerses us in the sheer silence of the heart-womb *kolpon,* pregnant, and birthing in this fertile present, speaking the Word, infusing Wisdom and awakening a Christ consciousness that beholds from within the holomovement of Trinitarian divine life. Only sheer silence knows, in this exquisite unknowing, how we are one in Love's oneing. Enabling a seamless reciprocal flow between our conscious awareness and this oneing Christ consciousness to stabilize, so we may truly be contemplatives in the world, is our task now.

Each of the mystics in this book have placed us in the ground of the heart and immersed us in contemplation, drawing on language that arises from the ground of the heart and returns us to the heart. Each has provided essential colours that illuminate, as the darkness of the present moment intensifies, and dawn waits for our readiness on the horizon. Each shows us how *love is God's meaning.* Our whole life and being is an expression of Love's oneing. Silently, delicately in *Beholding in Oneing,* we have beheld with Julian, savouring her multihued language of knitting and oneing that enfolds, encloses, ones us in Christ, as Christ encloses us. She opened the way for us to behold from within Christ our ground, in Christic ground awareness and for words to form in our understanding from this oneing point. Through teaching a way of beholding blindly and feeling nakedly, in this dark loving, the *Cloud* seer sensitised us to the *souereyn pointe* of Love's oneing, enlightening the spiritual knot of burning love that marks the transition point into our heart-mind's unitive vision within naked Godhead. Eckhart's single pointed desire for us to be one, in the simple One, awakened the spark of the intellect, or heart-mind, in the silent middle of our soul's ground, turning and releasing us so deeply into the birth of the Word within us, within God, that now we get nothing but this birth of God from all things.

In *Suffering in Oneing,* Mechthild's bridal mysticism showed us how sinking into suffering, can become the ultimate mystical union, when lived within the flowing *kenosis* of Christ crucified. Clare magnified how the luminosity of the icon of crucified love infuses, illuminating how we may become icons of contemplation, as each phase of paschal wounding, dying and rising, places us in the mirror of eternity. John of the Cross, refined our night seeing. He awakened us from our indwelling in the Beloved, Wisdom-Word, that luminously feels like an enflamed mustard seed, expanding into a sea of loving fire, enabling us to see from the caverns of our memory, understanding and will, aflame with divine light. Finally, in *Communion in Oneing*, Teilhard affirmed, "the fire spreads in ever widening circles till finally the whole planet is covered with incandescence,"[86] as Christic communal consciousness awakens in the noosphere. Beatrice confirmed how, as we concentrate our sense of who we are within our transcendent centre in Christo-Sophia Omega and see through the divine light flowing within, spondic radiance pours out mercy and compassion into the world. She prepares the ground for the future awakening of a oneing communion consciousness that sees within enstatic-ecstatic, *perichoretic* Trinitarian wisdom. Ilia places us in the holomovement of this Trinitarian loving, as we see with quantum eyes.

As Ilia prophesies, how we choose to create the future, depends on how we grasp this moment as the kiss of God.[87]

> May we behold and enjoy the kiss of presence
> in the incandescence of Love's oneing
> as creation's future wholeness in the flowing light of divinity
> evolves through our loving.
> In the silence of contemplation, we
> "live through love in Love's presence." (Eph 1:4).

---

[86] Pierre Teilhard de Chardin, *The Phenomenon of Man* (London: Collins Fontana Books, 1966), 182.
[87] Delio, *Making All Things New*, 200.

Praying Contemplatively

*Econoeisis is awareness of divine energy present in every aspect of creation,
from the grain of sand to the highest mountain and tallest tree,
and every leaf and the vein of every leaf of every tree.
"The whole creation is pregnant with God," Angela of Foligno wrote.*[88]

Embracing Stillness

Beloved Christ Omega
ever emerging in my/our consciousness,
as luminous risen presence
bursts into the beauty of the radiant colour of this day.
I/we come to embrace the restful colours of your silence,
your shimmering stillness, your idle tranquility,
your glistening peace,
your entangling energies.
I/we gather all my/our senses into a gentle rest and follow
your stirring within the centre of your heart.
Here I/we dwell in one love, with one awareness,

---

[88] Delio, *Econoeisis*, https://christogenesis.org/econoeisis-a-new-contemplative-paradigm/.

in one amorising creativity.
Here you are my Love, my Heart, my Womb of Creativity,
Omega.

Ruminating on Scripture

To those who have been called, whoever they are,
Christ who is the power and the wisdom of God.
1 Corinthians 1:24.

The Music of Silence

Creation shimmers with silent ripples of Love.

Contemplatio

I invite you to find a quiet place, become rested, silent, turn within, and centre in Omega Love in the still point of your heart. Feel yourself drawn into the ground of Love, into the oneing, into the holomovement of the amorising love of the Omega point. Dissolve into the point where your being and your awareness meet in the Omega point, in the flow of Love's oneing.

Softly, gently, expand your awareness out into the outer universe, beholding the beauty of the colours of the day, lingering and pondering the wonder of the book of creation. Sense the oneing of the outer universe with your inner universe.

Gradually, as the music of silence heightens, listen for Love's deep invitation to encircle and focus again within the ground of your heart, into your inner universe, in the Omega point. Turn into the inflow of love, releasing into your heart-self, into the heart-mind of Christ until your inner universes expands into the outer universe. Feel the pulsating love flowing, oneing.

In this flow of turning into your heart, breathe in harmony with Love's stirrings, until you come into an idle, calm, peaceful serenity. Continue to yield into the ground, into the oneing, into a oneing awareness. Attend to the flow of delicate, subtle, currents, rippling with amorising love, opening into a oneing, holographic vision.

Feel yourself part of the energetic inflow-outflow of unfolding wholeness, bubbling with evolutionary potential, becoming entangled with all the energies of life. Bathe in the energy of this cosmic hologram of being one in Omega love.

Rest for some time in the pure silence of essence pouring out amorising love in a dynamic evolutionary holomovement. Delicately sense pregnant seeds of grace, infinitely fertile with possibility and potential.

Gently open further, into our collective earth-body intuition and feel and release into the vibrancy of the amorizing love energy, giving yourself to you in the world, in love. Reciprocally, receive the world in love. One in one another, in a delightful evolving indwelling, feel love and faithfulness kiss. Feel the harmony, the peace, the power of the giving and receiving, intensifying. Sense the loving of this field of communion consciousness that includes humankind and the earth emerging in Christ-Omega and shower the world in love.

Throughout the day, be attentive to how the gift of this holographic seeing seeps into the day and enables you to turn into the world, seeing from your oneness in Omega.

Blessing

Luminous in the dance of inner and outer universe,
Unfolding and enfolding with evolutionary potential
I lean into your future fullness and
shower amorising love into the universe,
into the multiverse.
Joyously, peacefully, courageously,
I live in your incarnating creativity
loving the world that is your body.
Amen